MW01627515

My Quilts and Me

Gloria Curry Block -

June 5th - 92 - 8:00 to 11:00 AM 6:30 - 9:

6:30 - 10:00

NORA L. EZELL
MAR. 1992

July - 1st

" 2nd - 92 - 6:30 - 9:30 P.M.

" 3 '92 4:30 - 9:30 P.M.

July - 4th 92 - piano keys - 6:30 - 9:30 A.M.

My Quilts and Me

The Diary of an American Quilter

Nora McKeown Ezell

Black Belt Press
Montgomery

 Published in the United States of America by Black Belt Press, a division of Black Belt Publishing, LLC, P.O. Box 551, Montgomery, Alabama 36101.

General Editor: Randall Williams

Designer: Breuna Baine

Project Editor: Mary Elizabeth Johnson

Studio quilt photography: Harold Kilgore

[This manuscript has been subjected to a minimum of editing; certain portions have been structured slightly differently from the original for clarity's sake, and because of the archival nature of some of the materials included in the original. Editor's notes or additions are shown in brackets, author's are in parentheses. All photo captions are by the editor, who is responsible for any mistakes therein. Story and art quilt names are in italic, other quilt names are in quotes.]

Manufactured in China
Library of Congress Cataloging-in-Publication Data
Ezell, Nora McKeown., 1917–
My quilts and me: the diary of an American folk artist/Nora Mckeown Ezell.
p. cm.
ISBN: 1-881320-21-9
1. Quilting. 2 Patchwork. 3. Ezell, Nora Mckeown, 1917– , Diaries.
4. Afro-American quiltmakers—Diaries. 5. Afro-American quilts. I. Title.
TT835.E95 1996
746.46 ' 092—dc20
[B] 96-1815
CIP

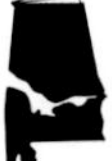

The Black Belt, defined by its dark, rich soil, stretches across central Alabama. It was and is a place of great beauty, of extreme wealth and grinding poverty, of pain and joy. Here we take our stand, listening to the past, looking to the future.

Frontispiece: *Children of the World*

Signed and dated "Nora L. Ezell, March 1991."

Approximately 67 inches by 83 inches. Cotton and polyester/cotton blend fabrics; woven tape; nylon and cotton laces; acrylic and cotton yarns; cotton fringe; silk ribbon; rick-rack with metallic thread; beads; embroidery floss. A written log on this quilt could not be found; Mrs. Ezell may not have kept one. Collection of Jimmy Hedges.

Detail, opposite page: "Migration"

Signed and dated "Nora Ezell, Aug. 1983."

70 inches by 94 inches. Cotton fabrics. Collection of Kathy Kemp.

This book is dedicated to my grandchildren
Beverly, Audrey, A.C., and David

My God Is No Stranger

I've never seen God,
But I know how I feel . . .
It's people like you
Who make him so real . . .
It seems that I pass him
So often each day . . .
In faces of people
I meet on my way . . .
He's the stars in the heaven,
A smile on some face . . .
A leaf on a tree
or a rose in a vase . . .
He's winter and autumn
and summer and spring . . .
In short, God is every
real, wonderful thing . . .
I wish I might meet him
much more than I do . . .
I would if there were
more people like you.

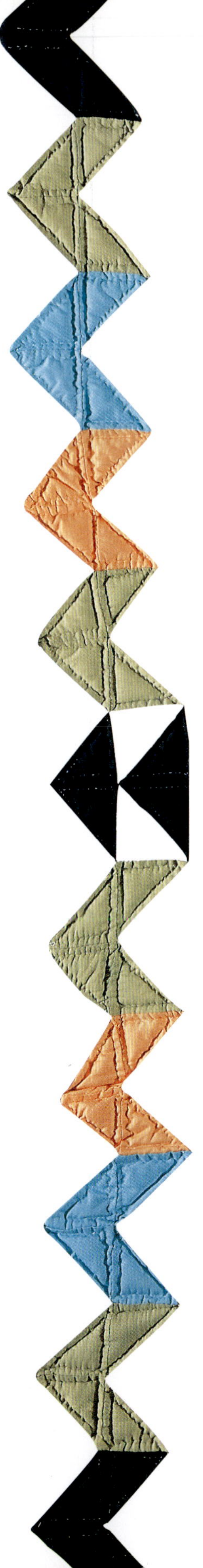

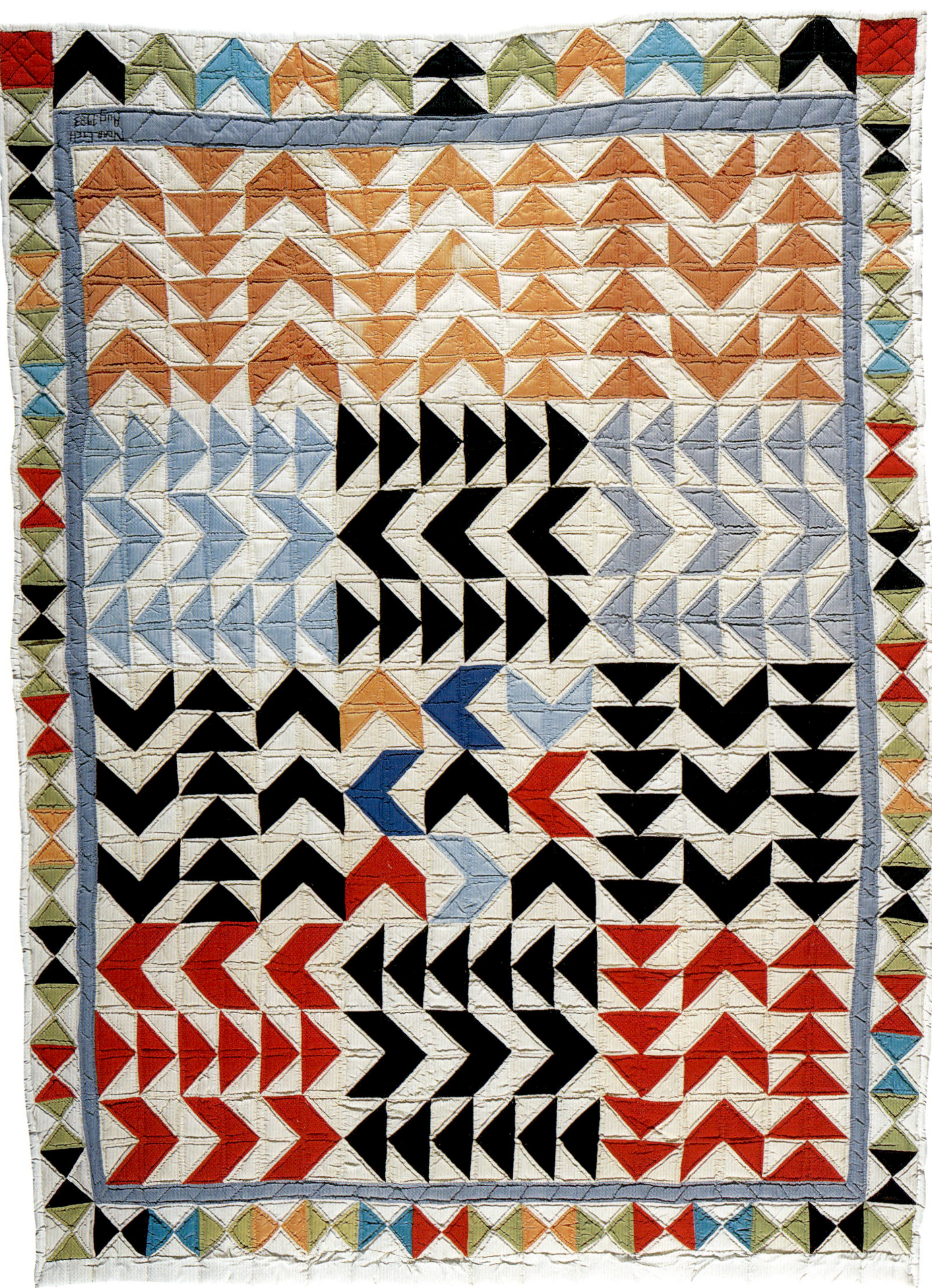
Nora Ezell
Aug 1983

Contents

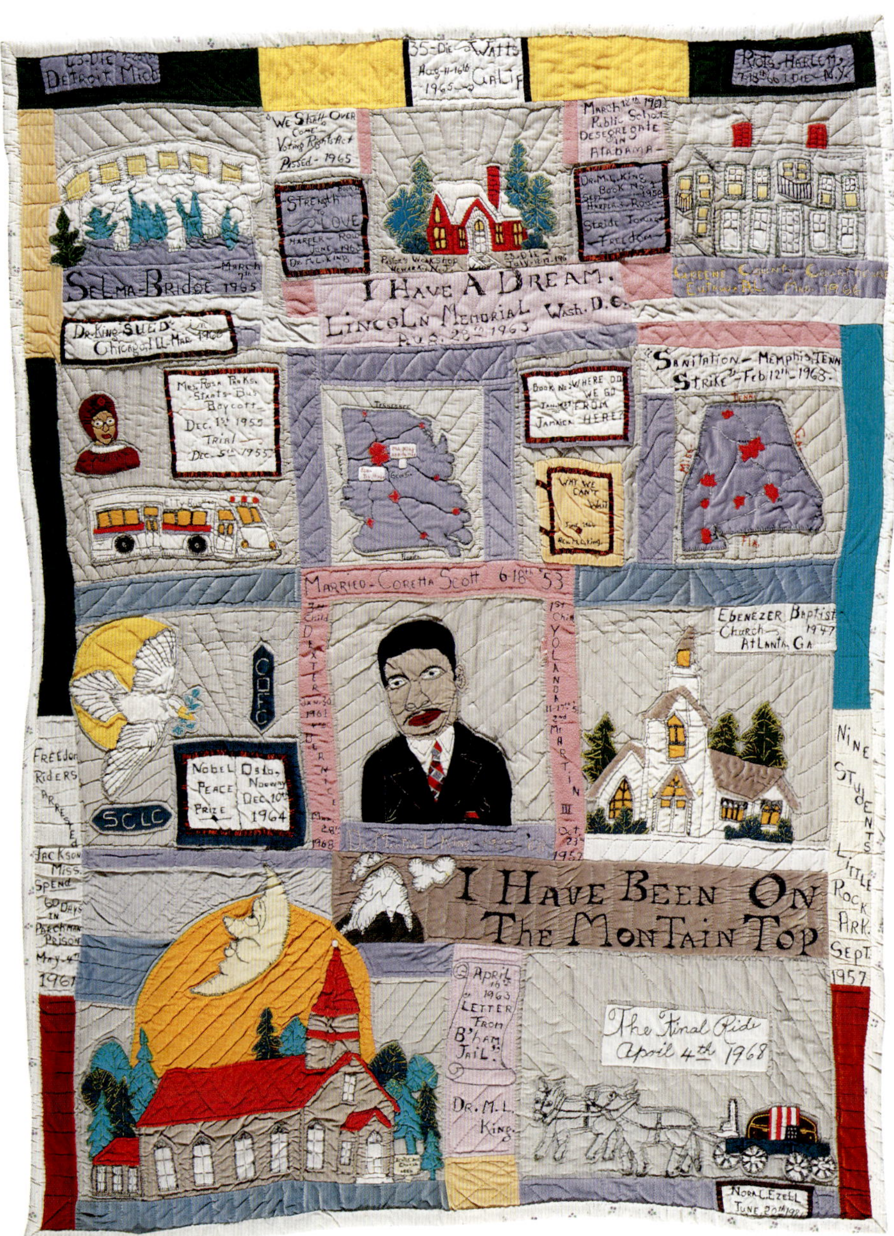

The Martin Luther King Life Story Quilt

Signed and dated Nora L. Ezell, June 20, 1986.

78.5 inches by 101.5 inches; primary fabric is nylon fleece; other fabrics include woven nylon, knit nylon, and brown satin ribbon. Detail on opposite page. Collection of Robert and Helen Cargo. Photograph courtesy of Robert Cargo.

Foreword

By Henry Willett, Director
Alabama Center for Traditional Culture
Alabama State Council on the Arts

Most people meet Nora Ezell through her quilts—colorful explosions of improvisation and visual delight—sculptural delicacies stuffed, tucked, and brought to life by the skilled hands that fashion them. Because Nora Ezell is an artist, her quilts speak out, as all good art does, across time, culture, and geography, boldly demanding to be noticed. This became particularly evident to me when, in 1992, I was in Washington on a National Endowment for the Arts panel, charged with making recommendations for National Heritage Fellowship Awards.

Our task was arduous. We spent hours reviewing the work of hundreds of traditional artists from across America—Cajun accordian-makers to bonsai sculptors—and, of course quilters, many quilters.

In reading over pages of support materials in preparation for this meeting, I had found myself frustrated by the very issue of quilters. They flourish in such abundant excellence, making it nearly impossible to single out one or two, or even a dozen, for this prestigious national recognition.

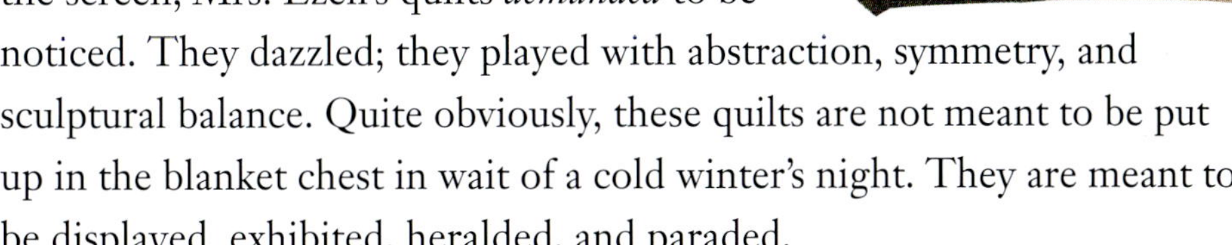

However, when the slides came up on the screen, Mrs. Ezell's quilts *demanded* to be noticed. They dazzled; they played with abstraction, symmetry, and sculptural balance. Quite obviously, these quilts are not meant to be put up in the blanket chest in wait of a cold winter's night. They are meant to be displayed, exhibited, heralded, and paraded.

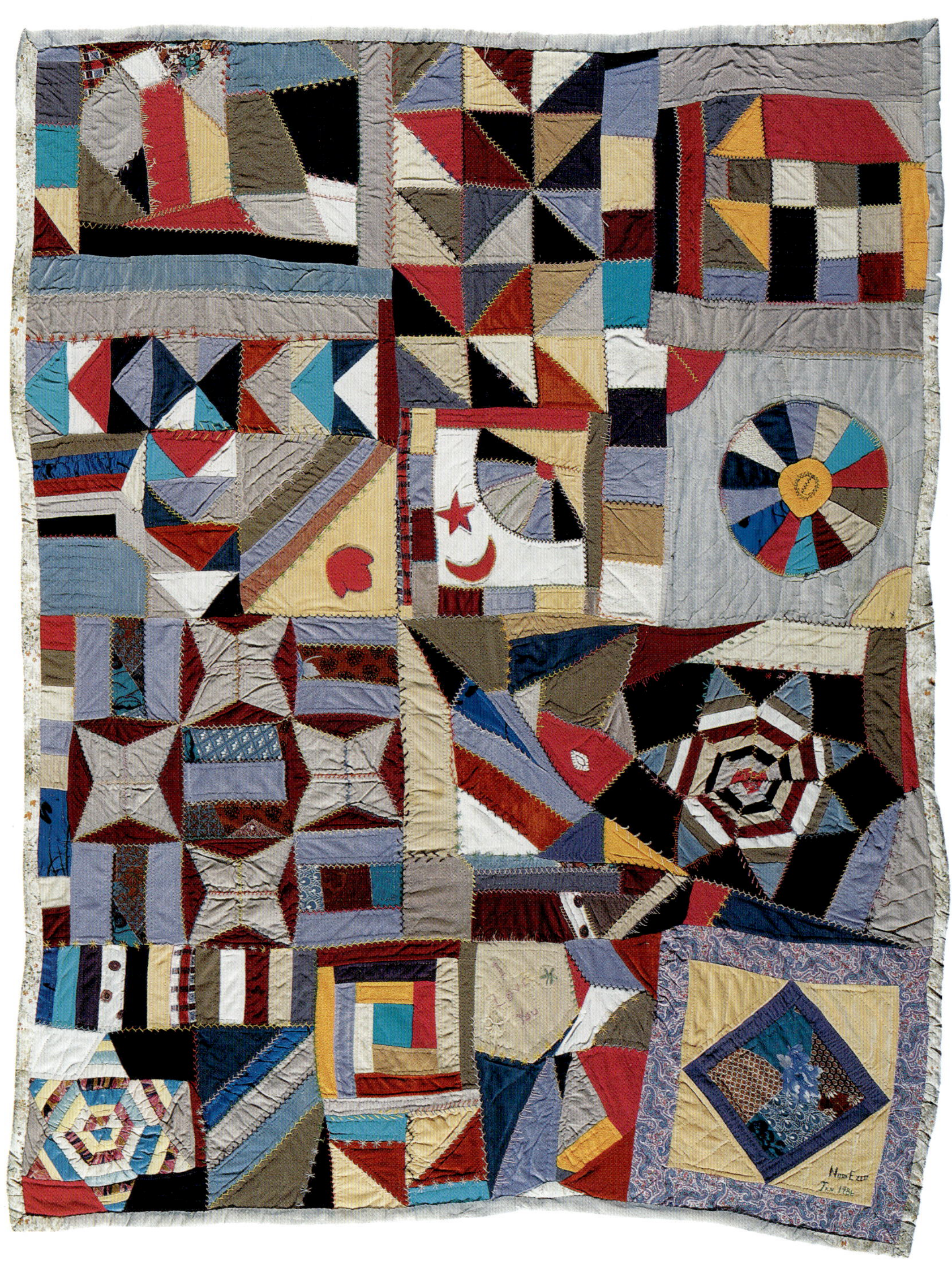

The finest of traditional artists (and Nora Ezell is certainly among the finest) don't simply carry on tradition; they *shape* tradition, often striving to imbue their creations with embodiments of their personal aesthetic visions. Nora's visions fairly explode from the surfaces of her quilts.

But, as becomes evident in the thoughtful words written in her journal, these quilts have a private side as well, reflecting this artist's life. The quiet hours spent quilting provide time for reflection—on health and aging, on faith and religion, or grief and loneliness, baseball and politics. Mrs. Ezell's writing is both eloquent and honest. Through her words, we are provided a window to the mind and soul of an artist of refreshing candor and originality.

Mrs. Ezell is fond of saying, "I put a part of me in everything I do." Her quilts are a part of her, and she is a part of her quilts. Her art is a dialogue with life; and through *My Quilts and Me* she invites us to share in that dialogue. To anyone who has attempted to stitch a quilt, admired, or simply slept under one, the experience will never be quite the same. Nora Ezell has seen to that.

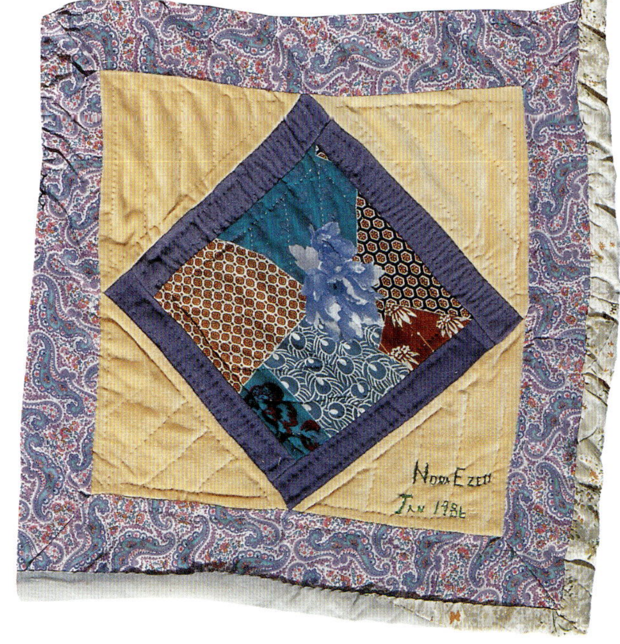

"Crazy Quilt"

Signed and dated "Nora Ezell, Jan. 1986."

72 inches by 92 inches. Made primarily from leftover pieces of nylon fleece used in the *Martin Luther King Quilt*, this quilt also contains cotton and cotton/polyester blend fabrics. Detail at right. Collection of Gail and Hayden Trechsel.

U OF A
ROLL TIDE
CRIMSON TIDE
No. 1
COMMUNICATION
GRADUATION
NORA L. EZELL
Oct. 1984

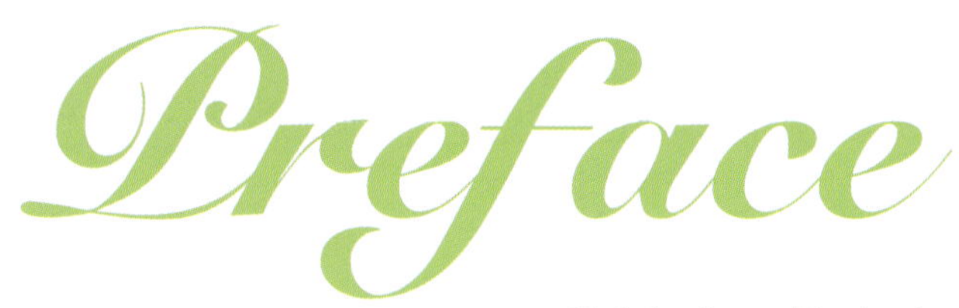

Preface

Gail Andrews Trechsel
Director
Birmingham Museum of Art

"I created my own style to do quilts in because I didn't want to do what nobody else did. I wanted to do something different. I never plan on making a pattern, I do whatever comes off the top of my head."

Those words of Nora McKeown Ezell express the essence of a quilting style that has brought her national attention and captures her personal spirit of individuality and self-confidence. During her quilting career, Mrs. Ezell has worked with incredible energy and drive, creating a large body of work that includes pieced and appliquéd quilts, both as commissions and as ideas that simply appeal to her. As evident from her quote, and from the following journal, Mrs. Ezell is stimulated by a challenge and relishes the task of translating a memory or event into cloth. Her curiosity and desire to continually try new patterns (or improve upon existing ones) lead her to create a wide variety of quilts. She

University of Alabama Quilt

The inscriptions read, "Life belongs to the living, and he who lives must be prepared for change. J. Wolfgang." "Inventing is a combination of brains and materials; the more brains you use, the less materials you need! C.F. Kettering." The titles embroidered on the books are: "Law School, Book I"; "Art, No.7"; "Music, Lee"; "Med School"; "Nursing, No.I"; "Psychology"; "Social Work Book V"; "Language, No.2"; "Drama, No.I"; "Accounting PL"; "Elementary Education"; "Computer Sciences, Book I, Hall"; "Engineering 1984 Edition."

Signed and dated "Nora L. Ezell, Oct. 1984." 78 inches by 92 inches, cotton and polyester/cotton blend fabrics. Detail on page 17. Collection of Robert and Helen Cargo.

Photograph by Gail Trechsel

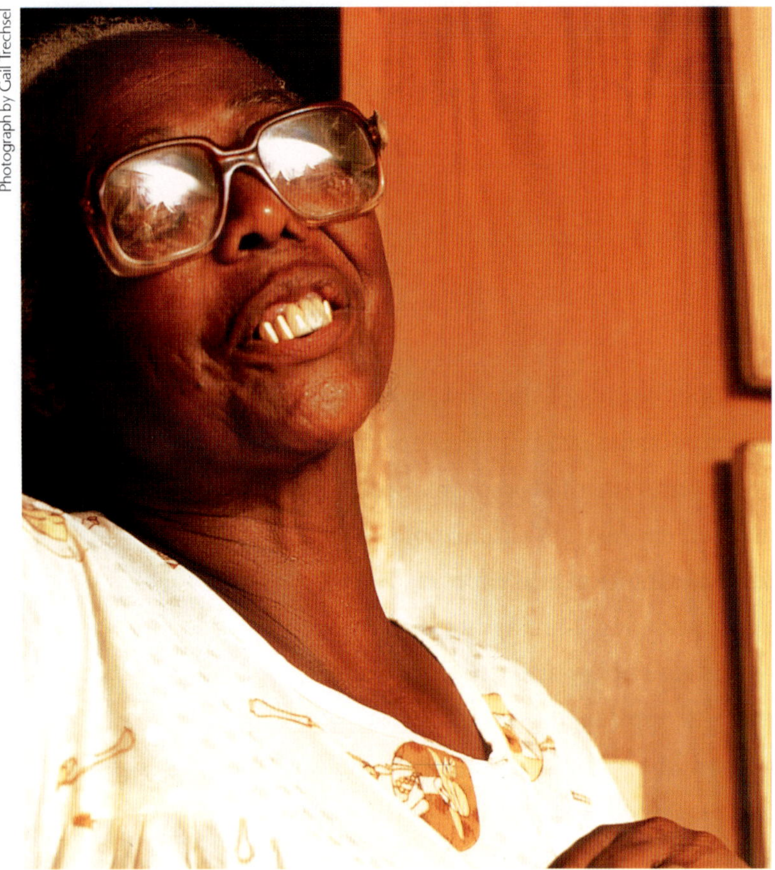

constantly challenges herself to do more, try more, and be more.

An additional desire is to prove that something can be made out of nothing. That is one reason she likes to make postage stamp and string quilts, "just to show you don't have to throw away nothing. You can make a beautiful quilt out of anything and everything you have." Mrs. Ezell is quick to add that you have "to do something to your quilts to make them show up...quilts is made out of anything, but you just can't put that stuff together and hope it will work, you have to think about it."

Mrs. Ezell did not invent the idea of narrative, or story, quilts, but she has made a distinctive contribution to the style. While it can be argued that all quilts tell a story, picture quilts use literal illustration, stitched in fabric, to communicate with the viewer. American examples date to the eighteenth century and continue to be made today; however, this type of quilt has always been comparatively rare.

In developing her style, Mrs. Ezell wanted to use her quilts to bring events to life. She sketches with needle and fabric, creating her appliquéd and embroidered pictures freehand, adjusting as the scene develops. "I just get the ideas and pin them on, can't tell what they will look like at the beginning. As a block comes to me, I do it as I go along."

Mrs. Ezell captures the essence of a moment with her ability to sift through various possibilities of images, using either actual photographs of events or her own fertile imagination, then depicting the one that best communicates the truth to the viewer. Her proficiency with the needle skills of appliqué and embroidery allows her pictorial genius to be successful. In her journal, she describes the time needed to create the individual blocks—the experiments with fabric and stitches, composition and shadow—as well as the effort necessary to craft the image. What she knows to be true is what informs her subject, but she must select from that wealth of information to formulate a design. "I have to decide what I want to use for a particular event. I try to do the most important things, and I have to decide what will look real, or at least pretty, good." And, she continues, "I try to express my own feelings and put down my thoughts with a needle and thread when I make a quilt."

Story quilts have the unusual ability to tell a story two ways. The quilts communicate one story to the viewer, but they also reveal the values, ideas, and experiences of the maker. When she decided to make a *University of Alabama* quilt, Mrs. Ezell designed the quilt to include more history of the university than "Bear Bryant's head and a football." Mrs. Ezell continues, "Now, Bryant made history, but he shouldn't get all the credit at the University. I wrote it on paper, because that's what I usually do when I'm coming up with an idea. I thought about the schoolhouse doors, and Arthurine Lucy and George Wallace—that made history. Then I thought about Lily Leatherwood, because she and I were members of the same church and she won a gold medal—that made history—and then I thought about the baseball team, because that particular year they won the College World Series, and then, naturally, I thought about Paul Bryant. How many other coaches done what he done? And then I thought about the song, 'Stars Fell on Alabama,' because that is a beautiful memory, and then I thought about the elephant, the mascot, then I thought about Denny Chimes, and the year Willie Lewis was at the

University. At the bottom I put all the books because you can get anything and everything there [from books]."

In creating the *Martin Luther King Quilt* and the *Tribute to the Civil Righters of Alabama Quilt*, Mrs. Ezell referred to publications and photographs, but she also relied on intutition and imagination to find her way through the projects. Memories of the Movement helped inform her depictions, as well. In making the *Martin Luther King Quilt*, she said, "I had no pattern—everything is just my perception of how things looked. I just came up with it all as I went along."

Excited about the commission for the *Civil Rights* quilt, she said, "I have so many ideas, I could create a quilt that would stretch from Greene County to Birmingham, with my memories of the 1960s." She tried to include the people and events she knew, such as the depiction of Woodlawn High school and the border of names. "I put down the people that I actually knew who were civil rights people around here. There are others, but these are the people I knew." [Photograph, page 74]

Mrs. Ezell has been included in several publications and exhibitions that have focused on African-American quilts and styles, some broadly, some more narrowly. In discussing some of the theories put forward about quilts made by African-Americans, Mrs. Ezell responds emphatically that she is an *American* quilter and is not inspired by African textile styles and traditions. Her reaction is similar to doubts voiced by some quilt historians concerning assumptions made about African-American quilts (indeed, about any group of quilts that share a common aesthetic) that can amount to aesthetic stereotyping. Mrs. Ezell insists that her quilts be studied and appreciated as unique to her individual vision and circumstances.

In reading Nora Ezell's journal, I am struck by the extent to which it reads like diaries written a century and a half earlier. Like those earlier records, Nora's journal witnesses struggles with failing health, inclement weather, the state of the garden, the meaning of Grace and of God in her life. It also exposes the reader to Mrs. Ezell's self-doubts and struggles with her work, her dissatisfaction with the composition of a particular block, some appliqué, or the quilting on a particular quilt. The journal opens the door for us on one individual's creative process and the effort required to achieve the desired effect. However, success ultimately is hers. She is her own harshest critic, and before the quilt leaves her hands, it will be right. It will also have brought her joy. Standing in her home sharing her quilts with a visitor, she sums it all up, "I just love to do 'em. I could just do 'em and do 'em and do 'em." Nora Ezell, her quilts and her words—eloquent statements on life's truths.

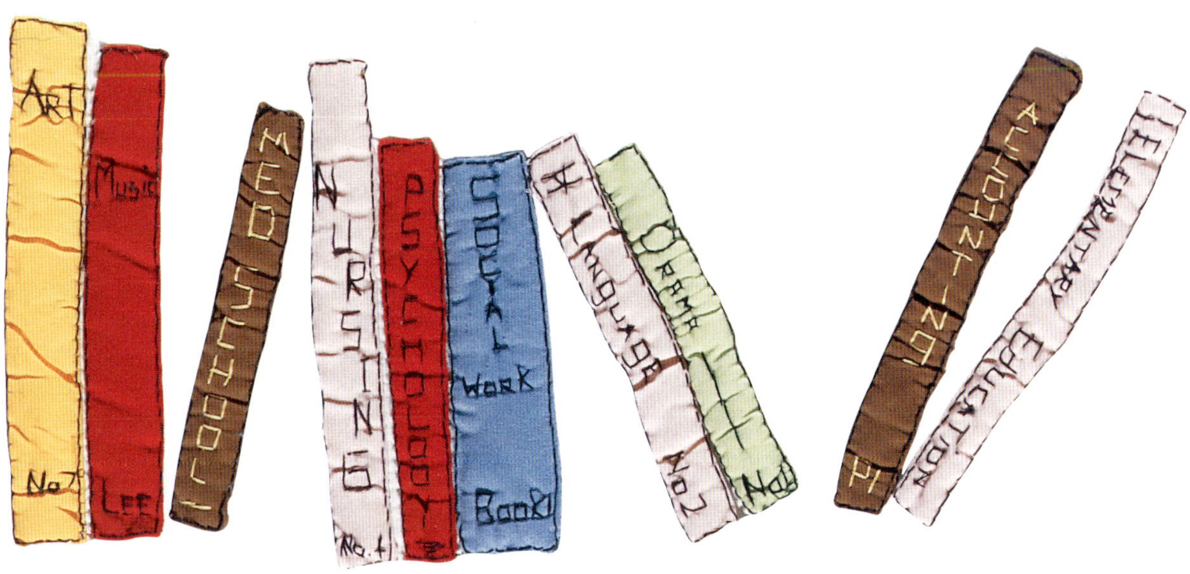

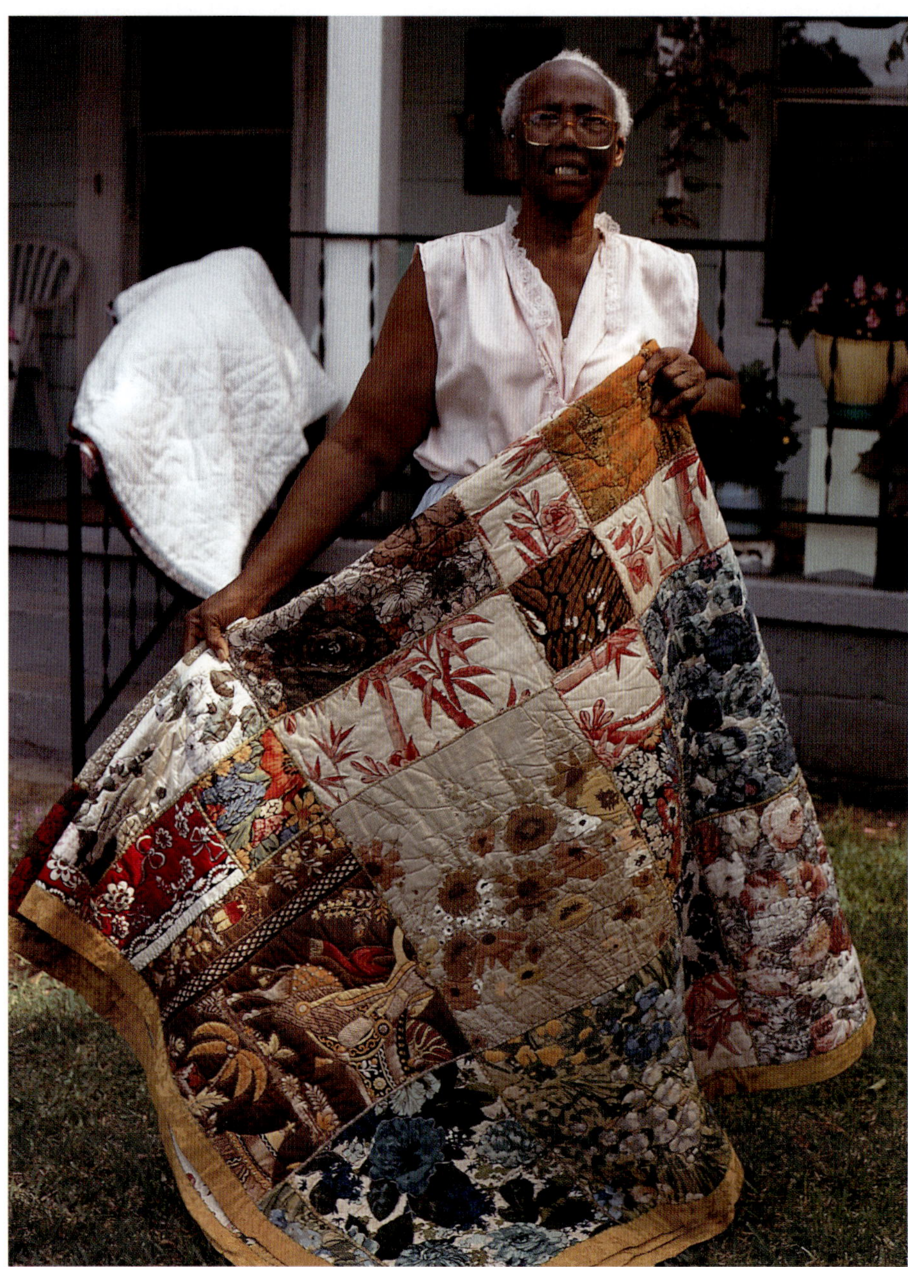

Mrs. Ezell holds a quilt made "before I learned how to quilt." This one is done in upholstery and drapery fabrics.
Photograph by Robert Cargo, 1994.

Collector's Note

Robert Cargo, Proprietor
Robert Cargo Folk Art Gallery

I have known Nora Ezell for some eighteen years now and have collected her quilts over that timespan. I consider Mrs. Ezell to be a friend, a great quiltmaker, one of a handful of truly original quilters who have actually contributed to the field. Certainly her picture quilts must be considered works of art. In her best work, Mrs. Ezell demonstrates a high degree of originality and inventiveness through the use of unorthodox materials—neckties, beads, discarded costume jewelry, feathers, upholstery fabrics, and such—combined with meticulous research and documentation prior to undertaking a major picture quilt.

Over the decade and a half that I have known her, she has presented to me for purchase an incredibly rich array of quilt types: quilts done in traditional patterns, picture quilts, "quilts I made before I learned how to quilt," a crazy quilt, a cathedral window quilt, a petal quilt, a biscuit quilt. While her best and most original works are, of course, the picture or story quilts, Mrs. Ezell does not shun traditional patchwork. Even within this category, the quiltmaker demonstrates an uncanny ability to look at a picture of a quilt and reproduce it with remarkable accuracy from patterns of her own making, or else she makes it with her own variations, which are even more delightful than the original.

Just the search for suitable fabrics, both in color and in pattern, for use in one of these "copies" would be a daunting task for most quiltmakers. But Mrs. Ezell, like all true artists with whom I am familiar,

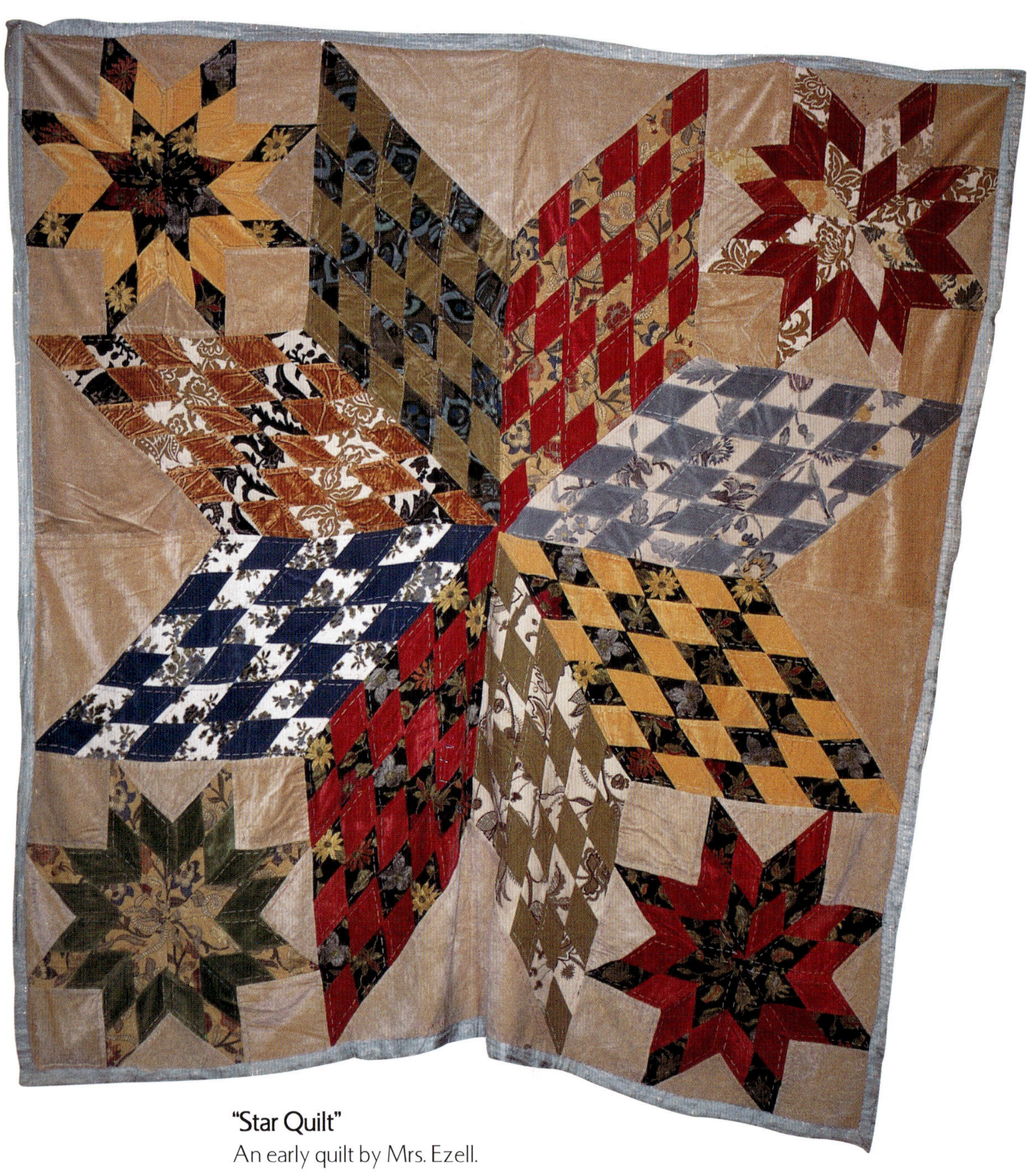

"Star Quilt"

An early quilt by Mrs. Ezell.

Photograph by Robert Cargo, 1994.

labors like one possessed. She goes about her work with determination and persistence, driven to create in spite of all odds.

On a personal note, Mrs. Ezell is outspoken, direct in stating strongly-held opinions. She demonstrates unswerving loyalty and devotion to her family. She works hard and tirelessly and seeks to convey her sense of pride in work well done to the young people whom she undertakes to train. She has no tolerance for what she considers inferior work, and is outspoken in her condemnation of it. Mrs. Ezell does not suffer fools gladly.

Rare is the folk artist who takes the quilt as a medium for artistic expression. There is an enormous difference in making a picture quilt and the production of a painting or sculpture. I know of no self-taught/folk/outsider artists working in other media who would be willing to invest the time necessary to do a picture quilt. It has been written that "African-American quiltmakers, such as Lillian Beattie, Yvonne Wells, and Clementine Hunter . . . have made exceptional contributions to the body of American quilt works."* I would submit that with her picture quilts, Mrs. Ezell deserves to be included in this group.

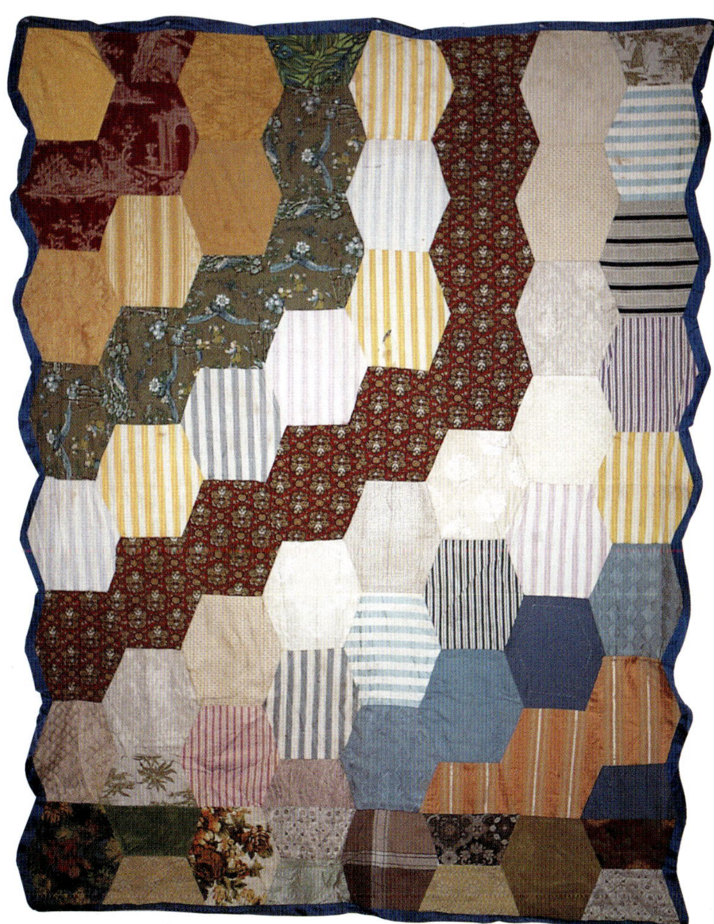

"Hexagon Quilt"
Another of the "quilts made before I learned how to quilt."
Photograph by Robert Cargo, 1994.

*Cuesta Benberry, *Quilter's Newsletter Magazine*, November 1991, no. 237, p.45.

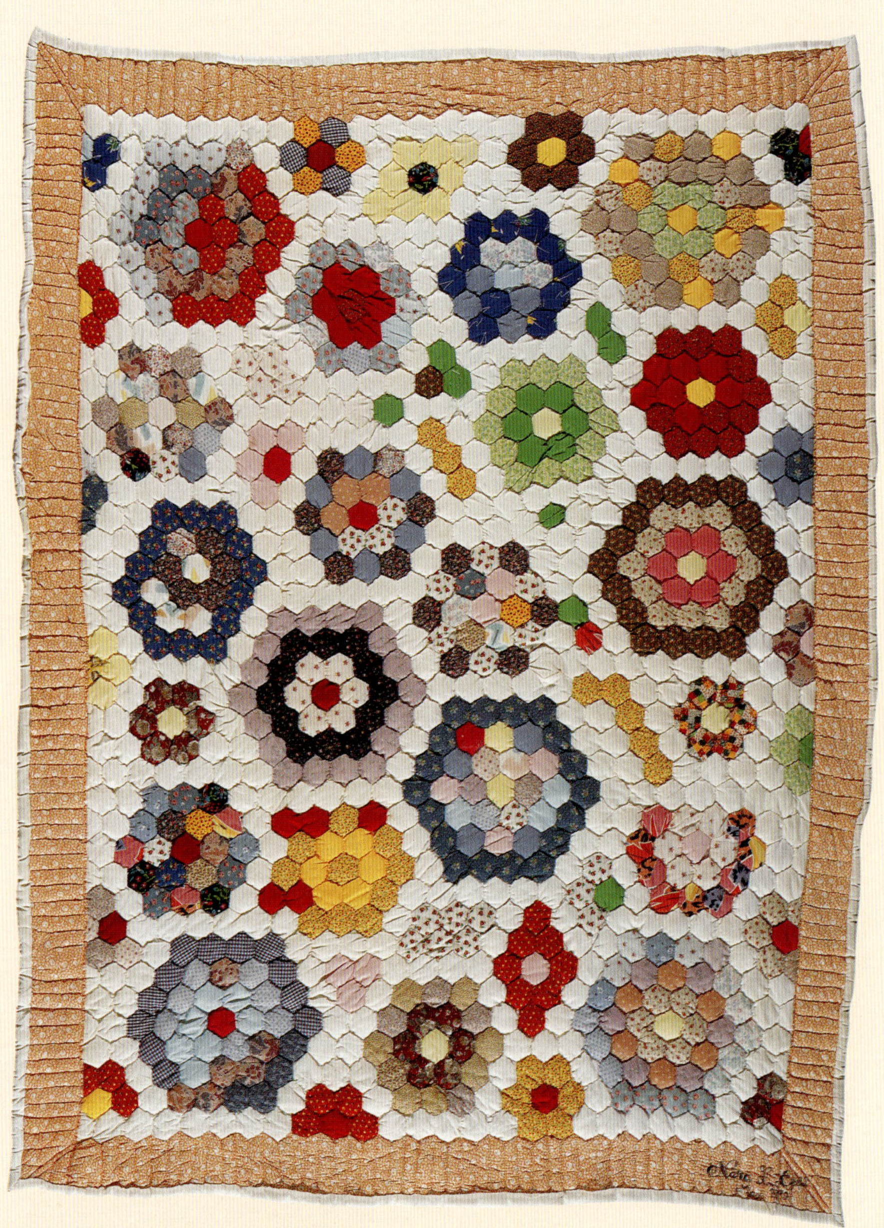

"Grandmother's Flower Garden"

Signed and dated Nora L. Ezell, May 1990. ["A real flower garden has flowers of all sizes, so mine does too," points out Mrs. Ezell.]

34.5 inches by 92 inches. Cotton and cotton/polyerster blend fabrics. Detail on opposite page. Collection of Henry Willett.

Introduction

Nora Lee Ezell
January 7, 1990

I, Nora Lee McKeown Ezell, made this book in my seventy-second year. I hope my family will always keep the original copy; I made all the quilts and took all the pictures. Some I still have and some I have sold. [In the original manuscript, Mrs. Ezell included instant color photographs, as well as black-and-white and color prints.]

I was born in a small town in Mississippi (Brooksville) on the 24th of June, 1917. The family moved to Birmingham, Alabama, in 1925. Later, after my father began work at the T.C.I. Steel Mills [Tennessee Coal & Iron, now United States Steel], we moved to Westfield, a suburb of Fairfield. I attended Westfield Elementary for eight years and Westfield High for two years. After getting married on May 26, 1936, I moved to Aliceville in May of 1938.

It was there that I became interested in quilts. After watching my Aunt Tony (Ethel Mack) do quilts, I decided I really wanted to learn. I had been around my mother piecing and quilting, but all she let me do was fan her while she made them.

My aunt had all kinds of quilt patterns. All the old ones. I guess it never came to her to do her own, but I'm a little bit jealous, and I wanted to do something no one else had done, so from the beginning I thought of "doing my own thing." (Sorry kids, I know how to say that too.) I wanted my quilts to be different. Eventually I wanted to do something no one else had done. Thus, even at that time, I wanted to make a quilt that no one else had made.

I would like to pause here and go back to my girlhood. First, I wish my mother and father could be with me to see some of my quilts. My mother worked so hard and did without so much to see about an education for us. My father worked and supported his big family without a "howdy-do" about being segregated or not. He went to the by-product plant (a portion of T.C.I.) and did his job. He must have been good, because he retired after 34 years, 10 months, and 16 days. Now after so many years I can look back and see and thank them so much for what they did for me, which I realize was the best they could.

When I first started quilting, I got fabric by selling boxes of candy for the "traveling salesman."

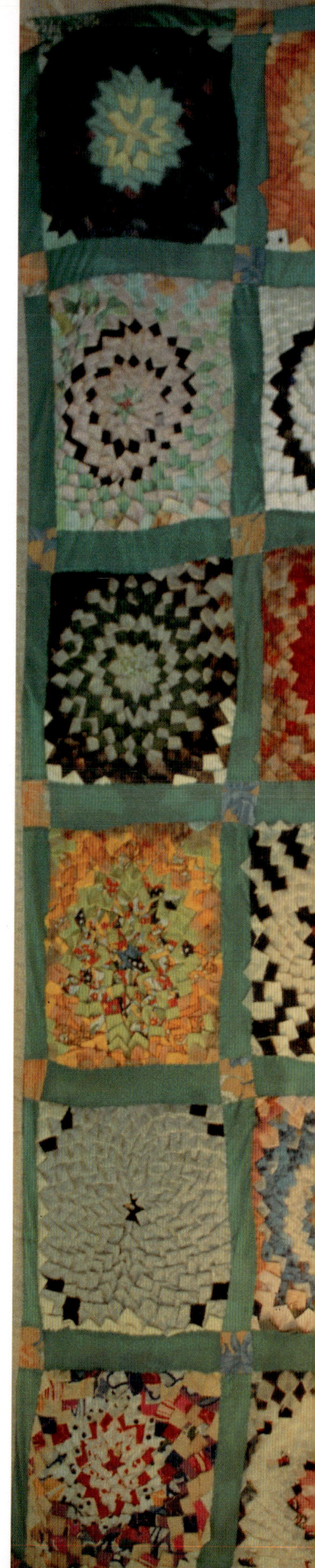

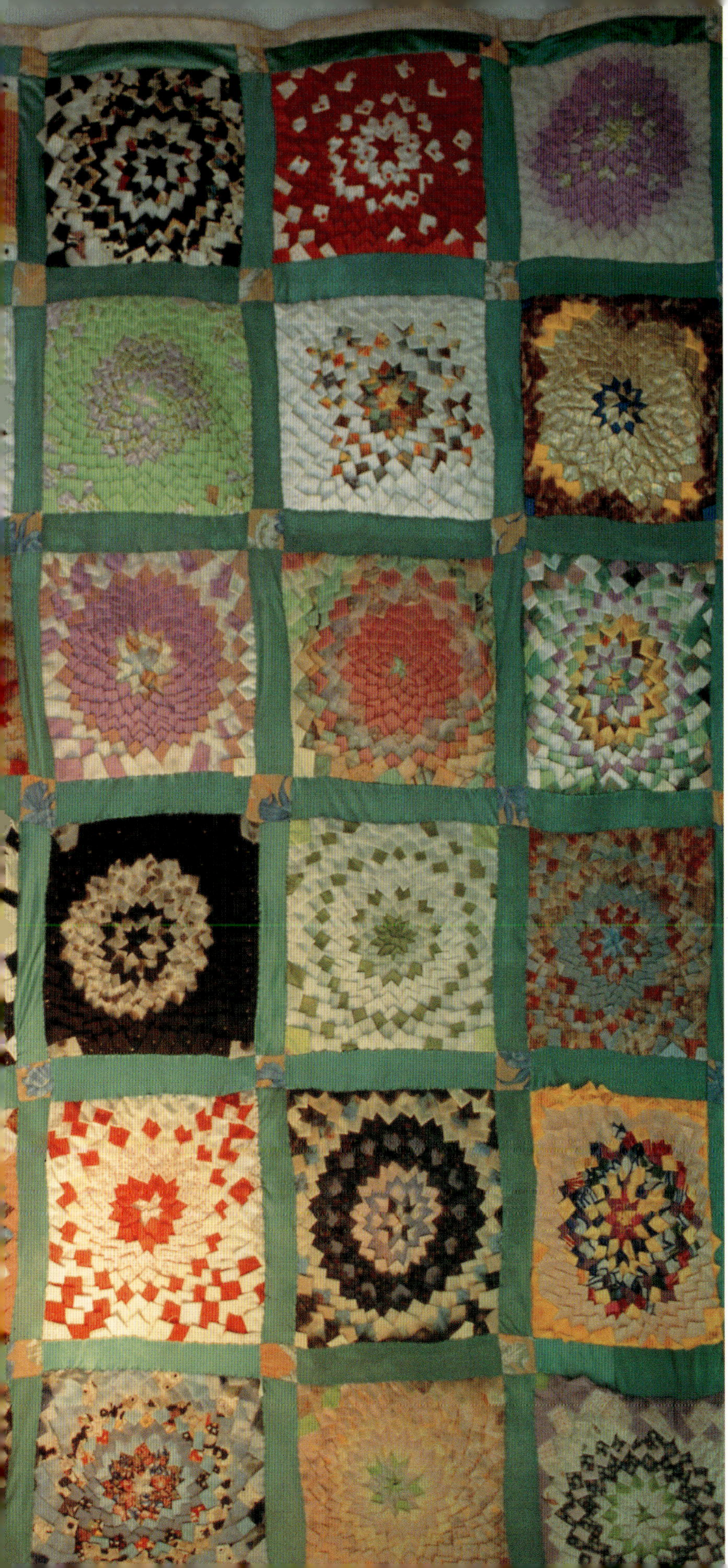

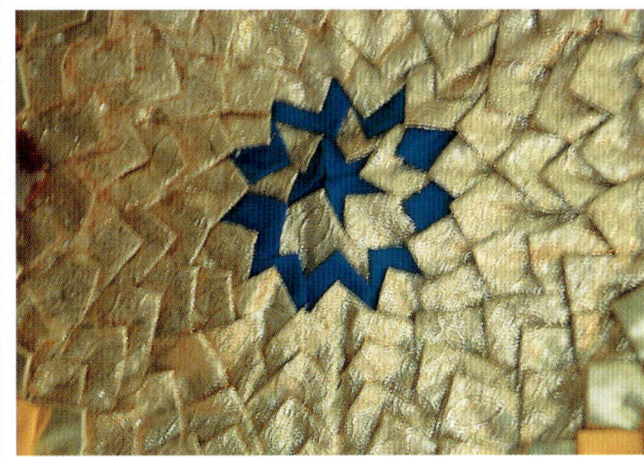

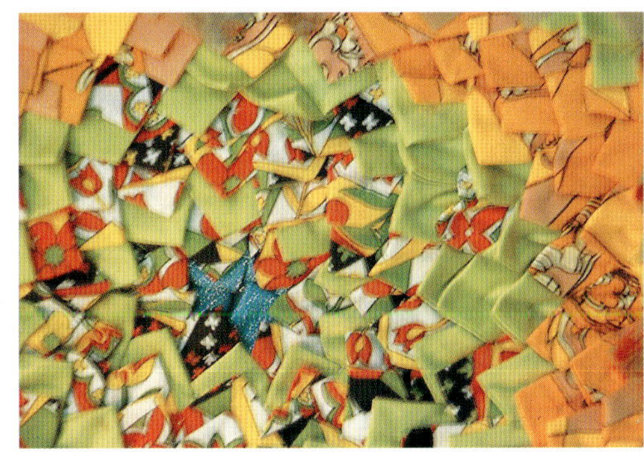

Once in a Lifetime, 1959.
The quilt is made from folded squares of fabric arranged in a circular design. It is very heavy. Details above.

From the collection of Robert and Helen Cargo. Photographs by Gail Trechsel.

Sometimes I would take the fifty cents I made on a box, but most times I would take cloth; we called it "yellow domestic," but now it is known as muslin. Sometimes I would take a scrap bundle. There were times when I split my money between Sears and National Bellas Hess. They had the best and prettiest bundles.

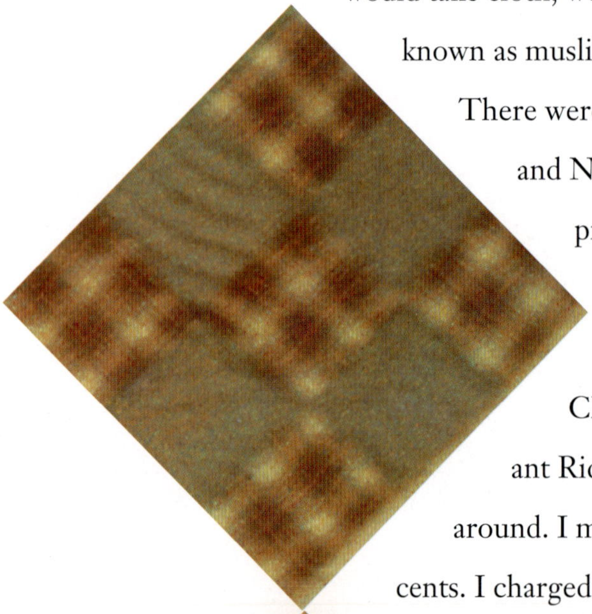

I sewed for everybody all over [Pickens] county—Vienna, up near Emory Chapel Church, Nolan Place and over the Ridge [Pleasant Ridge]. Then I styled everyone's hair for miles around. I made many dresses for twenty-five and fifty cents. I charged the same to style hair.

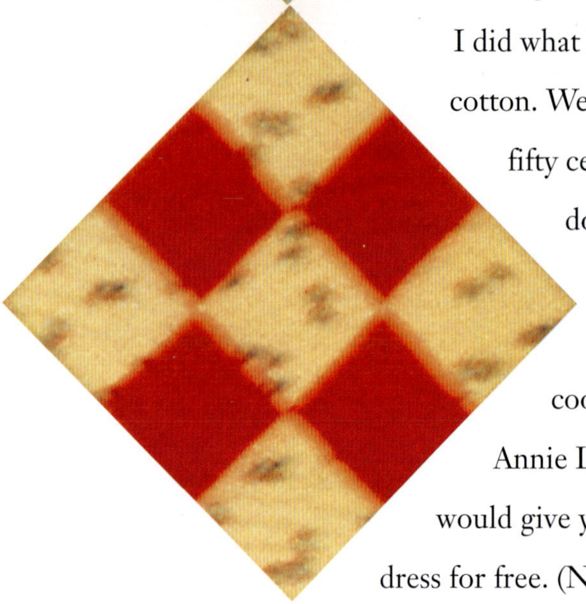

I did what I could in the field, chopping and picking cotton. We made only fifty cents per day chopping and fifty cents per hundred pounds picking cotton. That doesn't sound like much, but consider what we got for free: our rent, our doctor bill, some of our food, and all of our wood for heating and cooking. I remember the overseer's wife, Mrs. Annie Lee Mays, you could wash her dishes and she would give you and your family dinner and make you a dress for free. (Not mine because I could sew myself. But I would help her so she would give me quilt scraps.)

We got our cotton for batting by scrapping up the [leftover] cotton after [the owners] finished [picking] the field. At the gin, they took the seeds for ginning it. At Summerville's Gin, the guy that worked there would give me twice as much.

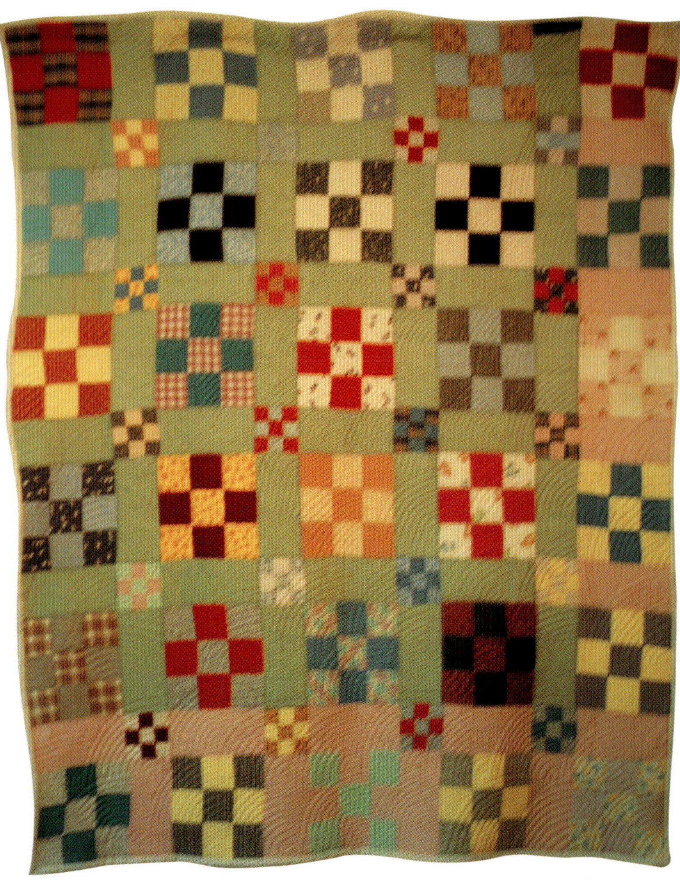

"Nine-Patch"
Ms. Ezell's great-grandson, Joey, asked her to make him a quilt like this when he was five years old. She doesn't take it to shows. She is saving it for Joey. It has "special quilting." Details on opposite page.

The Best Helper I Ever Had

My daughter, Annie Ruth, was born June 28, 1937. When she got older and I started doing quilts she would help me decide on colors. She taught me a lot about colors. She could see so straight, she would help me get seams and cut pieces very straight, which is very important in making a quilt. This I will discuss in another chapter.

Annie Ruth and I went to a fair in Greensboro, Alabama, and after looking at someone's version of the Alabama quilt, we decided "Bear Bryant" made history at the university, but not all of it. Several people played a part, so I came up with my idea of making my *University of Alabama* quilt, which was my first story quilt. Annie Ruth gave me the idea for doing the *Martin Luther King* quilt. Bless her heart, she never saw it finished. After fighting cancer for 2½ years, she died before I finished it.

I worked at Lloyd Noland Hospital about 15 years. On each section at Christmas, we would give each other gifts, so my daughter and I made a simple block quilt and put everyone's name on it. I gave it to my secret pal; I remember her name was Lorraine White. Everyone Ah'd and Oh'd over the quilt. The head nurse got little work out of the maids that day. Maids slipped off from the other sections to see it. I really enjoyed laughing and talking about how we made it. I wouldn't do anything as simple as that now, but I guess it started me on my way.

In 1959, I made a quilt called "Once in a Lifetime." [Photo on page 25.] I had been in the hospital, so I wasn't working, and I started this quilt. I still have it. I have been asked about selling it, but I keep it as a conversation piece at shows. I will talk more about it in another chapter.

I'm a Self-Taught Quilter

When I say I taught myself I mean I learned a lot of things by practicing. For instance, nobody told me what a difference the size of a needle and thread made. Nobody told me what colors to use, or if colors made a difference. Nobody told me to quilt this pattern a certain way. Nobody told me I could make a "Log Cabin" quilt look much prettier, or as if it was really logs, by quilting it in the ditches. By this I mean you quilt in the seam. Don't ever open the seam, as this weakens it; just push it to the side.

When I was in school, and my mother told me to do something, I always did what she told me, because you better ask the Savior to help you if you didn't! (smile) But I would always try to do this or that my own way. It was the same in school. I always did my maps in geography or my projects in science just the way I wanted. This has stuck with me down through the years. I sometimes say that maybe this is why I don't get a lot of followers. I have had some say my way is too hard or complicated, but most of the time I like what I do. Every so often I don't, but then it's usually the pattern I don't like. It's not the work! I'm a type of person that has to excel. I got to be up front, so I just keep coming up with something else on my own.

I would like to mention that in trying to do a good job, I will try something several ways, especially if it's a new pattern, to see which way I will get the best result. Most of the time I will go back to my original idea. I believe this is what has made our best quilters.

I remember how I would watch my oldest sister and her friend piece quilts and I would say to myself, "Someday I'm going to do that too." I remember some of the quilts they made are favorites now, like "Double Irish Chain," "A Basket of Flowers," "Double Wedding Ring," and "Fan," and of course, the "Lazy Woman's Quilt," and the "Nine Patch." I have never pieced some of these; they just don't appeal to me. I would if asked, but I must say again that I never do simple patterns and I don't like doing the same pattern over and over again.

I have quilts that I have gotten the pattern for from someone else; what I do is change the fabric, be sure I cut very straight on the wolf [woof] and warp of the material, and use a different color combination to get just the effect I want. I have some people tell me, when they see mine, that it is not the same pattern I got from them. I have been told that my color coordinations are so good. I like this because I know that we use quilts not only for coverlets, but several other ways—to cover a sofa in the family room, hang on the wall for a wall covering, use a certain pattern in a quilt for your kitchen table to get a country look ("Hole in the Barn Door," "Monkey Wrench," "Double Wedding Ring," "Coming Home," and the "Log Cabin" are just a few that can be used very well to get this idea across).

I like a good chair; it does not necessarily have to have a back, just so my seat is comfortable. Sometimes I sit on a stool. My mother used several pillows or cushions when she quilted. I like one, but not a lot. I try to sit as straight as possible and still be comfortable. I like a radio when I quilt or piece. You have to keep your mind on your work, so listening is good, and not looking.

When I make up a collection (which consists of twelve quilts) for a show, I never do more than one of each quilt. I have one or two I usually carry with me because they are good conversation pieces. I try to have at least six finished quilts, three or four complete tops, one, if possible, in the quilting frame. One I carry I will never finish or sell. It is a string quilt called "The Broken Stove Lid." [Photo on page 32.] The lining is feed sacks and the batting is brown cotton, so this is only for show. I like to show how far quilts have come. It is good to have all sizes on hand. There have been times when maybe I could have sold a king or queen if I had them. I try not to make too many though.

Setting A Price

Down through the years, I have made a lot of quilts, maybe two to three hundred; some I sold and some I gave away. Most of the best quilts I made I sold. The first quilt I sold, in Greene County, I got $85 for it, from a woman in Akron, Alabama. I kept [the money] and laughed about it for a year. I couldn't imagine getting paid that much for doing something I enjoyed so much. The name of the quilt was "American Centennial." Now I wouldn't make a "Nine Patch" for $85. I have one I made and quilted it in shells with finger rows. It was made from the scrap bag but I wouldn't take less than $495 for it. You have to think of all the work I put into it—about 250 hours to quilt.

Since 1982, the least I have ever been paid for a quilt is $125, and the most $1,500. That may sound like a lot, but I put 586 hours in the *Martin Luther King Quilt*. Some I can do fast, but on most of my originals I put in a lot of time and sometimes a lot of money. I will get to that later, but if you allow yourself only $3.00 per hour, and put 500 hours in the quilt, that is $1,500, right? Oh well, let's not get ahead of our story.

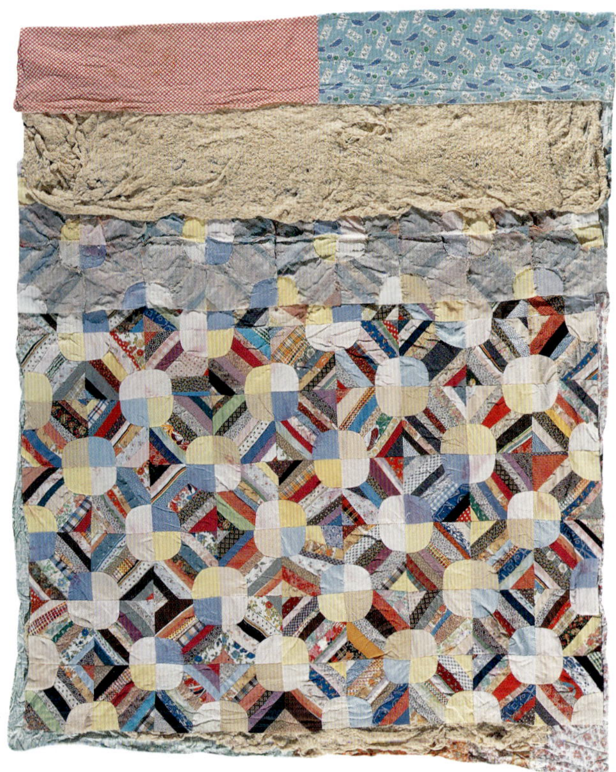

"Broken Stove Lid"
The top of this demonstration piece is folded back to reveal the brown cotton batting and the lining made from feed sacks.
Collection of the artist.

I have been told that my quilts have been all over the United States and some places in Europe. I've had friends who meet people from all over who know about my quilts. A very good friend, who is now dead, took my "Little Donkey" quilt to Israel, where she said it became a great favorite. I have sold six "Little Donkeys" in Israel and Europe, and every time I make one and take it to a show, it is one of the ones I will sell.

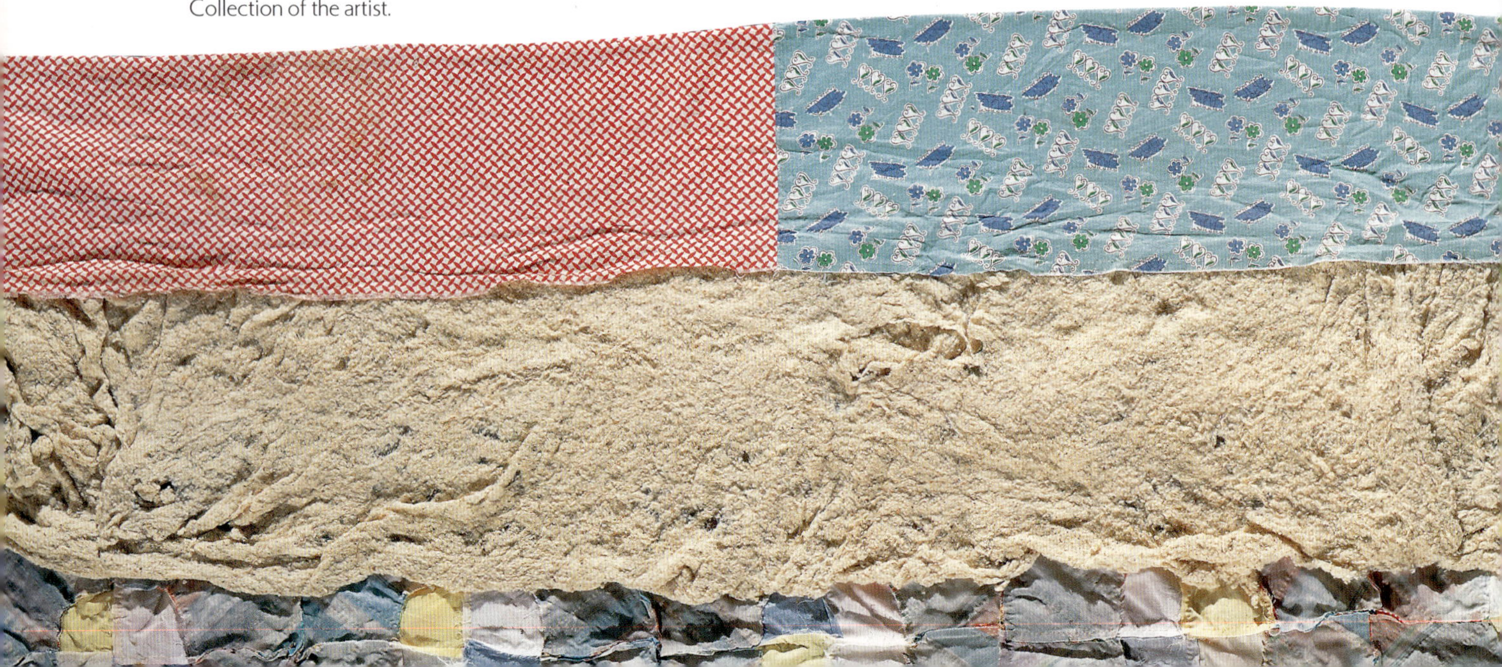

Some Thoughts on Finances and Fairs

In early 1989, I met a very wonderful lady who has certainly helped to change my work and life patterns. I don't mean my style of quilts and quilting, but little tips that would help me improve. In other words, some of her help and suggestions have made my work better. Her name is Gail Trechsel and she is with the Birmingham Museum of Art in Birmingham, Alabama.

One thing we discussed is that when you are invited, as a quilt artist, to come and help make a show a success, be sure to ask for a stipend before you promise to attend. As I live on a fixed income and most times at these shows or festivals I do not sell anything, I have to pay [my own] money for gas or transportation, buy a space to display, pay for electrical outlets (if needed), buy or rent a table and chairs, and lastly, buy or bring my own food. This is something that really should be considered!

I have just received an invitation to go to Moundville to help plan a fair for next year; that is not very far from where I live, but I do not have gas money. Now let me explain: if you are one of the ones that receive a grant from the Alabama State Council on the Arts (ASCA) you can sometimes go because they give you [money] to go with. But that is not always the case with me, as I sometimes need my grant money to buy supplies. I love quilts and I love to go to fairs and festivals to exchange ideas and talk with the other quilters, but I don't always have the means to go.

I'm so glad now that I work with the Alabama State Council on the Arts, because it has enabled me to buy a good camera that makes instant pictures and a 35mm camera that makes slides and a viewer that shows the slides. With the instant camera, if I see something at a show or festival that I like, I can get a picture. I also take a needle, thread, thimble, scissors and materials. Sometimes if I have time, I will make a block. One thing I always make a point of is to never copy anybody else's work ex-

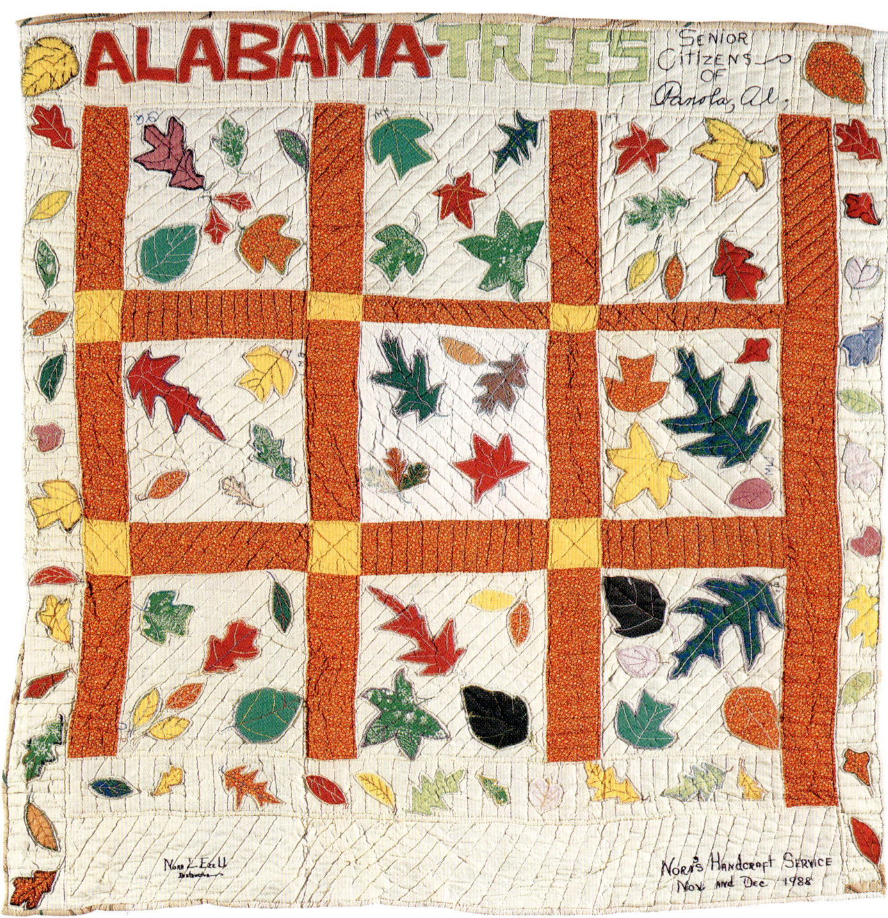

actly, because if they make a mistake, so will you. Most of the time I change it to a way I like; this way I put a little bit of me into it. I know all my ideas are not the best, but I find my notions and thoughts bring out the best in me.

Reflections on the Year Just Past

Winter is almost upon us, and cold weather drives me crazy: arthritis is going to take control. But I have learned, down through the years, to do whatever I feel up to. If I don't feel like quilting, I will sew or do something less taxing.

I live alone, so I'm lonely sometime. I'm also very nervous, so I never sit without doing something. I sew, knit, crochet, embroider, do crewel, macrame, petit-point, cross-stitch, needlepoint and, oh yes, I make lace with a hairpin. I do tatting, of course, most people don't know about that. Why am I so nervous? Because first, I'm old; I have worked very hard; I've chopped cotton all day with my oldest grandchild on my shoulders. (Because you didn't have a babysitter then, you just left your baby at the house nearest to your field. I could not stand for my baby to be dirty —

"Alabama Trees"

The quilt is inscribed, "Nora Ezell, Instructor, Nora's Handcraft Service, Nov. and Dec. 1988." Individual blocks are initialed: "E.H.," "M.H.L.," "O.R.," "L.M.B.," "M.L.J.," "J.I.D.," "N.L.E.," and "D.P.," the "Senior Citizens of Panola, Al."

79 inches by 81 inches. Cotton and cotton/polyester blend fabric, embroidery floss. Collection of Robert and Helen Cargo.

and that's what they would be when you were ready to take them home, so I just took my baby with me to the field.)

It has been a while since I tried to work on this book; it has been very cold and I have had all the great-grands for the holidays, so I have done nothing much but hollered "stop that" and "quit." Today is a rainy, cloudy day, but my granddaughter has men working setting up her trailer. I don't have a good feeling, but I am trying to get something done.

I must say that 1989 was some kind of year for me! It was not all good, nor was it all bad. I will just say I'm glad it's gone and I will not have to go through it again. I have done a few things that I'm very proud of and then there are some things I have done I will never, never do again. I'm sure I have said some things, too, that I'm sorry for and hope I've been forgiven for, and pray that they will not come up again.

I have made some very, very beautiful quilts this year. I am working on a "Grandmother's Flower Basket," king size, that I would not take less than $800 for. I'm also trying to finish quilting a very pretty sampler quilt. I have made some beautiful lace (tatting) for a sheet. I have been sick a lot, so I have not done as much work as I would have liked to.

A New Year (1990)

Well, this morning I'm witnessing a new year and decade. Yesterday was the last of 1989, a year I can look back on and see a lot of happiness I brought or made for a lot of people. I'm glad I made a little joy in the

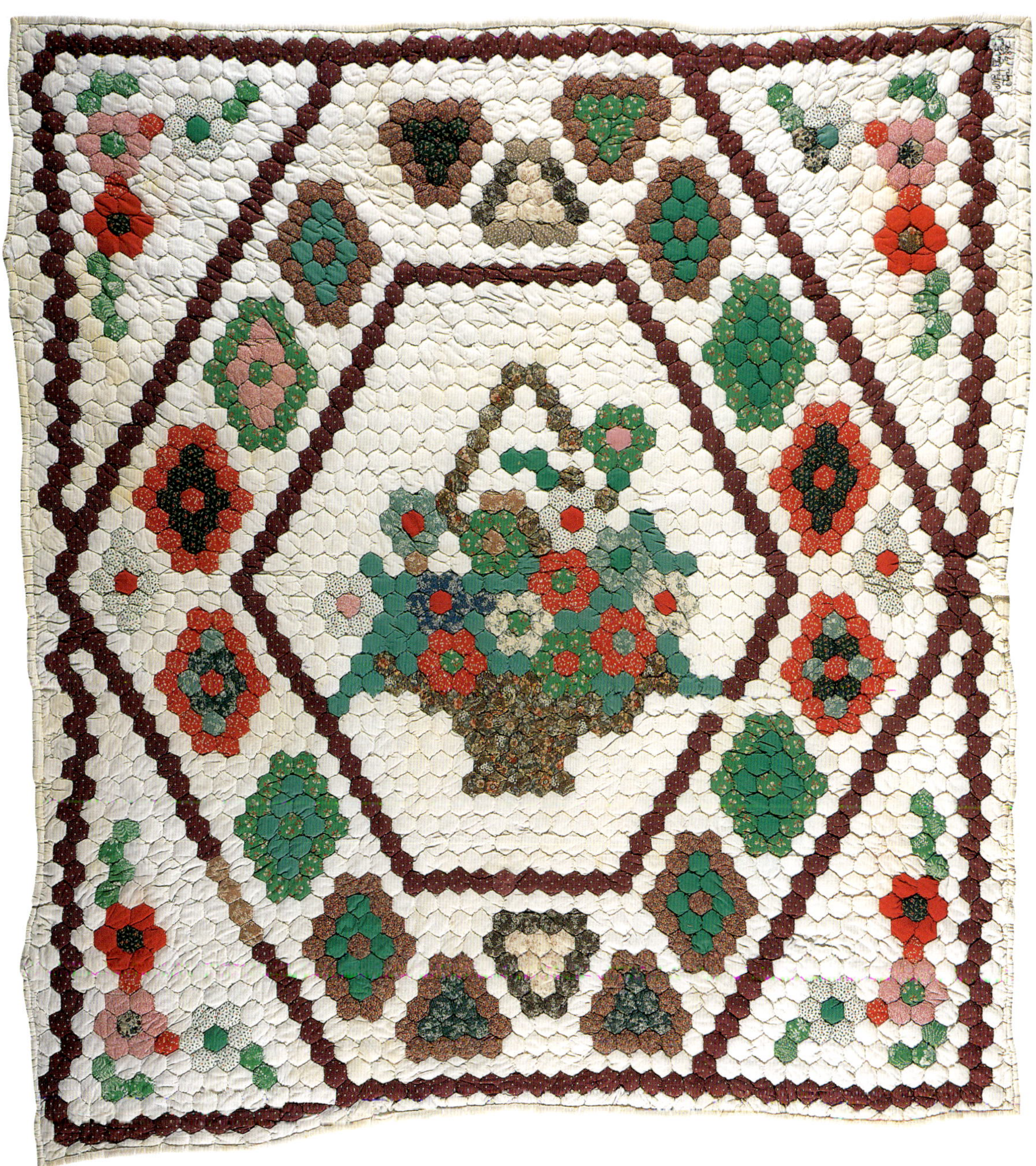

"Grandmother's Flower Basket," 1990.

Details on pages 30, 31 and 38. Collection of the artist.

world. I have done a lot of work this past year; I tried to teach a class, or better still, show some people what it means to do art with a needle and thread. Through the help of the Alabama State Council on the Arts' [apprenticeship] grant, I was able to do this. I didn't go as much as I would have liked to, but I'm happy to say a lot of my work made the rounds. The show that is touring the country from Williams College is still making the rounds. I wanted to go so much, but other things here just would not permit me to go. [The show was "Stitching Memories: African American Story Quilts."]

My plans this year are to go to more shows, even though I still have plans for one or two special quilts. I have decided to go to Birmingham, my hometown, for a show in March. I have an invitation for Dothan, Alabama, in February, and to go to Atlanta, Georgia, in September.

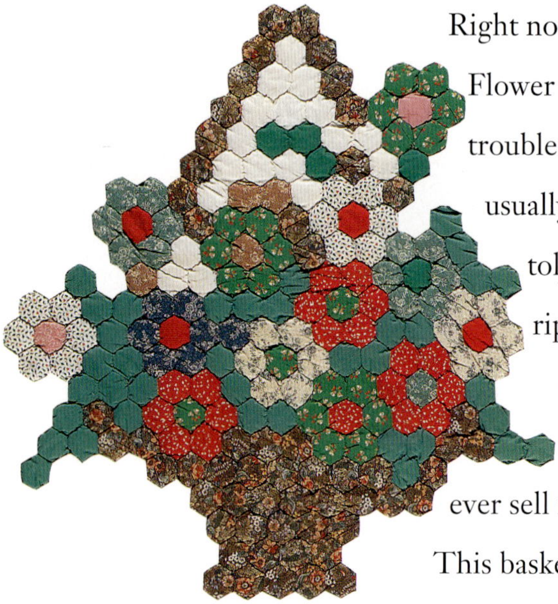

Right now, I'm still working on this "Grandmother's Flower Basket," which has given me no end of trouble. I only had a picture (to work from), which usually I can do, but getting a little older can take its toll on eyes, arms and quick senses. I think I have ripped more seams than I ever have, with the exception of a quilt I designed and made called "The Puzzle," but I finally finished it, and if I ever sell it I promise to keep the money forever (smile). This basket quilt is made by two-inch hexagons, which will be well over or between 1,500 and 2,500 pieces; I'm cataloguing this so I will know exactly when I'm finished. It is a very beautiful quilt and it is king size. This fall and winter I have made two kings and one queen size quilt. I don't do kings and queens quilts unless I'm asked, but I don't want to go to a show this year unless I have some.

Well, it is Sunday, January 7, 1990, and it's not like a few days, but more like some months, or maybe years have passed. I try to see what I have done with these 365¼ days; nothing much [of value] because I have done very little for the uplifting of the Kingdom! But sometimes I try so hard and it seems to me this is just what I should do; it is such a beautiful idea—I get started and all of a sudden everything is upside down. Tell me, Lord, "Is this the way it was with you?"

I know there is something different about my way of thinking; I can read a chapter or verse and I can see it as clear as a picture on one of the beautiful quilts that I make, although I don't always see anything materialized. I know men and women that do not live half as good a life as I do, but they can get the crowd to follow them—so I get back and I say, "What is this?" Oh, I wander off sometimes, I'm alone today. I have tried to do the best I could by example, but somehow that is not enough. I don't have much, but no one gave me this I have!

Quilting is not a hard thing to get into; it is catching, that I know. Once you get started, it's a thing that grows on you. It is such a joy and the one thing that I can do, I think, successfully, even though I have to do most of it alone. I have received a lot of invitations already this year and this is what I plan to do if I'm able. Oh Lord, do I need a new car!

I finally finished this "Grandmother's Flower Basket" (king size), a beautiful quilt. Now to get the quilting done. I have put together another sampler and have it ready to quilt too. I put 326 hours in the "Grandmother's Flower Basket"; it will take at least 200 or more hours to quilt. I shall catalogue it very carefully. I also have to figure the cost of materials. One thing about my sampler quilts, I don't put any money in them, except maybe batting and lining and sometimes I get that from the scrap bag.

I shall really pray for God to give me the strength and courage to get off my duff and do a few more constructive things this year, meaning for the religious side of life. I'm planning on getting something started Wednesday, January 11, 1990. Hope it pans out.

I have a notion to make a "Wedding Ring"; I don't have one. I also have plans for an upholstery material coverlet. This quilt or coverlet will be like making something from nothing. This upholstery material I salvaged from the furniture-making dump, so it costs nothing. We did it first out of necessity and now we do it for fun or profit. I'm sorry to say I am a shopkeeper, because I sell most of my quilts.

The most important thing is I have had a seven and one-half hour operation for cancer. Yes, over 20 years ago I lost a breast. But that does not stop me; I do anything I want to: get on top of my house and do whatever is needed, or under the house if I have a problem there. I've said these things to show you that if it is God's will and you are willing, He will take care of you — in Psalms Chapter 37 He said, "Trust in the Lord and do good and He will give you the things of thine heart," and I truly believe it.

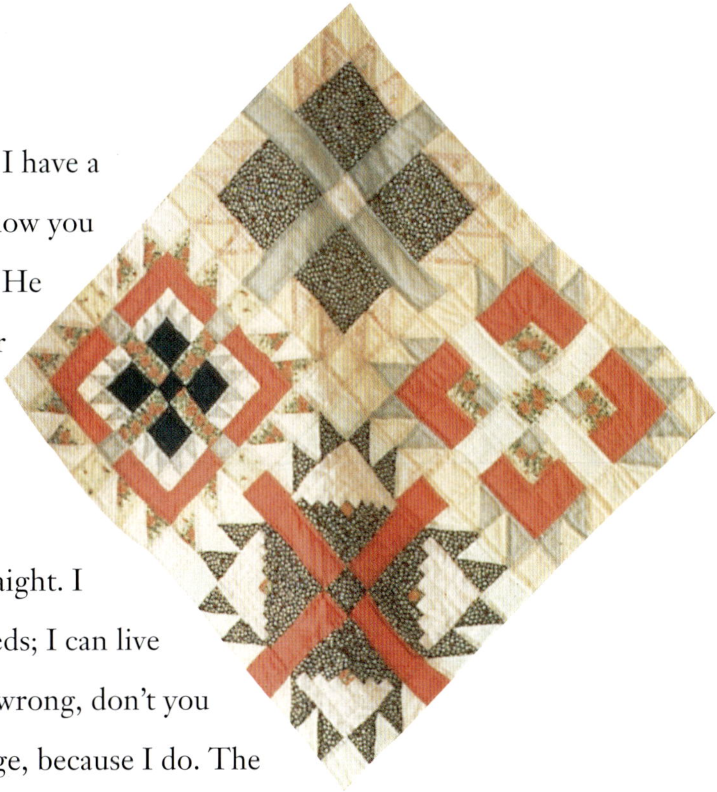

I'm so glad I've got my priorities straight. I can easily separate my wants from my needs; I can live in comfort on what I have. Don't get me wrong, don't you think for a minute that I don't want change, because I do. The point is learn to do with what you have and that's what quilts are all about. Taking nothing and making something out of it.

Thanks for All Who Have Helped Me

I'm very grateful to [Georgette] Norman, wherever she is today, for giving me The Alabama State Council on the Arts' address. She was the one who said my quilts needed to be seen outside Eutaw, Alabama. Thank God for the Alabama State Council on the Arts; because of them I'm able to do this. In doing this I can make someone happy for a day. If, at any time in my life, I could have thought for a moment that I would be in the position I am, I would not have believed it. When I used to watch, for hours, my oldest sister and her friend making quilts, I thought that I, too, would make them and do things with a needle and thread that I have seen done with pen and paint. Many thanks again to the people at the Council, especially Joey Brackner, who assured me when I was at a low tide.

My daughter, Annie Ruth Phillips, and my sweet granddaughter, Beverly J. Smith, as well as Ethel Mack—Aunt Tony—have all helped me get to this place, as you will hear. Dr. Robert Cargo has supported me from the beginning by buying my quilts. I am grateful to Ramona Lampell. I would also like to thank *all* the people who have bought quilts from me.

I can't think of too much more to talk about in the making of myself into what a lot of folks say is a good quilter, among the best in the Southeast. Maybe somewhere along the way I said a little something that interests you. If so, I'm very glad. If you would like to personally contact me on some point, please feel free to do so through my publisher. They will forward your letters and calls to me free of charge (smile).

"Dresden Plate/Bear's Paw Sampler"
Signed "N. Ezell, Nov. 1983."
Detail on page 41. Collection of Robert and Helen Cargo.

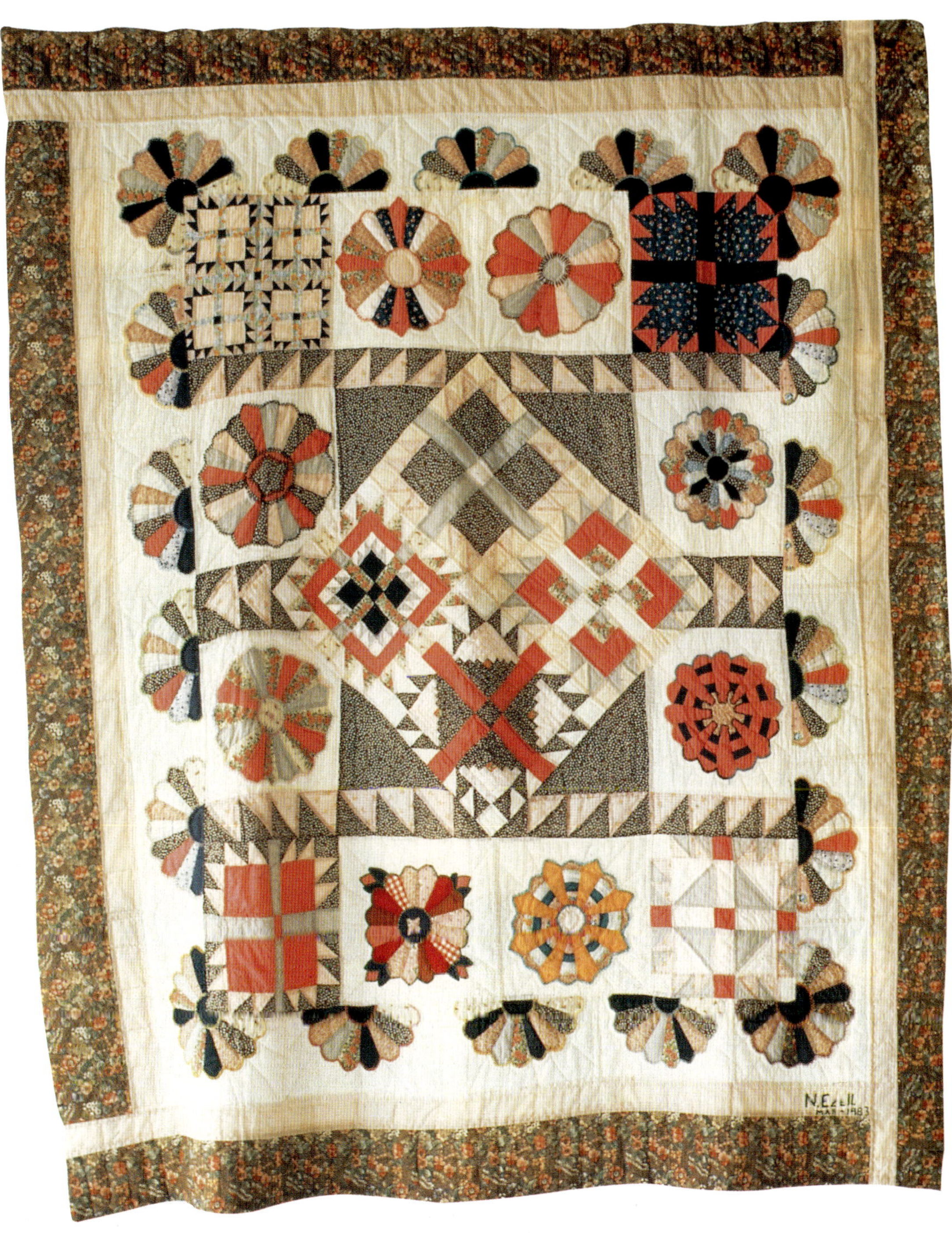
N.EZELL

Part One

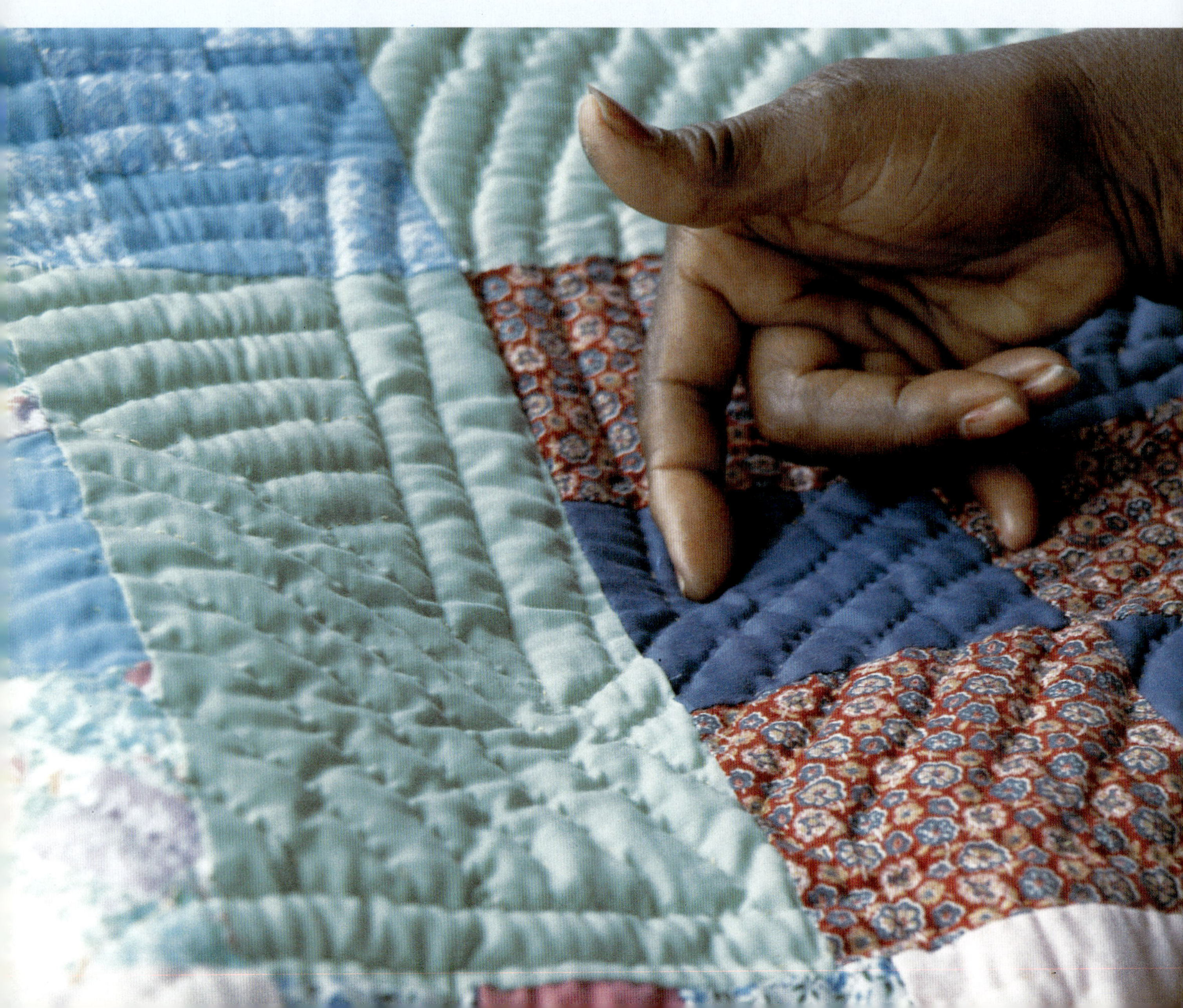

The How-To of My Craft

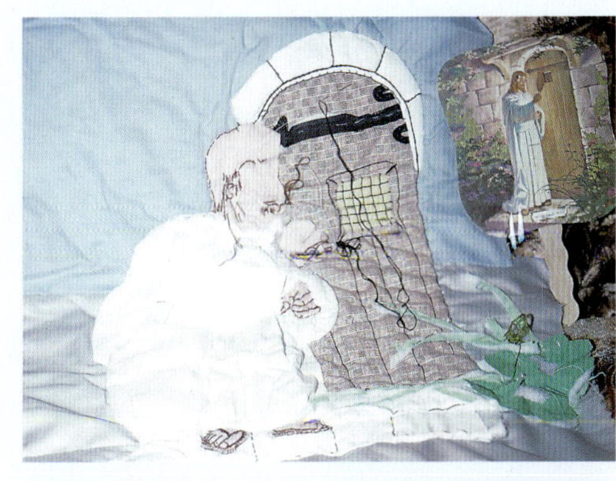

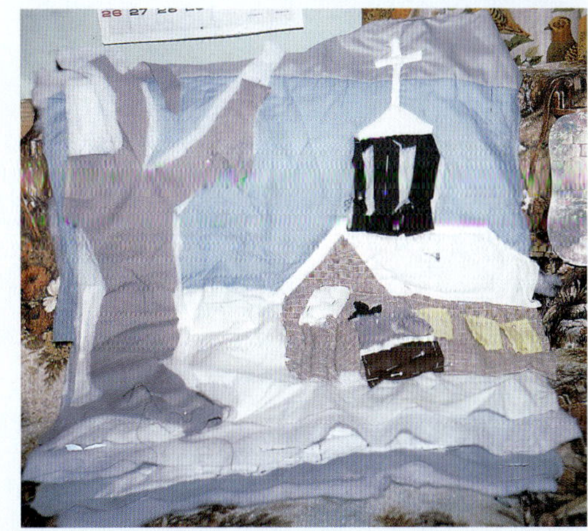

I Taught Myself

I have been asked many times who taught me, or did I go to a class, or did my mother teach me? None of these things; I say I taught myself. I had Home Economics at school; it was there I learned to sew. We did so much on the machine and so much by hand. This was on a treadle machine that you operated with your feet. In my last school year, we had electric machines.

I do not do quilts on the machine; I think it takes a very, very good quilter to do this. I have seen some that I would not have carried out of my house. You have to be able to alter your stitch, needle and thread to your fabric. You have to choose patterns and fabric that you can work with. I find that cotton is best to quilt with when working with your hands.

Creating both traditional and original design quilts, I work hard to tell a story with needle and thread. Sometimes I use photographs, pictures, and sometimes just what people tell me they want.

The hardest thing I know is to try to find a market for your quilts, especially if you try to do something no one has done. Although the Alabama State Council on the Arts has done wonders in getting my name and works out to others, the hardest job still is to sell. I must say also, thank God for Dr. Robert Cargo, who believes in me and buys my quilts.

I find that in creating or making a pretty quilt, you have to do like other artists: search constantly for materials and patterns, and have a

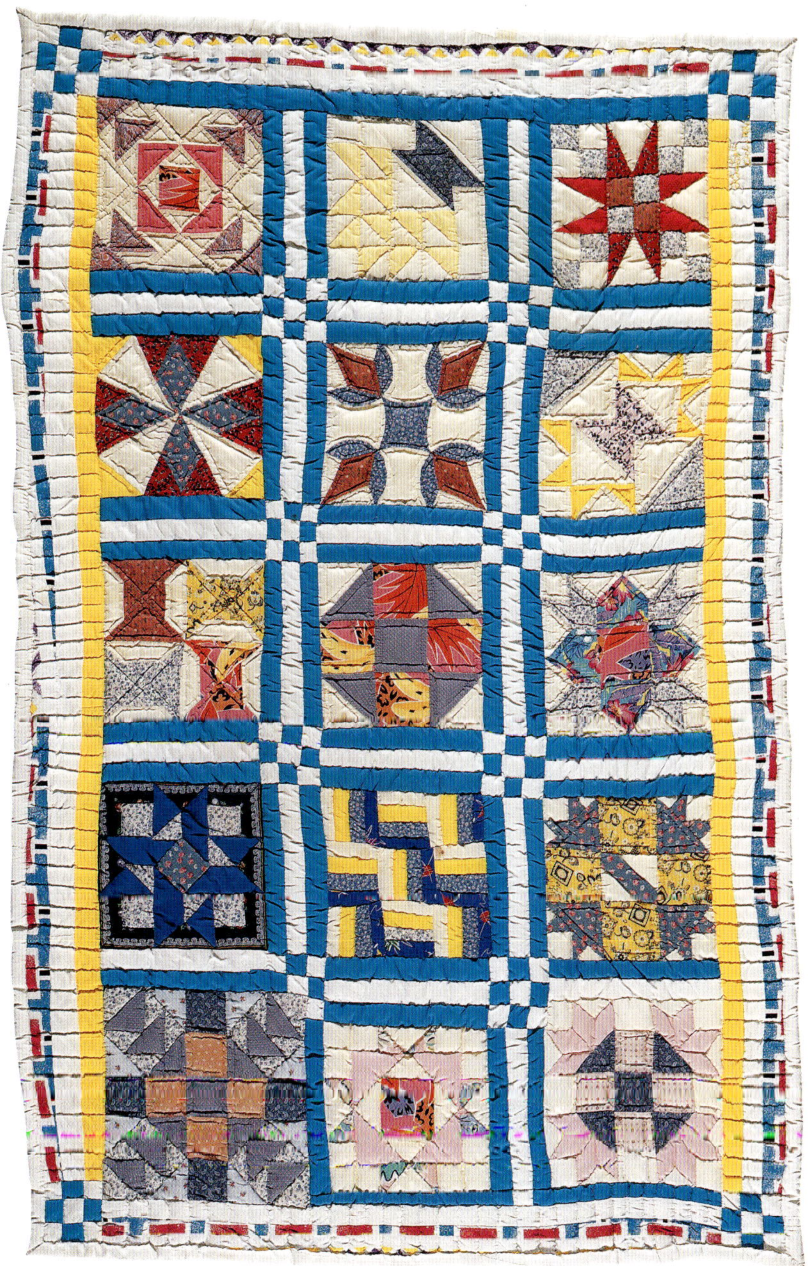

"Sampler Quilt #1"

Cottons, cotton/polyester blends. Signed "Nora Ezell, Oct. 1986." 57 inches by 86 .5 inches. Collection of Anne Kimzey.

creative flair. I work with this in mind. I also remember things I hear other people say or do, but I try hard not to do what they do. Copying was bad in school and it could be disastrous in your quilts.

Talking about teaching yourself, you have to know yourself when you have something no one else has, because you have no one to tell you when you do. I know when I have a buyer, I'm very satisfied with what I have done. Whatever I do, in my yard, in my house, or with my quilts, I have to satisfy me; I am my own worst critic. Maybe this is why I have no takers [as private students] — I'm a hard task master. I get that from my mother. She always said we could make an "A" as easy as a "B."

I like a quiet place to work, where there are no interruptions; I despise telephone calls when I work, because I lose my ideas and concentration. That's why I like my house and little shop to work in.

I didn't, as I look back now, find it hard to teach myself. I always knew what I wanted to do, and as a rule, it's not hard to teach me. I have a bad habit of talking to myself, and yes, answering myself back too.

I keep in mind all tips, points, and yes, God, mistakes, and this I think helps me a lot.

Tools Of The Trade

What, you might ask, what does it take to make a quilt?

First: you must have *a good clean mind.* (I might add a creative one!) You must be able to see beauty in what you do. You must be able to get

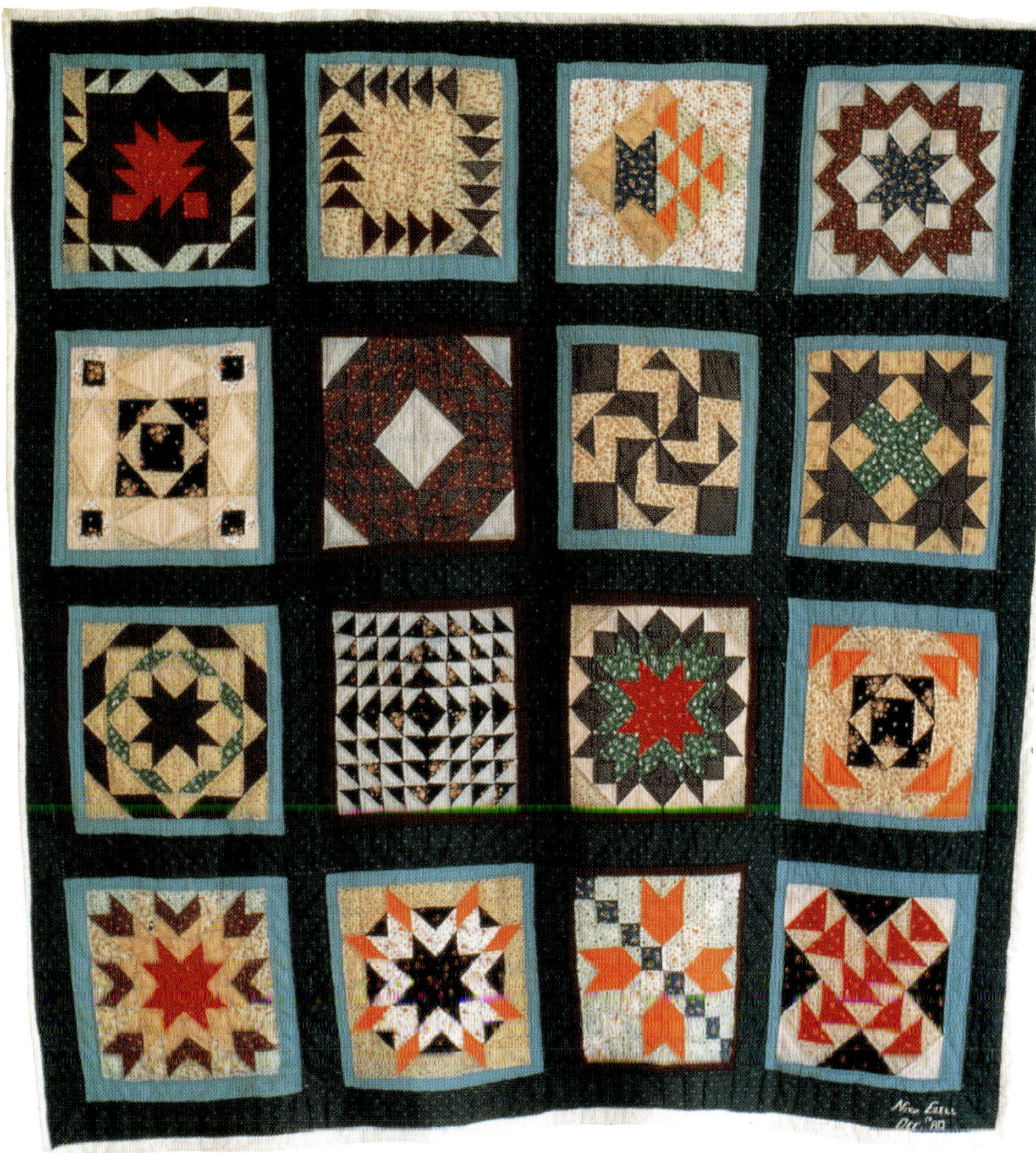

"Sampler Quilt #2"

Photograph by Joey Brackner, at the Birmingham Library Show, March 1990. Details on pages 50-51.

something from doing a good job.

Second: *Scissors*, at least four pair. You may ask, why so many? You need a good pair of dressmaker's scissors, the big, heavy kind, to cut a lot of pieces at one time or maybe very heavy material. Yes, you can use heavy material for some quilts, not all.

You will need a good pair of embroidery scissors, the small type with a keen point for clipping small notches or trimming seams. Be sure to keep these good and sharp.

A point I would like to make here is that you should always go to a good scissors sharpener. Don't try filing them yourself. I have seen my aunt (Aunt Tony) hold the kerosene lamp with her left hand and cut around the holder with the scissors and do a good job sharpening hers. But try as hard as I please, I could never do it. I have seen my Dad do it with a small file, but if you want to ruin your scissors, try this and that's what you will do.

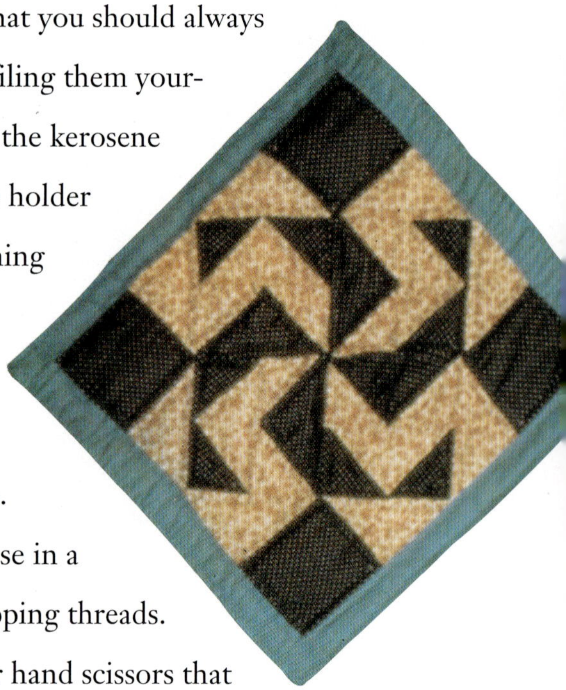

Buy yourself a pair of snips like they use in a sewing factory. They are wonderful for clipping threads.

The last pair should be a small regular hand scissors that you can hold on your lap, for cutting things close to your work.

Third: *Thread*—you might think any type will do, but I have found that this is not so. The worst type I know is machine thread, the sizes of

50, 60, or larger. It is not strong enough and it tangles too bad. Pulling it through the fabric so many times makes it unravel and split. I would never recommend it for hand sewing quilts. Likewise with heavy thread, even though when I first started, sack ravels was what I used. I must say that nobody knows the trouble I have seen with them. I'm so glad time changed all of that.

Use a good hand-quilting thread. Now I know this is expensive, about $1.40 a spool, but it pays off in neatness and good workmanship. At one time I used what we called ball thread, which worked pretty good; it was coated with something to make it easier to handle and not ravel up. You can hardly find this now. Sometime you will run across some spools at a small country store.

J & P Coats, A & E Mills, Inc., and American Thread Company make the best thread, I think, for quilting. There are, I'm sure, others, but these are what I use. I use this for piecing and quilting. Sometimes for some quilts I use number eight (8), which is good and strong and not as heavy as it used to be. I find that it is hard to find a store that carries it.

I use mostly white or off white for quilting, but sometimes on certain quilts, I use colored threads. Black thread in quilts is a NO-NO. If you want to go blind, use black thread! A pale pink works good and looks good in quilting. Lemon yellow, I have found, works well also. You can use other colors if you like, but what I'm trying to say is what works for me.

Fourth: *Yard stick (36")*, and *a foot (12") ruler*, *tape measure*, and if possible, a *see-thru dressmaker gauge*, *90-degree right angle*, and *a small (6") ruler*. These are not expensive and they are so much help. Now I must say that these things are for the person that does as I do, designs and drafts her own patterns. This is, of course, the quilter that does original quilts. Keep your rulers very clean; try not to use them for any other work.

Fifth: *Tacks and hammer*. Whatever for? Years ago they were used when we put a quilt in the frame, down on the floor, wiping it in with a big stick all the way around. This is when we used long poles and lifted them up to sitting level, resting the corners where the poles crossed on chair backs. Now I use a small square wood frame that my husband made for me, so that's why I use tacks and a hammer. I like upholstery tacks, as they are very sharp and leave a very small hole and no stain. I keep my hammer hid, because I don't want to use it for anything else but quilting. I keep it very clean. I use a very light hammer for this. I'll talk more about this in another chapter.

Sixth: A *good sewing machine*. I like a heavy duty machine because it sews all fabrics, and I only have to change the needle. Get one that has easy adjustment to the stitch length. A lot of quilters are doing quilts on the machine, but not me. I still like the good right hand, but I use the machine to sew on borders and bindings and to seam up fabric pieces to use on the backs of my quilts.

Seventh: *All of these come in handy when doing quilts:* paper, pens, plastic bags (save your stocking bags), good pieces of cardboard (save your boxes).

A Few Rules to Work By

Don't try to be perfect, just do a good job. Cut your fabric straight, sew your seams good and tight, but not too tight. Match your seams and corners; crooked seams look bad, and nothing looks worse than crooked quilting, and please, pretty please with sugar on it, DO NOT MAKE LONG STITCHES! Don't use a big needle nor big thread.

Measure! Always measure and mark your lines when quilting. If you use a light pencil this will fade out as you quilt. Never use a ball-point pen or a No. 2 black lead pencil. These will not come out and it will make your work look tacky.

Only make about 10 or 12 stitches to each inch. This takes time at first, but if you practice this, you will find it comes easier each time you sew. Never use a needle larger than size seven (7) for hand sewing, or size three (3) for hand quilting. Don't despair, you can use these if you try, and you will find the shorter the needle, the smaller your stitches will be. Just practice this. I'm sure it will work for you.

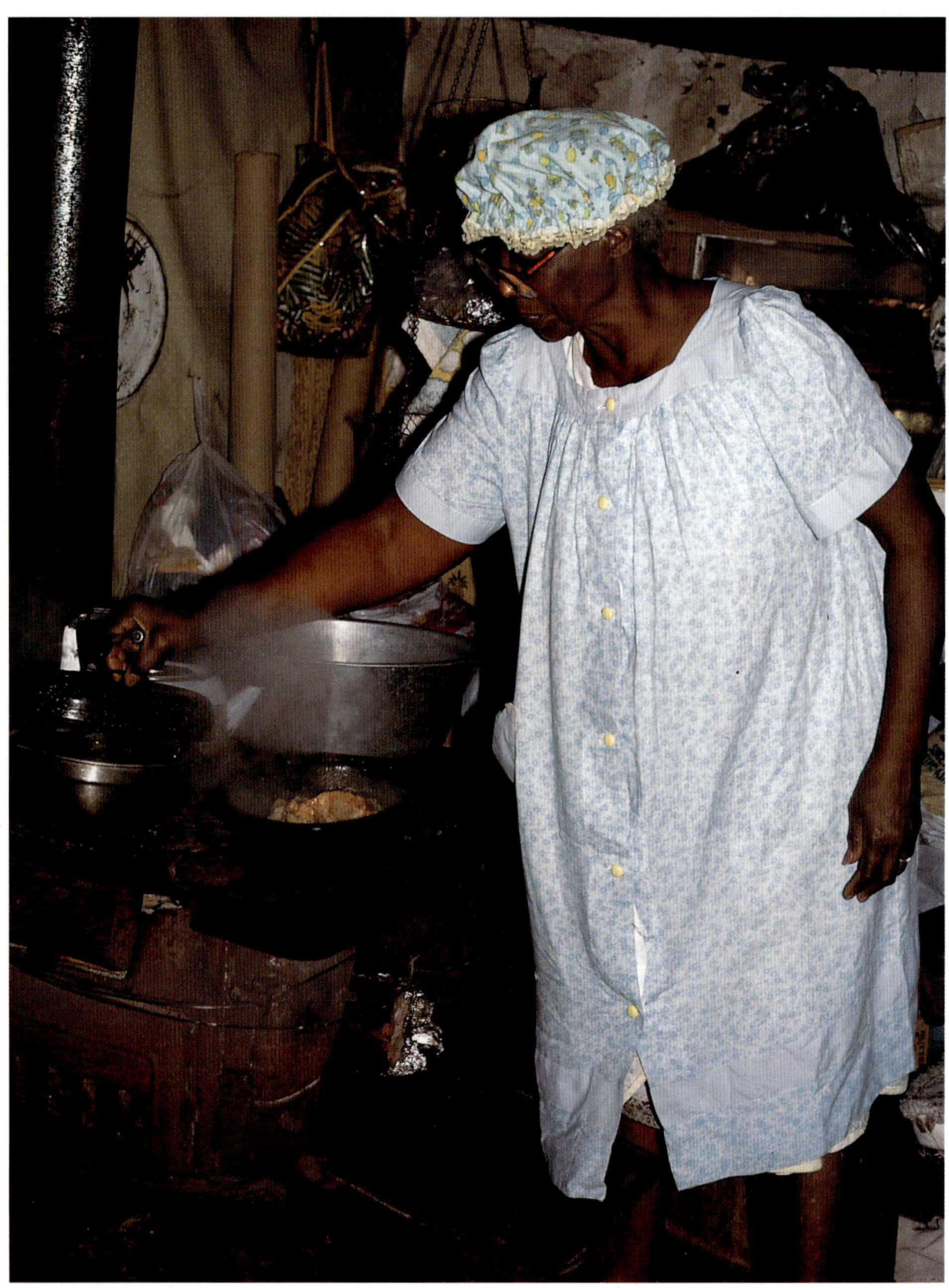

Mrs. Ezell cooks lunch on the woodstove in her "shop" for a guest.
Photo by Robert Cargo, 1988.

My Work Place

Anywhere in my house except the kitchen is my work place. If you work in the kitchen, you will come up with grease spots, water spots, and if you drink it, coffee spots.

I have a little one-room building behind my house that I call my "shop." I have an old wood cookstove, with the four eyes for cooking and a bake oven at the bottom. It heats the building. I also have a radio, television, clock and fan in this building. I have an old treadle sewing machine. Because treadle machines are so easy to handle, I use it when I try out new things: that way, I can be in complete control. I also have a dressmaker electric machine, but I can work buttonholes on my treadle machine.

I have all sizes and lengths of scissors. I have all kinds of materials. Some days I experiment with new patterns and ideas. I like this work place, as I can cook while I work without having to run back and forth. I do not have a telephone for the simple reason that I don't like being disturbed when I work. Usually I lose my place or needle, thimble or scissors, so I don't have a phone in the shop.

My other favorite place is the family room: I use it on cold or rainy days. I like this room for the same reason I like the shop; I can get up and leave everything. I have everything you can imagine. I buy all kinds of sewing and handicraft items when I'm out shopping. I have things I have had for years.

How I Choose My Fabric

What types do I use? Whatever suits my fancy. I have made quilts from old clothes, especially overalls, cotton sacks, feed sacks, fertilizer sacks, old draperies, upholstery scraps, acrylic, wool scraps, silks, satins, organza, cottons, cotton blends, knits (both single and double), velvet, velveteen, fleece, and sheath lining, just to name a few.

I like 100 percent cotton, but it is expensive. One of the reasons I like to work with 100 percent cotton is that it is very soft but strong. It works so well. It also quilts well, and looks very pretty when finished. I must say the only time I use it is when I'm doing special orders, as it is always expensive and since I live on a fixed income, so I only have so much to put into my playthings (quilts).

I also like mixed blends, you know, like poly cottons. The only problem is they are prone to ravel. This is bad for some patterns that might have curved edges.

You can make a quilt from anything, because I know in the beginning that's what we did. Now there are so many beautiful fabrics. My suggestion is to keep your pattern in mind. Use fabric and colors that will give a little something to your quilt. I have a bag of beautiful fabric, some type of rayon, but pretty, in very strong colors. I'm toying with the idea of a "Stain Glass Window," or maybe a "Spool" from the scraps.

I use whatever I get, and believe me, I get a lot. Even at flea markets.

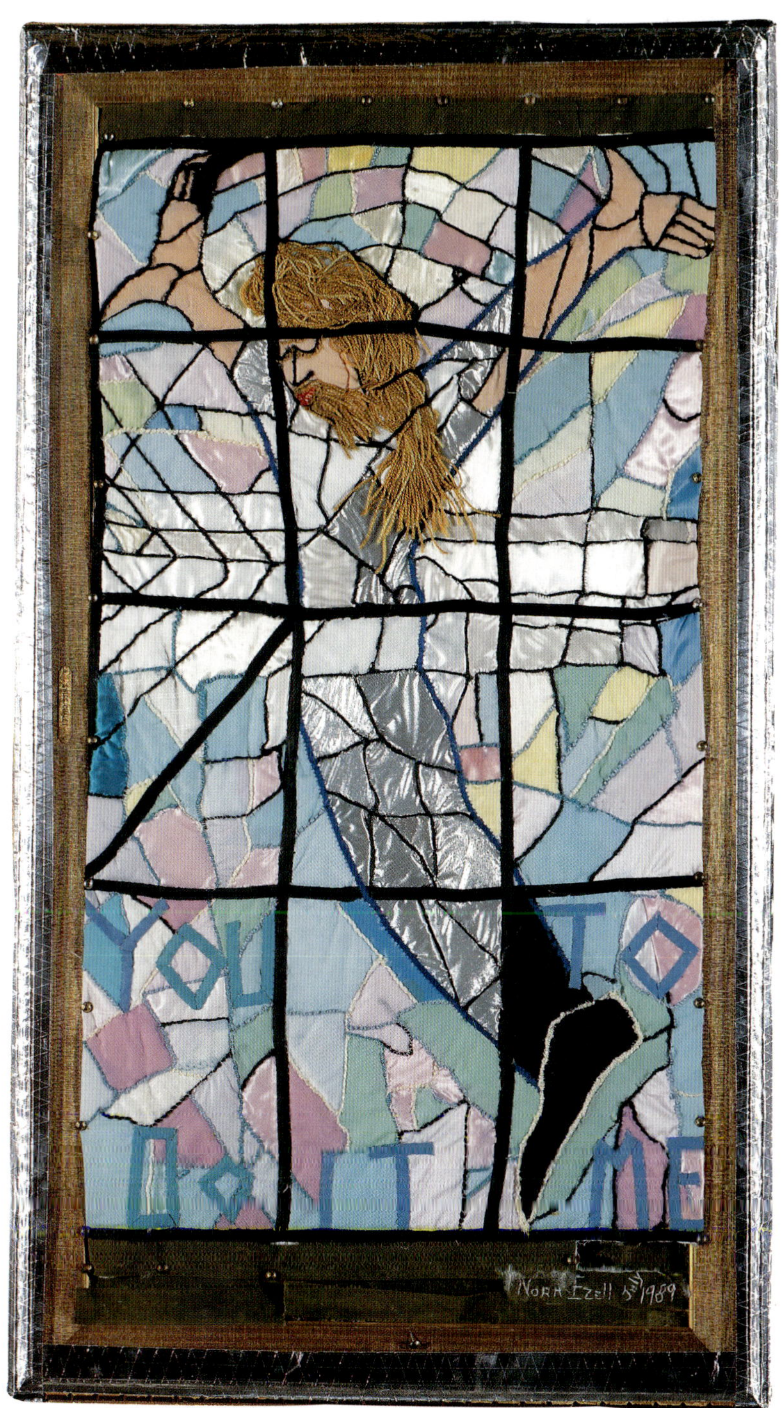

You Do It To Me

Signed "Nora Ezell, July 1989."

235 inches by 46 inches. Worked in the "stained glass" technique of patchwork and appliqué, using rayon, satin and other synthetic fabrics. This quilt is a close adaptation of the stained glass window given by the people of Wales to the Sixteenth Street Baptist Church in Birmingham after the 1963 bombing in which four children were killed. Gift of the artist to the Alabama State Council on the Arts, 1995.

I love this work and the life I'm living right now!!!!

I shall try this year to do something very special with the last of my upholstery fabric, because I can't get any more.

Making Blocks

How many times have I been asked what is the secret of making a pretty quilt? First, do a pretty block, square, row, or whatever you are going to make. Well, you might say, what makes a pretty block?

You can make a quilt about anything or anyone. I like houses, churches, pictures of plants or buildings. I try to use colors that express what I'm trying to make, and I always choose colors I *like*. I look for colors that show my quilt ideas to the very best.

The way you put it together makes a big difference. Choose a fabric suitable for your quilt. Cut your pieces as straight as you can. Sew your seams neat and straight with very small stitches. Keep all edges very even. Make all corners match; nothing looks worse than some seams that are going one way and the others going another way. It certainly requires a lot of measuring. Of course, in the beginning this was not so. We, bless our hearts, didn't know about that. We tried just to make something to keep us warm. Now we do it for a variety of reasons.

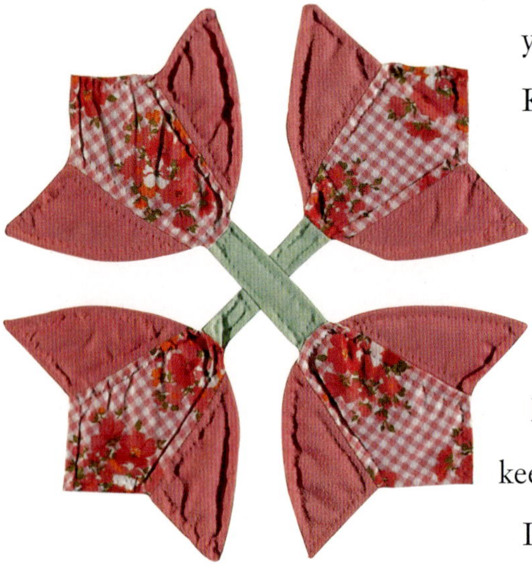

I have bought so many books and still buy them every

once in a while. I never cut them up. I buy templates and make my own patterns for traditional quilts. I never make patterns for originals, as I would never do two of them. I do not sell or give away my original patterns; maybe this is unusual, but I just don't like to do it.

A lot of people are trying to get into quilt making on the machine. If you want to, your best bet is to do something simple, like "Nine Patch," "Double Irish Chain" and a few others. The first and only quilt I have made on the machine is the "Arkansas Tulip." I used double knit, because I found that knits stretch just right around corners and curves. Tulips are very bright, so I used bright colors to bring my idea out. I tried to make the block and strippings very straight. This is another

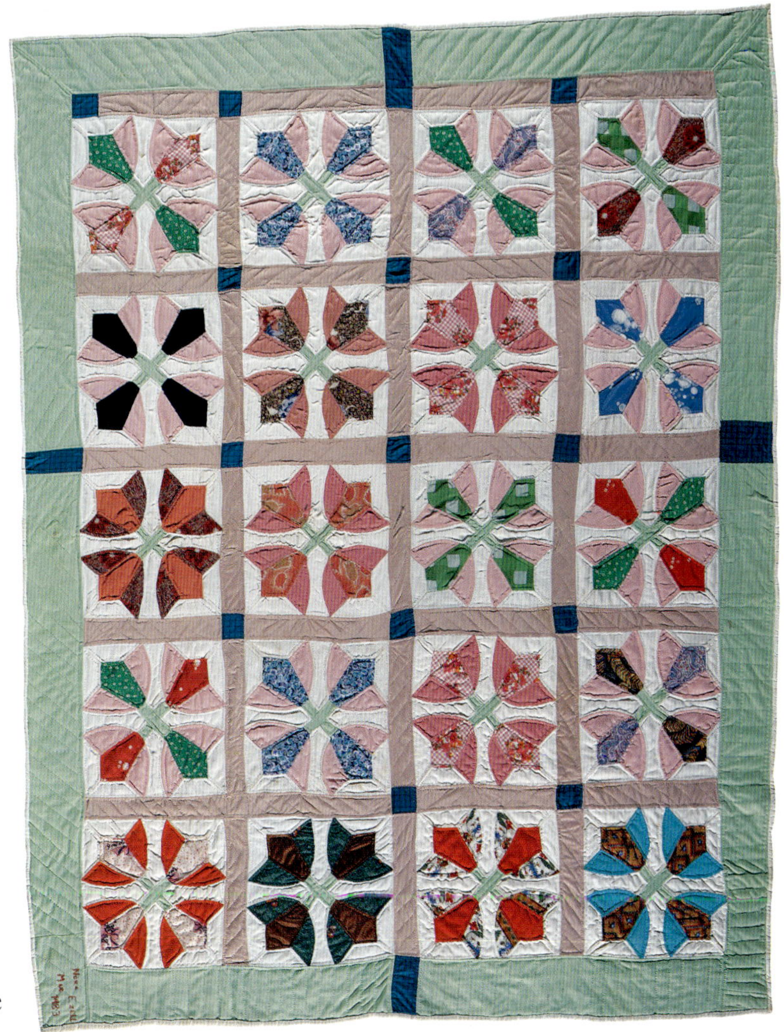

"Arkansas Tulip"
Detail on opposite page. Collection of the artist.

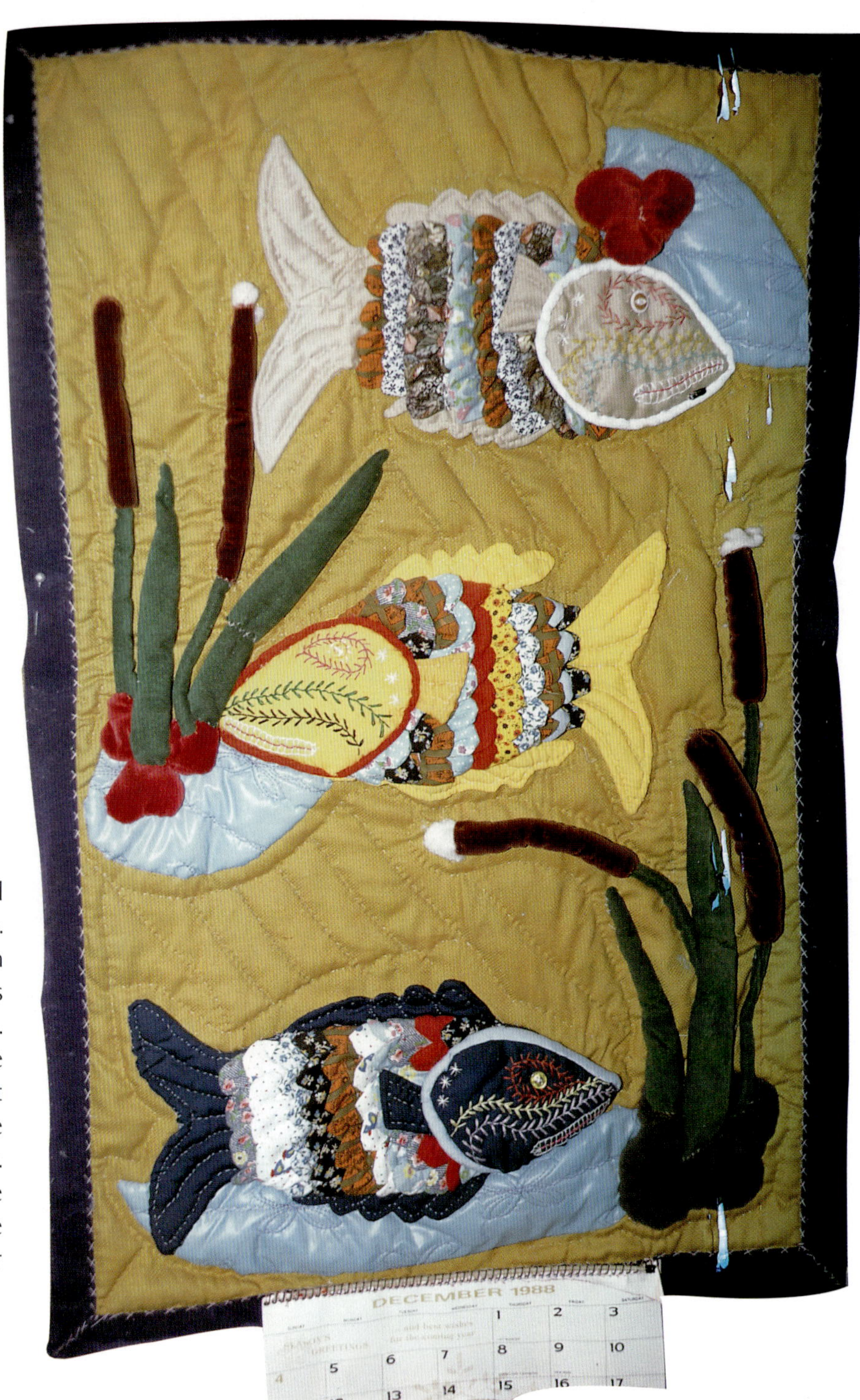

A calendar, made by Mrs. Ezell for her husband, who liked to fish. He would mark his fishing days on the paper calendar that is attached to the lower edge. Mrs. Ezells comments, "The fish have separate scales, which makes it very unique. I wouldn't advise [this project] for the beginner. The cattails look so real, you have to see them to believe it. I have made only one, so it is not for sale."

Photo by Gail Trechsel.

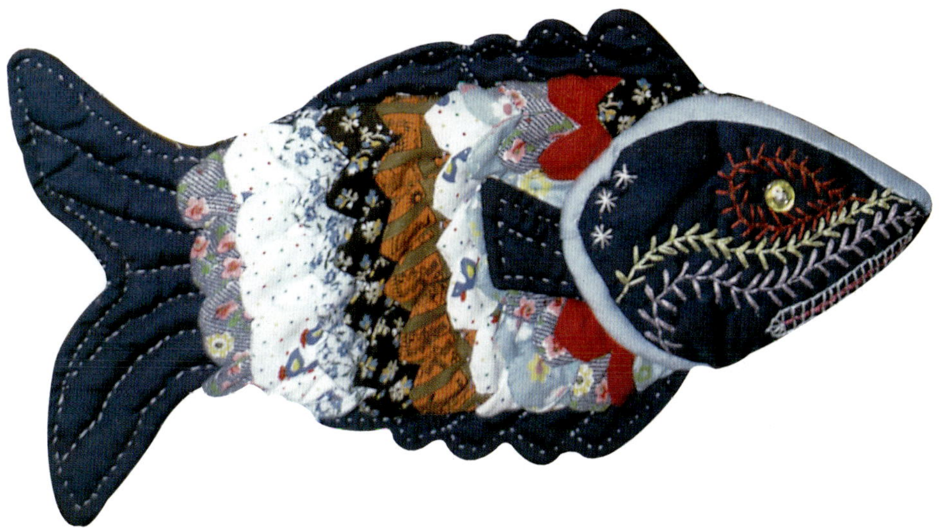

quilt that makes a good conversation piece at shows.

I wouldn't suggest you begin machine quilting with the "Arkansas Tulip" [See page 59] pattern unless you are like me—experienced.

I don't try to be perfect, but I have to excel; I never could satisfy myself by doing something simple. Another thing, *I never practice*; when I start out to learn something I have to make something. I had a friend that rode the same bus with me each morning. She was trying to learn to crochet and she made a chain about five miles long. The last time I saw her, she had not learned to make anything but that chain. So, I say, if you want to learn to make a quilt, make a block, put it with some other blocks, and quilt it.

When you do enough blocks, you can put them together and make your first quilt. We'll talk about this later in another chapter. The popular "Sampler Quilt" is a good quilt to use all your blocks, so once a year I make a sampler. This is known also as "The Friendship Quilt."

My Quilt Frame

Oh, how far we have come! The way most of us learned to quilt was to use four poles and put the quilt on the floor and whip it in with a needle and thread (my goodness, I could never do it now). Then we would pull it up to sitting height and hang it from nails or hooks on the ceiling of the house.

We spread our lining down wrong side up and laid in our batting. When we used cotton from the gin, my Aunt Tony used three peach tree switches and beat it out all over the lining. I remember she used to laugh about the switches and say that one was for the Father, one for the Son, and third was for the Holy Ghost, so she could beat the devil out of the cotton. She was right, sometimes it would be so knotted that you had to do something to it.

Now we have individual frames that can be used in your lap, as well as small frames. I really don't care for either of these. In all the ways I have tried, I like my way the best. I have a 30-inch frame on 36-inch high legs that my husband made for me. I never have to move my chair; I can turn the frame whichever way I like. I learned a while ago that it is best to start quilting at the center of the quilt and work out to the edges.

There are several other ways, like lap quilting, which I never do; I don't like it.

Quilting

There are several ways to quilt. My favorite is quilting around each piece. You might want to know what is so important about how you quilt; I have seen some beautiful patterns that were spoiled by the way they were quilted.

The oldest quilting pattern I know is quilting in shells (most people say shares). I have heard my mother or aunt say they were doing "corn rows" or "potato rows." "Corn rows" are rows made about one inch apart as far as you can reach, and bring the rows toward you until you get to the frame. The "potato rows" are made one big and one small until you finish your shell.

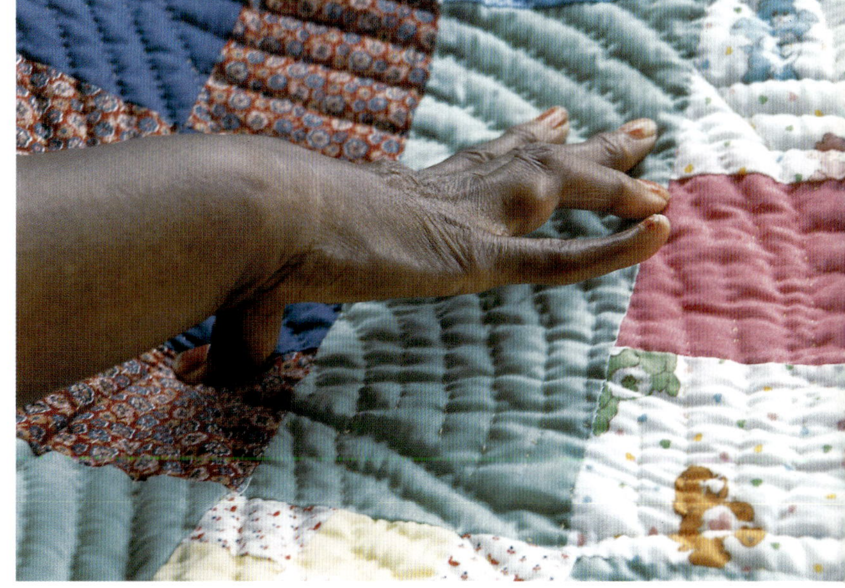

Mrs. Ezell demonstrates shell quilting done in "corn rows." Photo by Gail Trechsel.

When we worked in a quilting party, the best quilter laid off the shells and you had to follow her row. But down through the years I have found this spoils your pattern. One thing you have to learn is what works best for you.

If you teach, you will find yourself leaning toward your own methods, while, at the same time, you are trying to get quilting as a whole over to your students. Work out your idea, but be sure to try to do whatever your students want, as well. There are few that want to do what you do.

The best and prettiest quilting is done with very straight and very small stitches. Use a very small needle; a size 3 is what I usually use. I'm noticing lately that my hands are very stiff in the morning, so I do my quilting later in the day. I have been asked if I quilt at night or if I quilt *all* night? I must say I never quilt at night unless I'm pushed. I try hard not to let myself slip into that position. As well as I love quilting, I never work at night.

How I Arrive At A Price

Someone asked me, "How in the world do you arrive at a fair price when you put in so much time?" I worked that out in a way that was easy for me. When I do a special quilt or original, I catalogue very carefully. I start with the month, day, and year, then the hours, and do this until I finish. I save all of my sales tickets for purchases, which helps me to keep up with the price of materials. I can be sure to keep up with whatever materials I use.

The only quilts I don't catalogue are quilts from my scrap bag. I only keep up with the price of the lining, padding, and thread. I don't usually keep the hours.

So much time and thought is put into each quilt that it is hard to set a fair price. Most people are so unfair; they think of quilts as something cheap. A good quilt made by hand from beginning to the end couldn't be cheap. Thread and other materials have gotten very expensive. I put in so much time because I would like for you, if you buy one, to look back in future years and see a little bit of me in it!

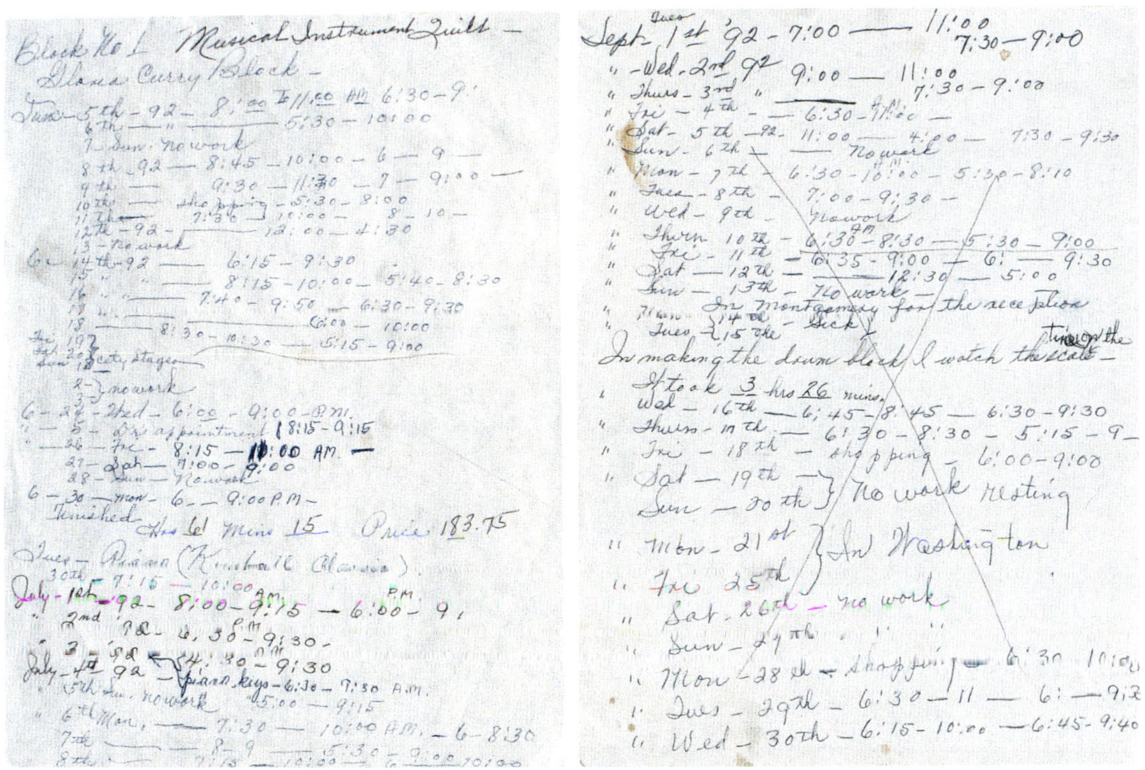

Mrs. Ezell keeps a time log like this one for each commissioned quilt.

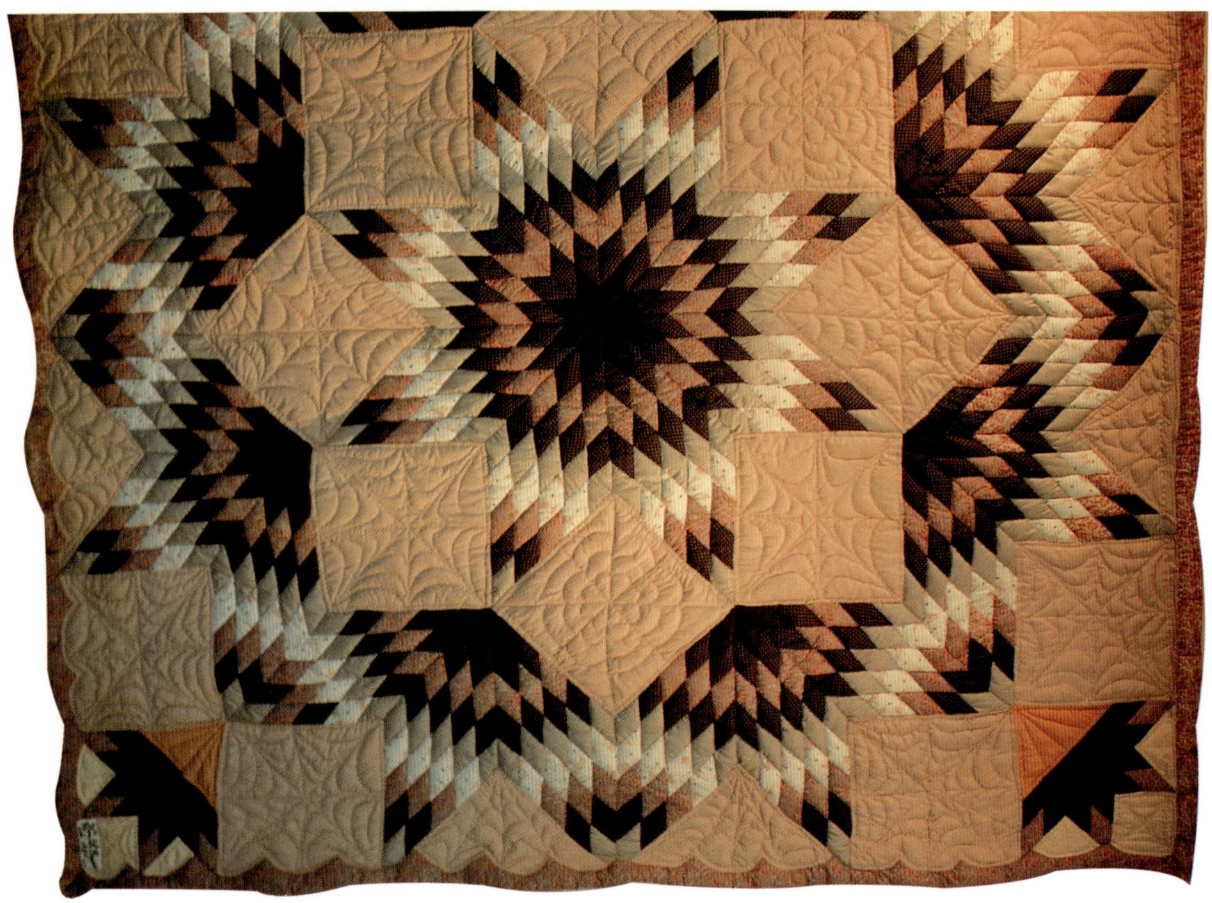

"Broken Star,"

May 1981. Mrs. Ezell notes, "The material was purchased at the T.W.L. store in Aliceville (Alabama). The manager was Dorothy Thomas, and my favorite clerk was Sarah Gibson. This is one of my best quilts!"

Photo by Gail Trechsel at the Birmingham Public Library show.

The Broken Star Quilt

Monday, May 4, 1981

I started this quilt today. I am going to make this quilt for Mrs. ___________. Last week Mr. Bobby Grayson and Mr. Elijah Spencer's wife died. I was too caught up to get going last week. So I'm going to start today. A very pretty day. I am having to really push today, as it's one of my bad days, very nervous; yesterday I ate and drank everything in my house.

I finished this quilt on Saturday evening, May 23rd, in two weeks, five days. Watching the young Dodgers' pitcher. I have been sick all day. Took a laxative and really feel it.

Love this quilt, it is beautiful. Hope I can sell it, don't care if I don't. (Smile)

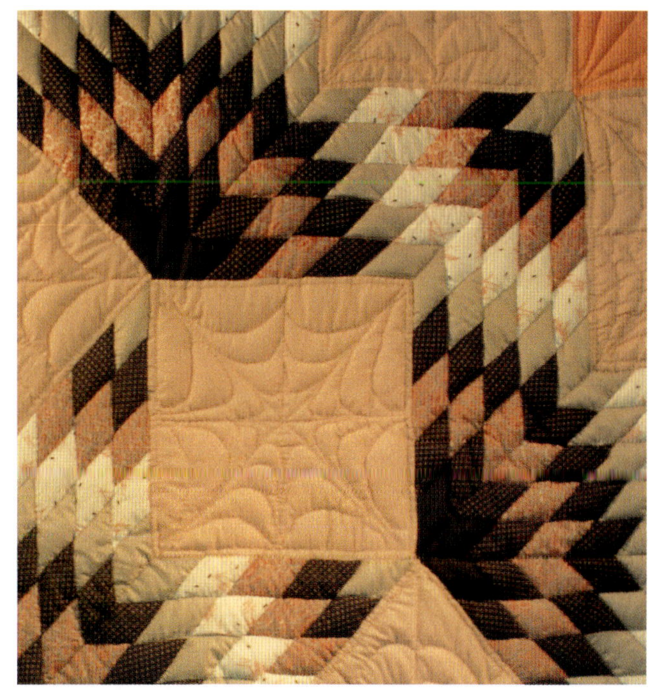

Cil is graduating the 7th of June, David graduated the 21st of May, Mike is getting married the 20th of June. I'll have a birthday the 24th, Ruth the 28th, Mama died the 9th, 1958, so many things to remember.

The first "Broken Star" very pretty and I thought a good job. And wouldn't you know she was too cheap to pay $295. But I sold it to a lady in New Jersey who also bought four other quilts.

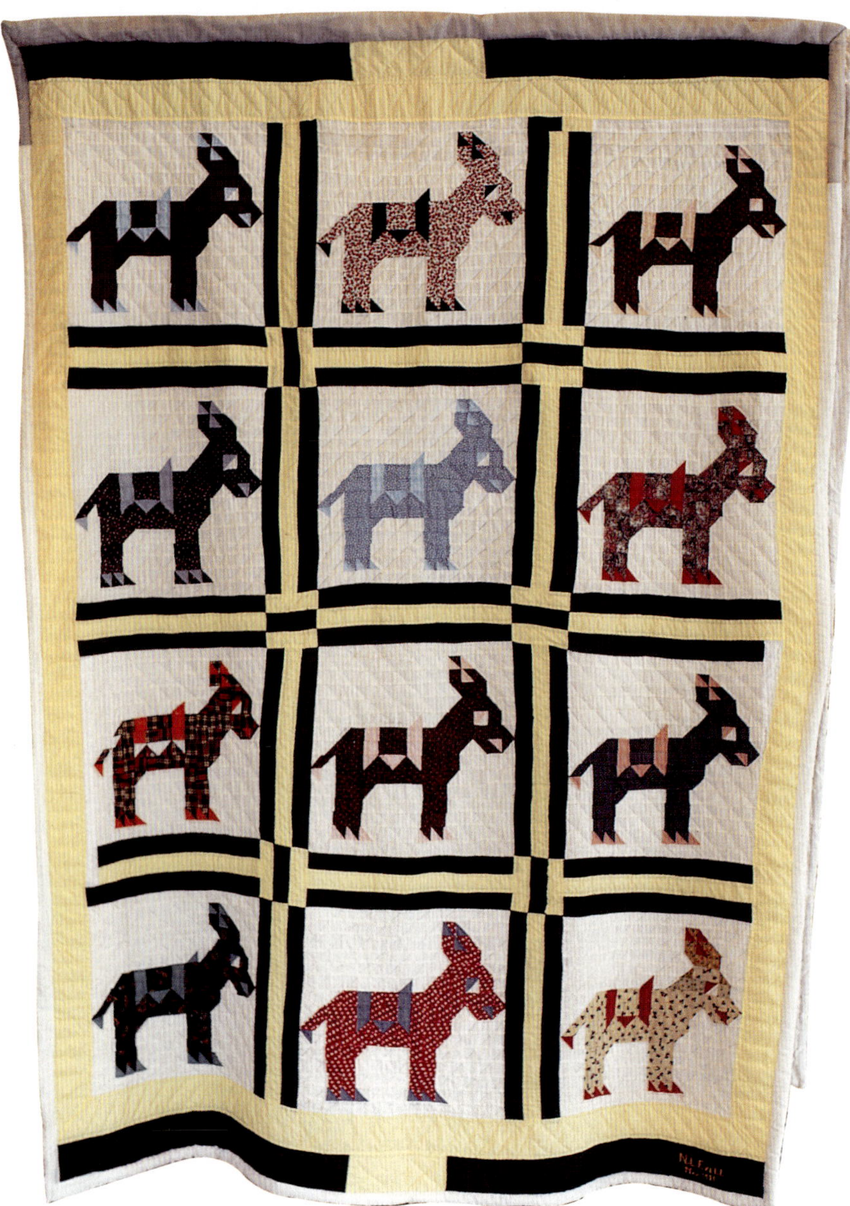

"Little Donkey," 1989

Mrs. Ezell points out that there are 270 pieces in each block, making a total of approximately 3,240 pieces in the entire quilt. At right, Mrs. Ezell takes a question from a visitor while demonstrating quilting at an outdoor fair.

Photograph by Gail Trechsel at the Birmingham Public Library show.

The Donkey Quilt

One night (seems like an eternity ago) my daughter and I were trying to get a "Double Wedding Ring" together. It was giving us all kinds of problems, plus my baby grandson, David, had a sick spell. I remember we had carried him to the hospital and come back.

My oldest great-grandson drew something on a piece of paper. He came over and said to us, "Mama, make a quilt like this."

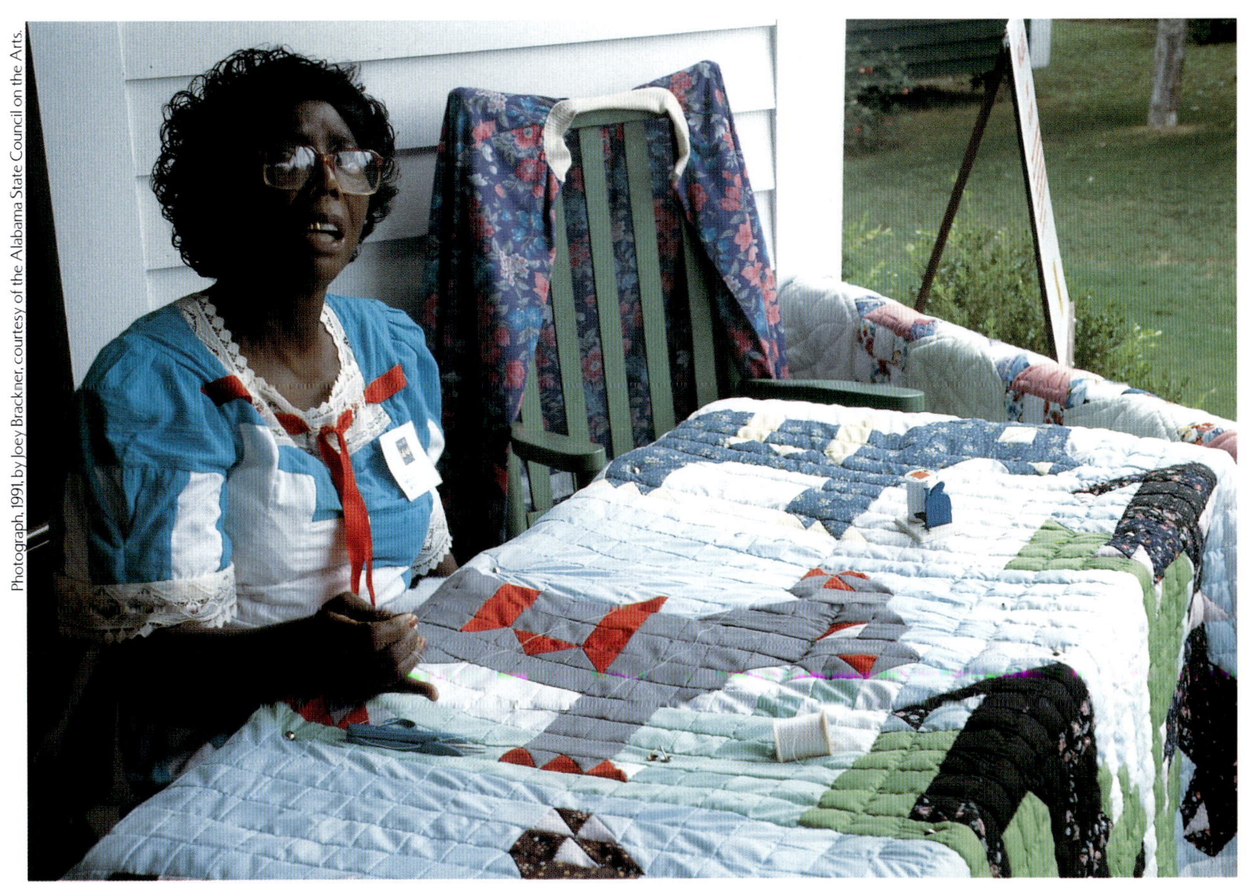

Photograph, 1991, by Joey Brackner, courtesy of the Alabama State Council on the Arts.

We laughed and asked him, "What is it? A dog?"

He said, "No, it's a little mule."

We laid it aside, but my mind stayed with it; later we decided to try to come up with something. We put it on one-inch graph paper, then decided we didn't want it round in places, so we made it match the lines on the graph paper. We liked what we saw, at least I did. My daughter had me to make a few changes. (Oh how I miss her. She is the one that really helped me to do as good as I do with this.)

We finally made a block, with 15 rows each way, 15 pieces in each row with the exception of 10 rows, where we added half pieces to form the donkey, his saddle, feet and tail. We ended up putting 270 pieces in the block, made out of three colors. I warn you right now that unless you are an experienced quilter, don't try this. There are several little catches to it.

It has been by far my best seller. How many have I made? Seventeen. How many have I sold? Sixteen, six of which went to Israel and Europe. How much money I have made? I'm ashamed of you! Enough!

"Donkey Quilt Variation"

Signed "Nora Ezell Dec. 1991, #17"; cotton broadcloth, polished cotton, cotton/polyester blends; 73.5 inches by 85.5 inches.

Collection of Georgine and Jack Clarke.

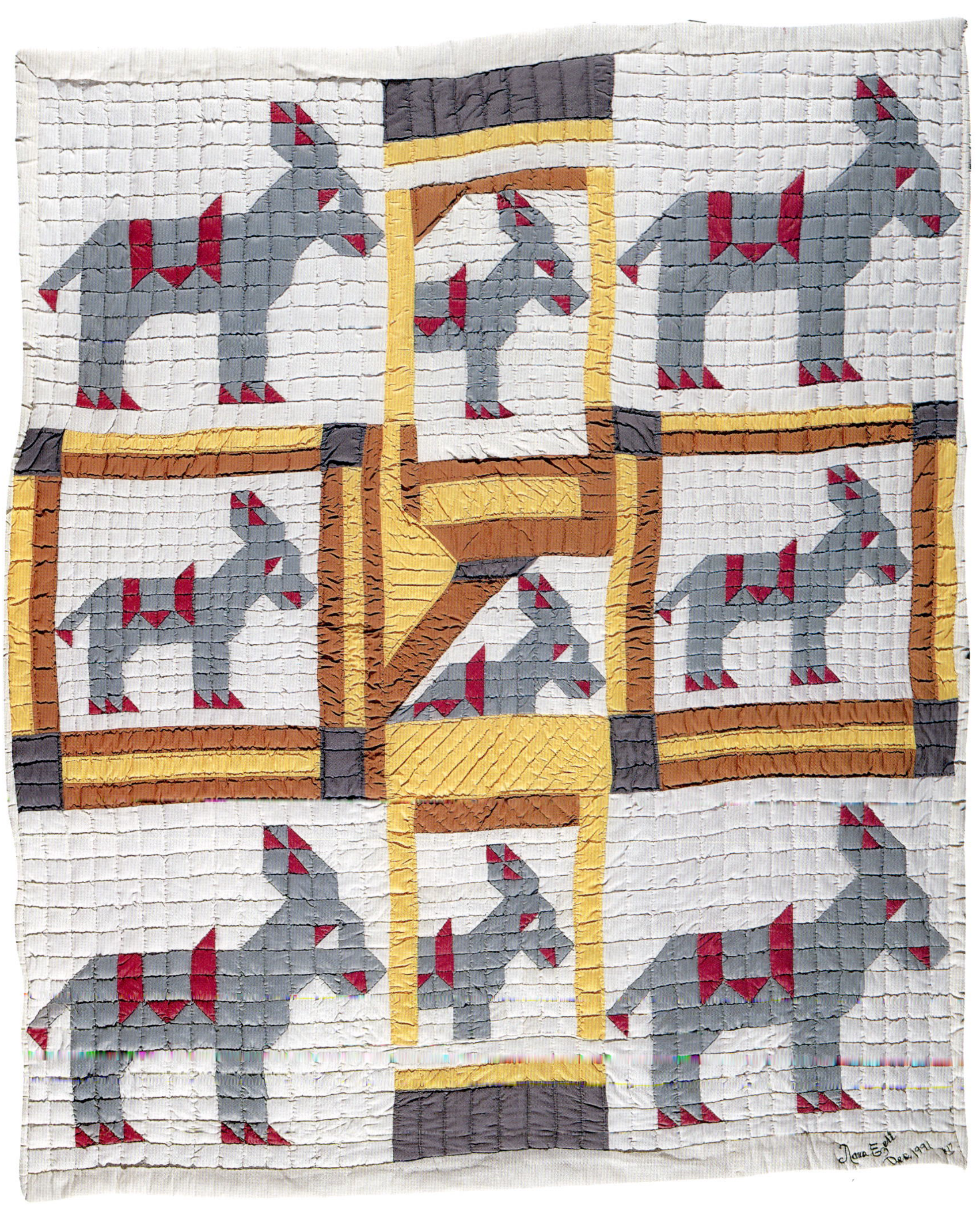
Dec. 1991

Part Two

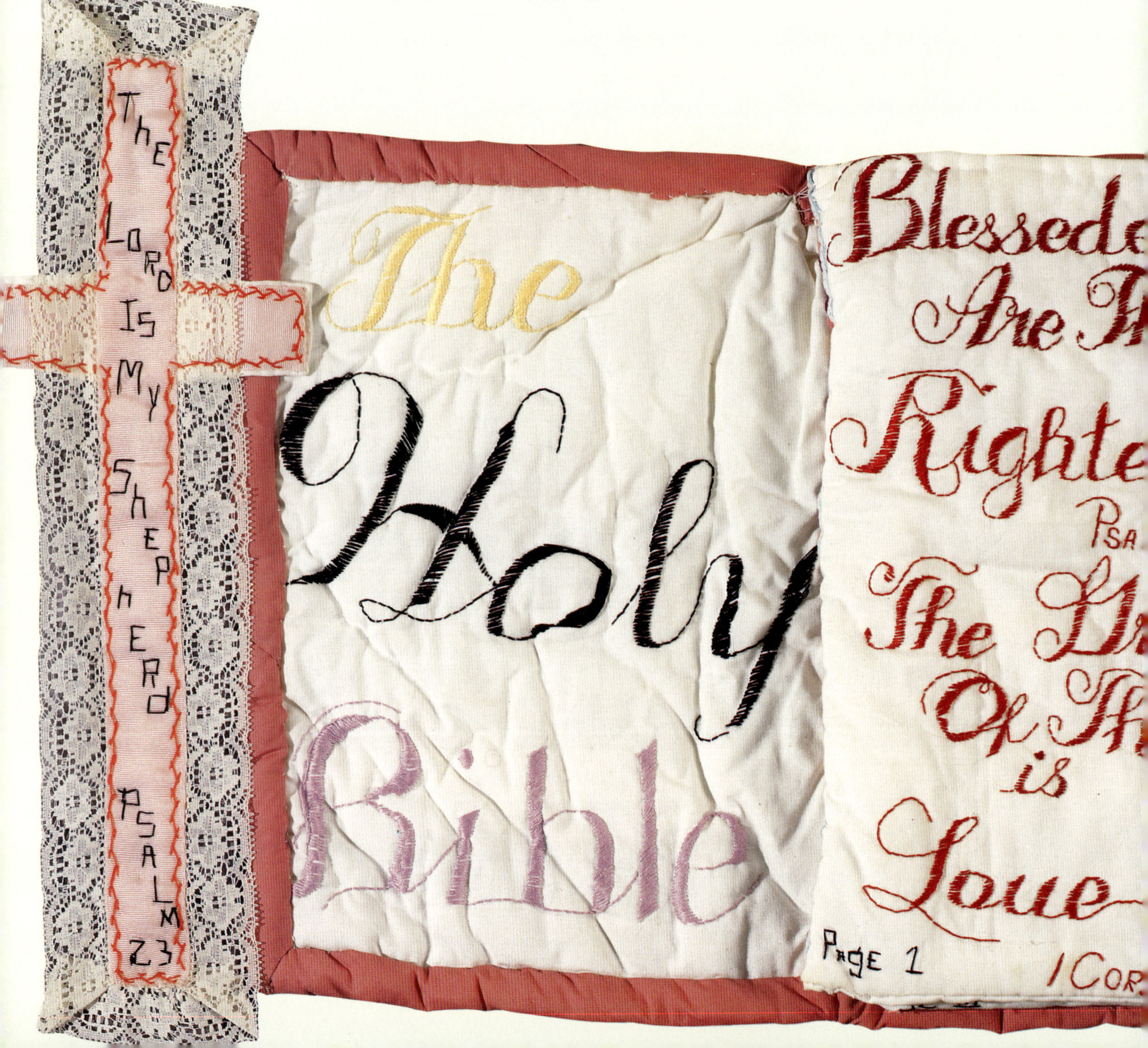

The Story Quilts

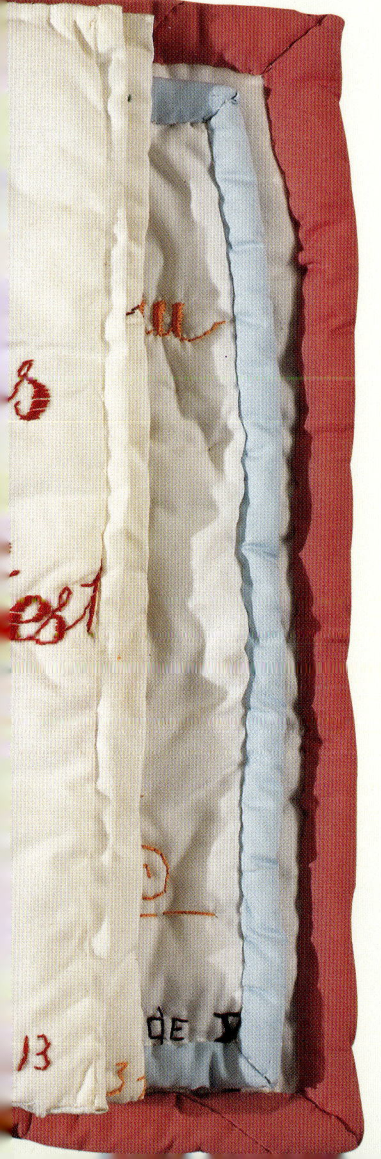

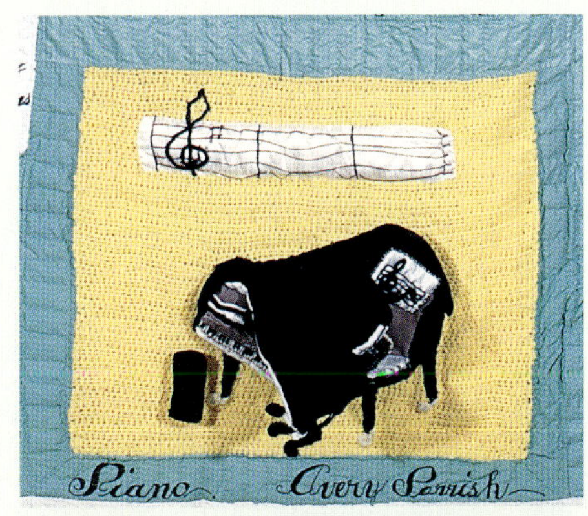

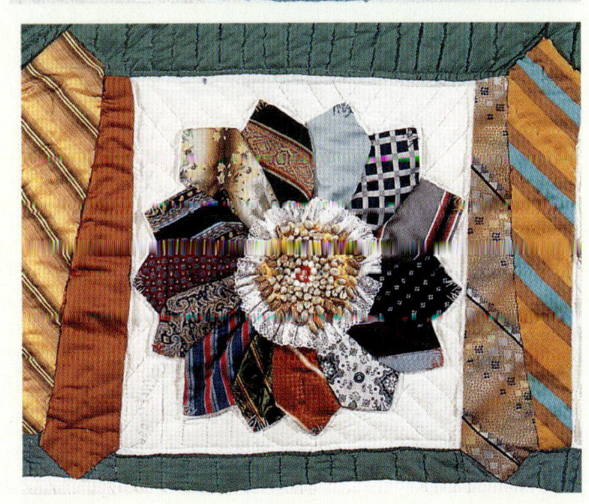

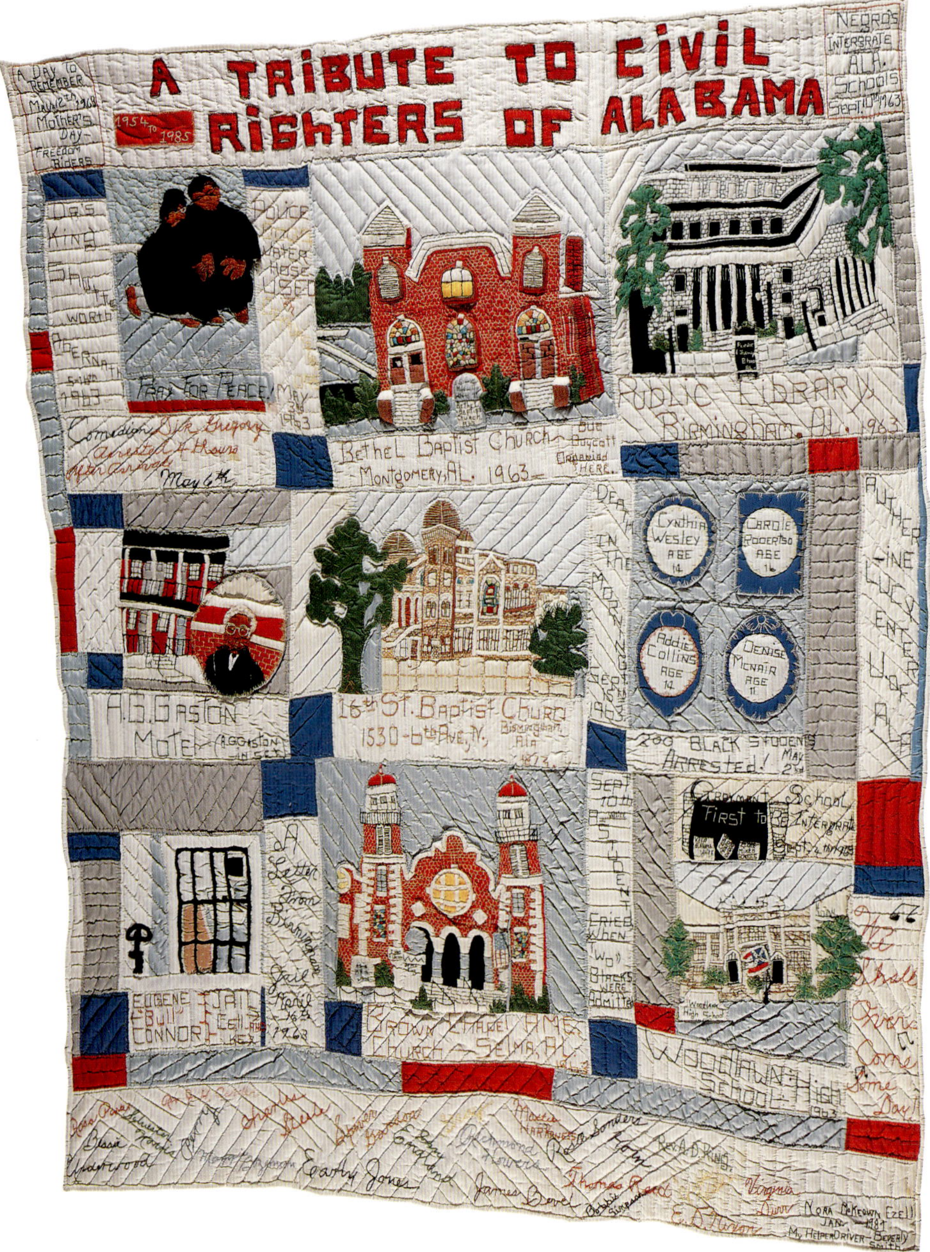

A Tribute to the Civil Righters of Alabama, 1954-1989

Signed and dated, "Nora McKeown Ezell, Jan 1989. My helper-driver: Beverly Smith."

70 inches by 106 inches. Cotton and cotton/polyester blend fabrics, cotton embroidery floss. Detail on page 70. Collection of the Birmingham Civil Rights Institute, Birmingham, Alabama.

A Tribute to the Civil Righters of Alabama, 1954–1989

I started this quilt Monday January 23rd, 1989. Beautiful day, a little cold, me and my ulcers having a bad time. Determine to get started, I do not find it easy to work on this quilt, somehow the *hurt* is still there.

Name of the quilt—*A Tribute to The Civil Righters of Alabama (during the years 1954 to 1989).*

Trying to work, no spirit, which makes it hard to do. I'm really concerned about my girls. One sick, the other with child problems. Been having lots of dreams about my husband and daughter (both dead). I'm deeply religious but not a fanatic. I can [always] feel when something is not quite well with them, as I love my grandchildren very much.

Well, a rainy Sunday and I'm kind of down in the dumps. Funny dream at two this morning. Read a portion of the Scriptures but fail to get an understanding. Have to pray another way I guess.

January 25, 1989

Started on the 16th Street Baptist Church block. Hope I can concentrate. Trying to give my granddaughter a hand with her baby son. Put him in school at Eatmon 1-8-89. He is almost as nervous as I am. Hope I can help him, God's plans must be carried out. I wonder if I am always destined to help somebody? God please help me to do the best I can!

February 5, 1989

Started the Woodlawn School block. (Such a sad day. On this day a few years ago, on my way home from work, I saw the poor people, especially the children, being drenched with water hoses. I thought, "My God where art thou?") When I started on this block I remembered that. After a visit to my doctor, I felt a little better, no recurrence of my old ailment. That was good news.

February 8, 1989

I started the Brown Chapel block. I'm up bright and early—feeling not too good. Got a good mind to do the jail cell block, along with Bull Connor. Trying hard to get started—very nervous today. Worked on the quilt awhile, quilted on another quilt I have in frame. Ended up going to bed. Wondering again why I can't do what I want to do without outside interference. To do all in my mind and carry out God's plan — I like King's "can't afford to wait." I just have to keep going—not feeling good, but very excited about Brown Chapel block. Monday I worked 3 hours and 10 minutes on the stain glass window. So do you think I could teach someone else to have this kind of patience? I never plan on making a pattern; I do whatever comes off the top of my head. (Smile) So you don't believe it? I'm sorry. Could I, or would I do this again? Yes, but not for the same money!

February 15, 1989

Still not feeling very good. Don't seem to be able to shake this cold, aches and pain, trying to work anyway. Finally finished Brown Chapel Church. Almost finished the coordinated wallhanging. Got back to the 16th Street Church yesterday. Very cold, hand and arm almost too painful to work. Skipping about on lots of things. Hope to do something worthwhile today. The weather is about to get me, still I'm pushing on.

February 20, 1989

Pretty good ideas on the 16th Street Church! Finished with a rush! Decided on Bethel which is really a push. Besides sinus, my mouth and jawtooth has been where I couldn't eat again. Oh! I'm so hungry! (smile)

February 23, 1989

Well, today I'm still suffering along. Don't feel like doing nothing, just pushing. This church is something else. I like my idea— no pattern, nothing, just as it comes, I do it. Crazy or creative, you be the judge.

February 27, 1989

I have been very nervous for several weeks, just going through the motions, no energy. So many problems—Gosh! Where is the end? Still want to live somewhere else.

[She was living in Eutaw, Alabama, in Greene County as she wrote this.]

Saturday, March 4th

About one-third done on quilt. Still very nervous and tense, trying to work, doing a very poor job, not at all satisfied with some things I have done. Trying to do [too] many things at the same time. Grandchildren still getting on my crazy mind.

March 6, 1989

Today I'm very tired. So you don't have a garden? I do flowers and vegetables. Kind of nervous but getting the Gaston block started. Coming pretty good.

March 25, 1989

Finished Gaston block today! Just three more blocks to go. One large Woodlawn school, two small. Very hot so quick! Hope to finish by the end of May. Hope it goes well, some things I like, some I don't. Can't seem to do tedious things as well as I like.

April 10, 1989

Ann and the group didn't come yet. Don't know what happened. They called and said they were coming to make pictures and all. Nearing the end of this job. Not bad but not as good as I would like. Have house cleaning on my mind. Plan to finish all projects by June 15th.

April 25, 1989

Vacation? I have saved money but not sure where I will go or if I will go any place.

May 1, 1989

Not going to Massachusetts [for the Williams College exhibit], did not like the write-up, think it could have been better. I gave a long interview, hope they do better with this project. Finished Woodlawn school block. Lost most of my ideas worrying about family problems. Said over and over that I would not, but I can. School will soon be out and I will be through with that. Don't know about David, just want to throw him from me! I want to do my thing (which is odd and pretty quilts) without so much interference.

MAY 4, 1989

Starting the last block, "a prayer vigil" with King, Abernathy and Shuttlesworth. Beginning the last strip. Hope to finish this real soon.

MAY 7, 1989

A few miserable days ago I finished the quilt!

MAY 8, 1989

Put in frame, hope to finish by June 15th. Really feeling bad, legs and feet hurt so bad. Sinus continues to be very worrisome. So much rain and wet weather. Lately I don't seem to be able to concentrate. Went to church Sunday and on a plain flat road drove my car off into a ditch, nobody coming or going near me. It really shook me up, don't even remember how it happened.

MAY 15, 1989

Today it's raining again, will quilt some later. Going to bed now, very nervous. Worked pretty good on quilting today, not much, but good work. Praying for the end (smile). I have worked so hard, been sick so much, just pushing and praying. Well I see the end, and I am glad.

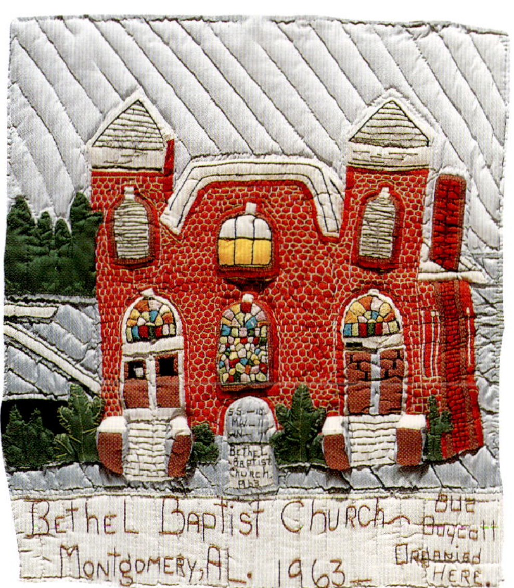

The "Bethel Baptist Church" block is carefully detailed to represent the brick of the building's construction and the stained glass of the central window and door transoms. The sides of the steps are three-dimensional.

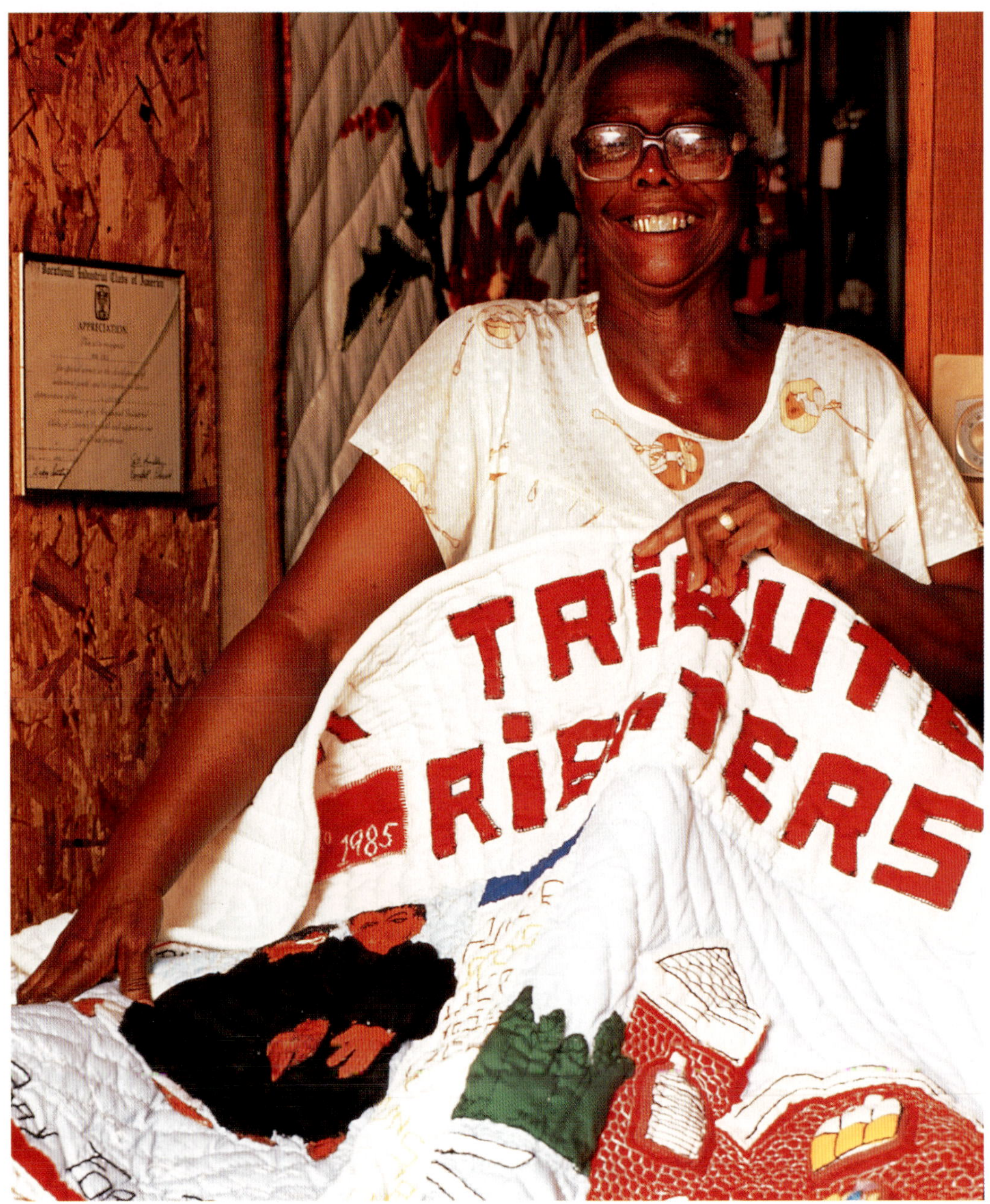

Showing off the *Tribute to the Civil Righters of Alabama* to a guest.
Photograph by Gail Trechsel.

May 20, 1989

Quilting on civil rights quilt. Finished the pattern for "Broken Star" for a class I hope to start at West Alabama College.

May 21, 1989

Not one person showed up at the college, so I will do this "Broken Star" at home. There is no way to keep a person that is as determined as I am "down."

May 23, 1989

Not doing the best with my work but pleased with my quilting. See so many things I missed, some will have to do. Didn't realize I missed so much, but when you work from the top of your head, I guess you will do that.

But after all "a job is a job" thank God for that.

May 27, 1989

Well, working hard to finish. Quilting every minute I can. Legs and feet stiff, so much sitting I guess, but I still don't understand. Lady called last night from California, Mrs. C. Gardner. Wants lots of quilt tops straightened out. Some I know, most I don't. As I said earlier, can't seem to concentrate. Will try to do them, I'm sure she will pay well, she seems to be so honest. She said like others, "I wish you would come out here." Plenty of money to go, but no time. Can't find time to go to Massachusetts either. I got a lot of brochures and write ups. Much better this time around. My good friend and quilt buyer Dr. Robert Cargo went. He told me the quilts really stole the show. So much for that. Would love to go someplace, and relax, wish my church had a retreat.

Planning a trip to Birmingham on the 17th, trying to finish so I can take it with me. Need tires for my car, also a tuneup. I have put so many miles on it this year. Had to finish the "Ohio Star Quilt," that's another project that didn't work out. I don't seem to be able to get help, I think they find my style too complicated. So I think you have to be able to do something different. Got to I think "be able to do your own thing."

June 1, 1989

Today I crossed another milestone in my working career. This has been both a joy and a hurt. I worked hard to make this program a success. I tried to do things would appeal to everybody, but somehow it didn't go over. Almost everybody liked the ideas or things I made but nobody wanted to try them. Very disappointing. I planned to try ten projects, I made quilts, rugs, pillows, towel holders, tissue holders, bill holders, coverlets, soap holders, embroidered and hemstitched pillowcases, Christmas tablecloths, hemstitched, tatted and lace edged handkerchiefs, covered umbrellas, gowns, slips and panties, Mexican-embroidered aprons, and pillows, oystershell ashtrays and soap dishes, pantset made from upholstery scraps, crochet-edged washcloths on holder, knitted socks and afghans. It is good for me to believe that so many people like my work, but so few wanted to actually work with me. Anything anybody asked me about I tried to set up a project. I spent money buying materials for projects but found that no one would show [in Greene County].

This has been both a joy and a hurt. A joy to make so many people happy to see this world's current events brought to life in a quilt. I try very hard to live up to the name — "an artist with needle and thread." (smile) A hurt because it brings back so many unpleasant memories. I have enjoyed working indirectly with others, it wasn't too hard to do with so much help.

June 15, 1989

Finished quilting and hemming this quilt on the 9th. Like most of it, but some [places] I wish I could have done better. This credit I would like to give to my mother and father. They were just the opposite [from one another].

My mother was an old school teacher, who taught her children that it was as easy to make an "A" as a "B." My father, with little or no schooling, taught us to use our hands and mind.

My oldest sister Edna, taught me beauty in work. My second oldest sister, Etoil, taught me how to do domestic. My third sister, Birdnell, taught me to stand on my own feet.

The fourth sister is me.

My fifth sister, Bernice, taught me how to read and understand what I read. My sixth sister, Bessie, taught me independence. My only brother, the seventh child, Cecil, taught me to *live*, whatever I did.

My eighth sister, Waltzena, taught me courage. My ninth sister, Christine, taught me to live wherever I stayed. And last but not least,

Jettie, the baby, taught me possession and cleanliness.

So I gained something from each of them.

Many thanks to: Ann Adams, Dr. Marvin Whiting, Barbara Nunn, Odessa Woolfolk, my sweet granddaughter, Beverly Jo Smith, and the Alabama Council on the Arts, Montgomery, Alabama.

Time spent [on the Tribute to Civil Righters of Alabama Quilt]:
414 hours & 30 minutes—to piece
121 hours & 55 minutes—to quilt
14 hours & 30 minutes—to hem & finish
$107.54—worth of materials
580 hours & 55 minutes—total hours to complete
This done—June 12th 1989

The Christmas Story Quilt

June 21, 1989

Well, my mind is on the "Christmas Story Quilt." So I guess I better get going.

Oh Lord! These quilt tops came today from California—oh no! A "Dahlia," the hardest top I know, but with a little bit of everybody, I'll do it.

Pretty soon I'll be another year—June 24th.

Do you like this quilt? Thanks.

Beautiful Birmingham

Thoughts and ideas as I made the *Beautiful Birmingham Quilt* for Carol and Jim Sokol, Birmingham, Alabama.

May 28, (1991)

Dear Carol and Jim:

Today I started work on your quilt. I'm sure I shall love doing it for you. Some blocks I could pick out right away, but others I'm having a little problem deciding on. All the pictures are so nice, of the house and dog. I was hoping for the church, as I love to do them.

May 29

Don't feel like looking around, but have to go to Birmingham to see my brother, who is not feeling too good. Praying and hoping, as he is the only man in my life right now. (smile) Starting this block on this lovely house, gee, I love it! It's an overcast day, which makes it a little hard for me. Hope you will like this It is such a pretty house. It is the one thing I have always wanted, as I love to keep [house].

May 31

Last day of May, raining, which always depresses me; I think of all the wrongs I have done and that have been done to me. I'm listening to the Gospel Program and trying to carry on. I'm going to start stitching on

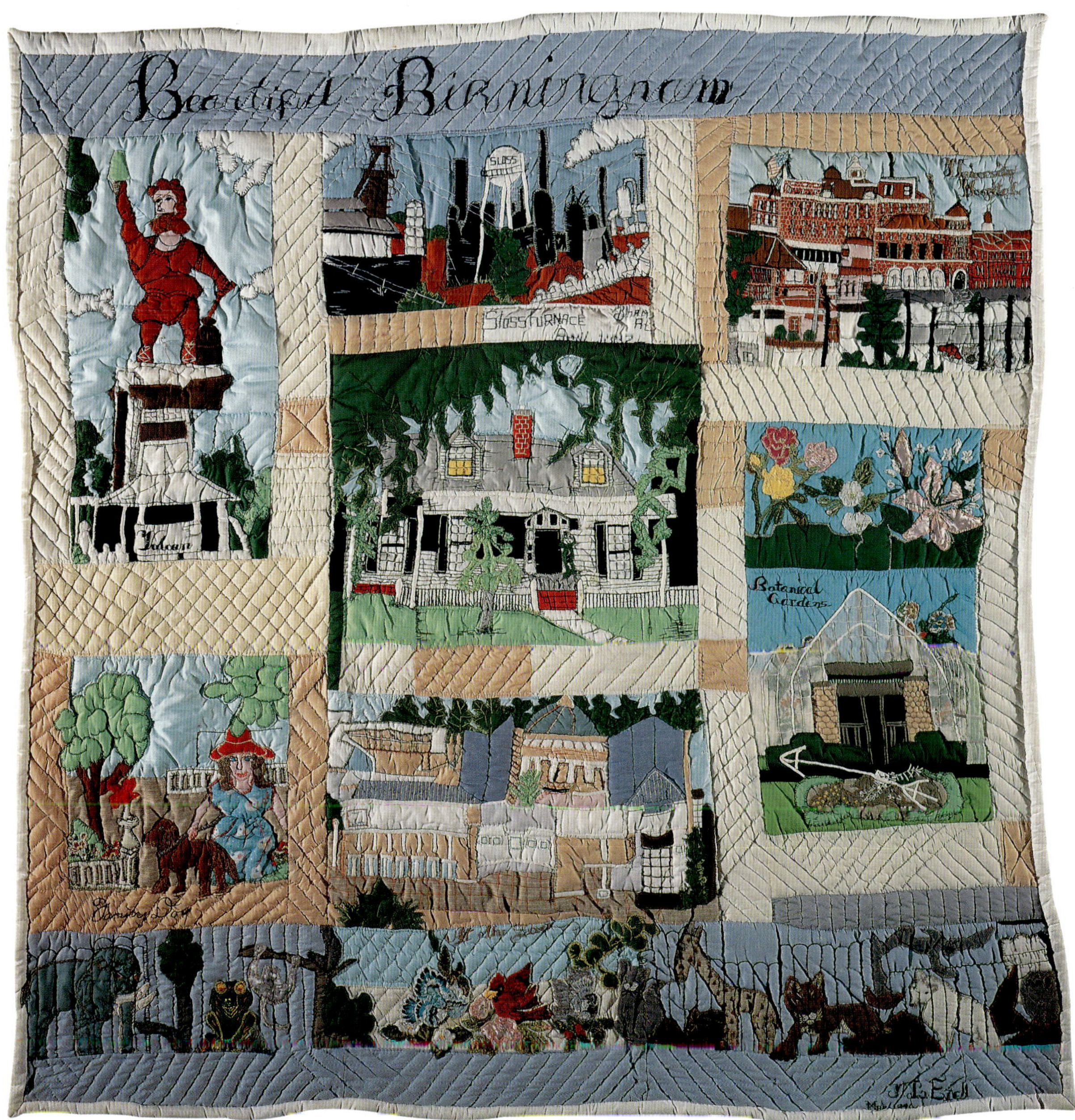

Beautiful Birmingham
Signed "N. L. Ezell, May 1991."
Collection of Jim and Carol Sokol.

your quilt. I hope I can do something I will be pleased with. As I am my own best critic, if I do to please me,the work will pass. I love, again, your house.

June 1

So the year is passing on, six months already. I know I should do more for the uplifting of the Kingdom. Sometimes I wonder what I can do, when the good Lord does so much for me.

You didn't hear? I won the Black Heritage Award!! What is it? Oh my goodness, $1,000!!! Amazing!! As I often say, this year is making up for all the years when nothing came my way. Oh, thank God for Jesus and the people He made, like you, who believe in me and my work and give me a chance to express myself in a quilt.

June 8

Almost half of the year is gone, and I'm still wondering what my job in life is. Maybe I'm like Paul; don't know it when it comes. This morning I have a very annoying headache. I think my allergy is acting up again. I hate to take so much medication. Sometimes I can work on something I like and lose my bad feeling. I finished the two dormer windows and the chimney. I like what I've done—headache, please go away!

Saturday morning, June 9

I have to say good morning. Trying to work a little, don't think I will do much. Don't feel too good, have to keep kicking. I like what I've done!

June 19

Been a little while since I worked. So much time and water has passed under the bridge. It's a good day to be alive and back at work. I was quite busy with the show in Birmingham. Sure am glad I met you there. Feeling better, not so tired. It was a beautiful two days. So many people and so much to see, do and hear.

June 20

What a wonderful morning to be alive! Thank God for the day and the mind to work on your quilt. This end of the house keeps bugging me, but I'm going to finish it before I quit. Trying so hard to get myself together, still worrying about losing so much weight.

June 21

Good morning, Carol and Jim. How are you this morning; good, I hope. I'm kinda hopping on one leg and jumping on the other. Thanking God for this beautiful day, trying to work on your house. Still hoping I will get a chance to see it. Haven't had a chance to read my book; it's doing the grandchildren circuit, but I will get it back soon. Please say hello to your daughter.

[The following note was enclosed in a book Jim Sokol gave to Nora; she includes it in her diary.]

Dear Nora,

I hope you will love this book as much as I do! I think about you often when I read it, perhaps because your quilts are so special.

"Why a Quilt? Because quilts are about caring. Quilts are about comfort and about physical and emotional warmth. Quilts are about relatedness, connectedness, intimacy. And in their color, design, scale, and variety, quilts are about human creativity, human imagination, and the richness and fullness of human life itself."

Come to think about it, Nora, maybe you belong in this book.

Jim (James) Sokol
April 4, 1991

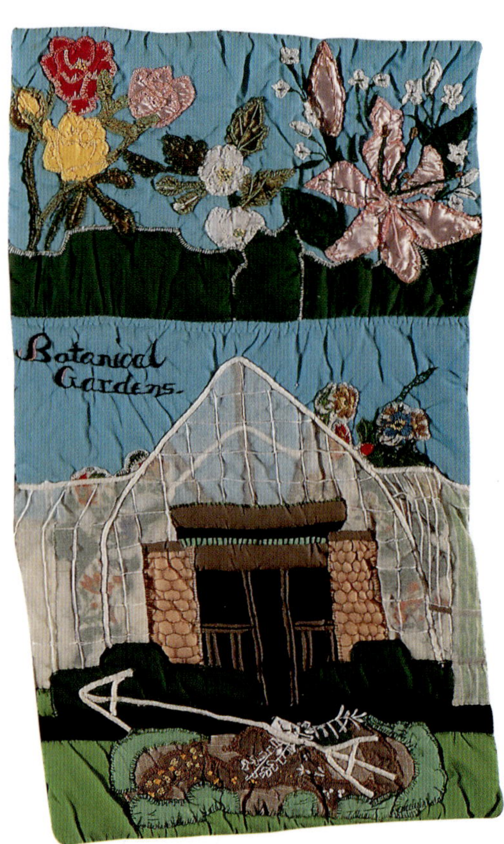

The Botanical Garden block from *Beautiful Birmingham.*

June 22

Feeling pretty good this morning, thank God. Work is slow but it looks good. Sometimes this [the way the work looks] is what I care about, even though I know I have to finish the quilt. Sure hope you will like it. I was so glad to see you, and to know you didn't mind me showing the started block.

June 26

Two days after my 73rd birthday, I feel pretty good. Much better than I have in two months. The main thing I have gotten is a lot of rest. My work looks to suit me, and I think it will please you. Good morning, dears, I have gotten together another block with your dog and your daughter.

June 27

Another beautiful day!! Tomorrow would have been my daughter's 52nd birthday; I loved her but God loved her best; so sadly missed. Well let me get on with my work. Going so slow, but love the work, looks very good. Praying much for the people of Iran, but God's work must come through.

July 6

So it's July, hot July, so soon. Still a little under the weather. Haven't worked in a few days. Thought I had shingles again, but I got the rash under control. Just couldn't do anything but eat a bite and sleep. Up early this morning, 3:00 to be exact, had coffee and started to work. Still love the work, just going kind of slow. Well I've gotten to be old. Oh, how I hope I can do it gracefully. Not a lot of complaining, but it is not easy to go from young to old. (smile)

July 14

So it is getting late in the year. Not doing too much. Went through so much, hate to keep reminding myself. But I'm sure this is the result. God help me to carry on. Trying to get a little work done. Where has the month gone. Well, get going girl, you have to get the job done!! Raining and depressing, but so what.

July 31

Well, Carol and Jim, this morning at 9:15 I finished the block of your house, Block No. 1. Worked 329 hours, 25 minutes. What I decided to do is keep a log of each hour worked and allow myself $3.65 per hour to arrive at a price for the quilt. This hourly rate also takes care of setting up the blocks.

Somehow this has not been a good period of work. The work is good, but the feeling is terrible. I have been sick so much, and I have had to work so slow. Hope I can finish at least by Christmas. I have two more shows scheduled for this year. In Montgomery, I have to evaluate my work for the Council. I have some more work I must do on the house. Oh my God! How I have worked this year. Still canning and freezing, have lots of nice late tomatoes to can. But I enjoy everything I do, (or I don't do it). Have to buy tires for the old car, always something to use my money for.

August 6

Feeling pretty good, not so shaky. Sometimes I'm so tense, I worked hard late Saturday trying to quiet down. Didn't feel so good, but went to church. Enjoyed the service; Reverend Fulgham spoke from First Samuel the 17th chapter, 44th verse. His subject was "He Won't Leave You." Seems like that was the confidence I needed. Felt very relieved and quiet. I went to see a friend that has been sick. So all in all, my day was made. Have to run to do something else. Oh, by the way, "Sloss Furnace Block" is coming nicely. (smile)

August 8

Hello! Another beautiful Saturday morning! I've worked since 6:40 a.m.; couldn't get up this morning, sinuses so bad. It's unusually cool, my resistance is low, as I have worked very hard this year. Like this "Sloss Block." Coming pretty good. Hope you will like it too.

August 9

Oh, what a beautiful day! Work is going good, but I must break for something else. Have so much to do; grass, oh my goodness, to cut. Other work too. I'm enjoying this very much, working on the Sloss Block from a picture card and using my imagination. Thank God for the gift of creating. I love this, maybe this is what God saved me for. I love to do something like this for people like you. Sure hope you will like it.

August 14

Cloudy Tuesday morning, so depressing for me. Trying to work. About to finish the "Sloss Block," which came pretty good, but not as good as I like though. I'm always striving for perfection; well, not quite, but as good as I can. How are things with you? Very good, I hope. Still looking hard at the Middle East, hoping God will keep us in His loving hands. Please have a good day!

Friday morning, August 17

I finished the "Sloss Block" after 24 hours and 55 minutes, approximately $73.50. Thank you Father!! So, on Monday I shall be ready for V U L C A N ! ! ! ! !

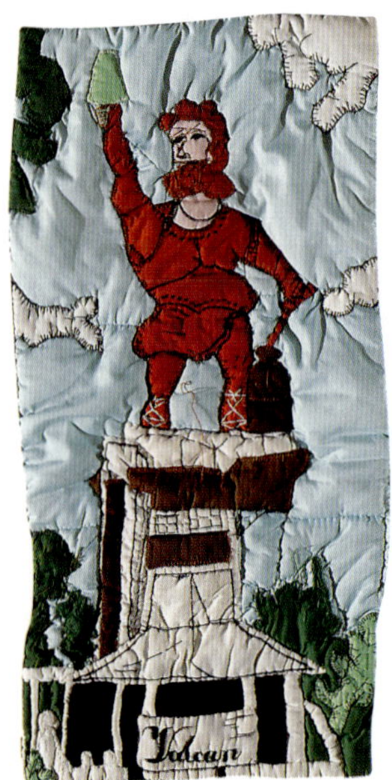

The Vulcan block from *Beautiful Birmingham.*

August 20

I started this block with a bang! I love this. I think maybe I'm doing my best work. Sometimes I get the feeling that I may not do this type of work again. My fingers just simply refuse to hold the needle and my eyes don't see the needle's eye! Are they trying to tell me something? I don't know, but I shall pray God will give me the strength, as I have the want to do a good job. Cloudy day, yesterday we had rain, Thank God, but it is a depressing day for me. So I must push real hard. How are you two this morning? Just fine, I hope. Maybe, just maybe, by December I shall have this finished.

Help me pray!

August 27

What a morning! I haven't been able to do any work since Thursday. I have a sick arm and leg. I was in the bed for 2½ days, but thanks be to God, I'm able to get on the job this morning. Hope you had a nice weekend. Working hard and good on the "Vulcan Block," and coming along nicely. Like the work, I keep telling myself, this is my best yet. Truly hope you will like it.

September 1

So it is September. Trying to do a little work. Have to quit early, as I have a little shopping to do. Don't feel too good. Mind won't stay where I want it to. So I will get back to this soon.

September 11

Got going on Carol and the dog. Trying to get the block together, nothing to go by, just an idea. Didn't have much of an idea, but worked with what I had. Sometimes this happens.

September 14

Not too good this morning; under a little stress this week. A big show coming up. Thinking and working, trying to get ready. Finished this "Vulcan Block" on the 8th, and I'm glad, very glad. After 27 hours and 5 minutes. $82.85 is not much, but a lot too.

September 17

Hello dears, this evening I started another block with Carol and the dog. I'm making up the gazebo (hope it's there). Feeling a little low. Got my first speeding ticket in Alabama, going to Montgomery for a quilt show. Kind of excited, not paying enough attention to details. Finally got to Montgomery and did the show, met some interesting people. I love doing these shows, and enjoy the glad look on the people's faces.

October 3

No work on this part for a long time. Worked otherwise. I've had no mind to write, but in between I have finished the "Carol and Dog Block."

October 12

I started work on the "University Hospital Block." Love the work but I must say it is very tedious. Coming along pretty good. In fact, it's about half finished. Had the baseball playoffs to keep me company. Cut a little grass. I guess that is what has me so tense. My feet and legs always break out. Maybe I will have to give it up.

I'm working on the "Civil Rights Institute Block." Found this among some old newspapers I had saved. I'm quite a packrat. I had thought at one time that I would do it for a wall hanging.

Coming pretty good on this "Civil Rights Block." I like what I've done. I say again, this has been my best work on this quilt and I'm so glad. Even though sometimes I say this is the last? I wonder, experiencing a depressing and bad time now. Old something that happened $3\frac{1}{2}$ years ago, keeps coming back to haunt me. But I'll live through this and come out smiling like a rose.

November 3

Haven't written on this in a long time. I have had a few worries, nothing serious, but nagging, aggravating things. But thank God, I feel

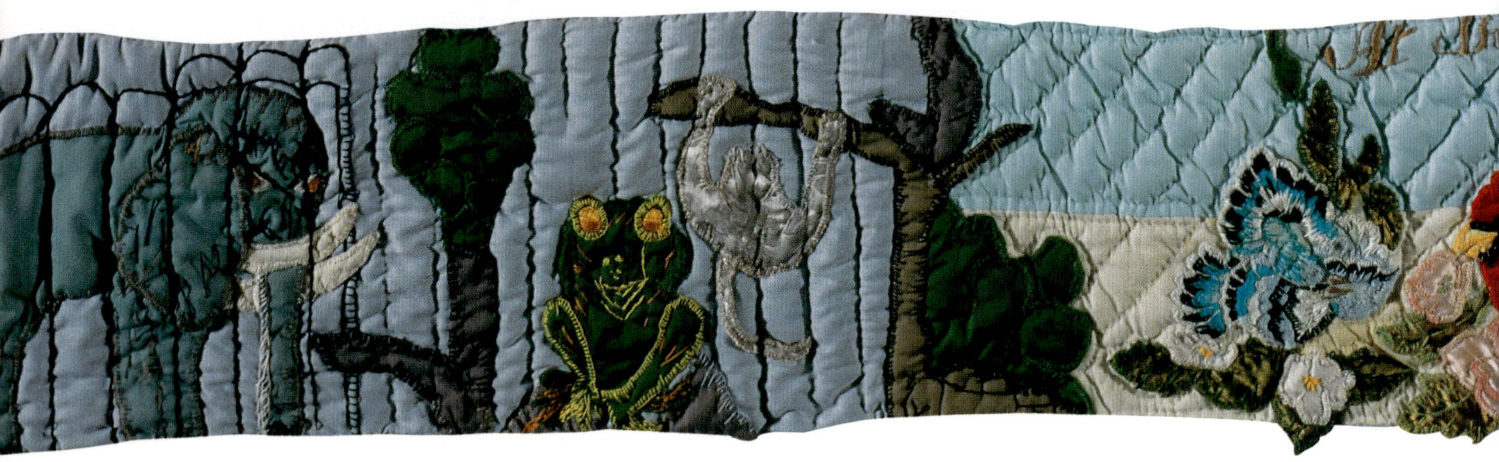

much, much more secure in my God's love. I'm going to try to go on. I have been working but not writing. I have worked hard on the "Civil Rights Building" and the "Botanical Garden Block." Just had no mind to write. Hope you all have been A-OK.

December 12

Today is not one of my best, I'm very depressed. It's cold and I feel so crippled up. I have not done a lot this week, just kind of hopping along. Funeral in the family, one of the last two aunts, made me wonder. Still have this court mess on my mind. Not actually worrying, just kind of thinking.

Working a little on the "Botanical Garden Block." Like what I've done, just going so slow. Very tired, I have worked so hard this year. But trying to keep going. I don't want to stop, I might never start again. Hope you two are in a good mood this morning. Hope to have this finished before Christmas.

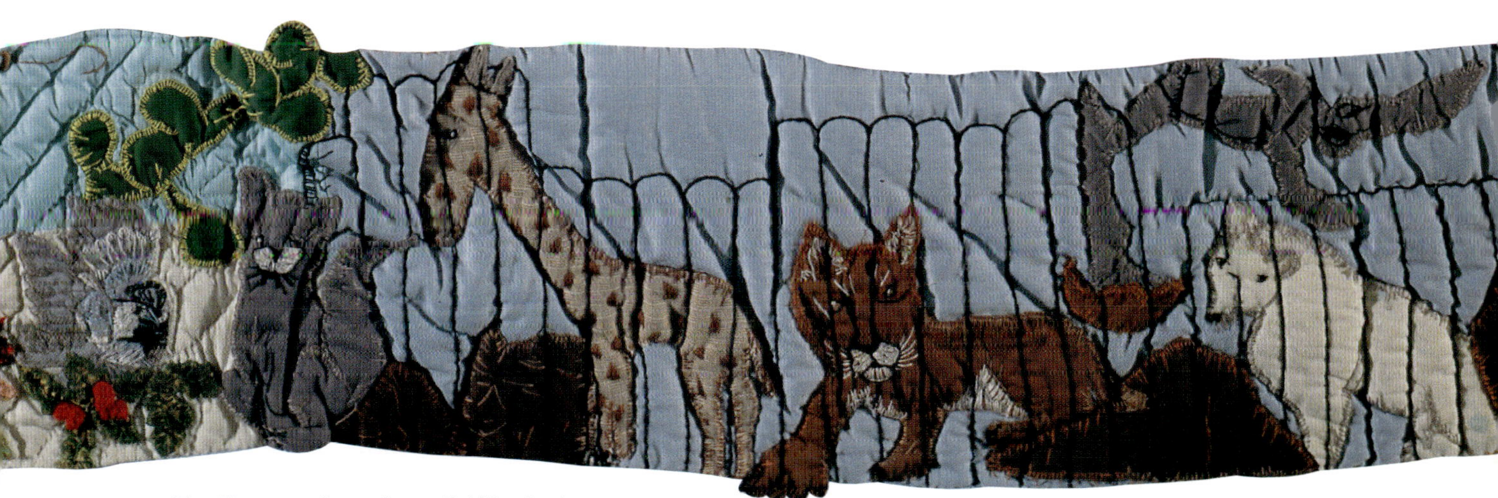

The Zoo strip from *Beautiful Birmingham.*

Today again is a depressing day, when it is hard to get anything done. Just pressing [on], waiting for whatever is coming.

December 27

This is nearing the end of a year that I have done a lot of work. Quilts and otherwise. I have stopped wondering and trying to decide what tomorrow will bring. Just living in hope and trying to go.

I try not to think about it but my hand is getting worse and worse. It has been almost a year or two since I had surgery done. Now the knot is larger than ever. Beginning to pain me, but I shall certainly finish this quilt.

December 28

This morning I feel better! I'm so tickled, the little bit I [have done] on this block—the zoo—I like. I'm going to visit a little today, my only true friend in Greene County (smile), Mrs. Lillie Barnes. How are you two guys today? I guess your daughter was home for the holidays. Would you believe I have not had a chance to read my book? I love doing this quilt. It is indeed a work of history.

December 30

Haven't written in a long time. I have finished the "Civil Rights Block" and the "Botanical Garden," two very tedious blocks. Didn't do as well as I would have liked, but finished the "Civil Rights Building Block." Couldn't get my mind to stay with the idea, just pushed hard to the end. Work on the "Botanical Garden Block" was a little better, playing and experimenting with new fabric. Hope you can see what I thought I saw.

January 1, 1992

Very cloudy and depressing day. But thanks be to God, I'm alive and have control of my faculties. Slept so late because I couldn't sleep last night. I have these nights. I finally went to sleep at 5:00. Sitting by myself watching a little of the Rose Parade. Never cared for parades to be a participant or a spectator. Working on this "Zoo Block," took me a while to come up with something, but now, not too bad.

Lonely night, spent a part of the day with my favorite granddaughter. Sometimes I hate to leave them. Crazy? I know, but that's the way it is! I guess because I was never nobody's favorite.

January 11

Trying to work a little, not much spirit. Rainy weather makes me crazy. Taking so much time on this "Zoo Block." Like what I have done, hope you will too.

January 14

Well, what will tomorrow bring? Have no thoughts, that's what the scripture says. It will bring whatever is God's will. We just hope we will like it. One thing I'm going to do is the best I can today. This zoo strip or block is getting on my nerves. I can't get it finished. Sometimes this happens. I just keep adding on until I go crazy with finishing it. Oh help!

January 17

Oh, what a beautiful morning! My God what a beautiful day.

A Word from Jim Sokol

Alex Haley, who passed away in February, 1992, was a great storyteller. Haley's *Roots* combined many elements to paint a vivid and proud picture of a peoples' history.

Nora Ezell is also a great storyteller. Ezell takes bits and pieces of cloth and imposes upon them an ingeniously creative imagination, producing a pictorial story of great power, emotion and beauty.

Nora's story quilts are special . . . perhaps because they reflect a lot about her roots. They are about subjects of which she knows and feels a great deal, and she stitches much of herself into them.

For example, "Beautiful Birmingham" (made for my daughter Caroline) includes designs that are both unique to Birmingham and special to Caroline. Nora's presence is there, too. You can see her steady hand and fine eye along with her humor and sense of history. What I like most about the work of both Ezell and Haley is that their work overflows with great humanness and spirituality.

Jim (James) Sokol

The Bible Story Quilt

Monday, June 17, 1991

Hello Mr. Hedges,

Today I started to work in honest on one of your quilts, the Bible Story Quilt. I don't keep a log on traditional quilts, but on the story quilts I like to see how long it takes me, how I feel as I work on it, if the work suited me; as I often say, I'm my own best critic. If it suits or pleases me, usually it will others. It is a beautiful day, so I had to work outside a while, cutting grass and working the grass out of my flowers. Next to quilts I think I love them, then my grandchildren. As you see, I have no living children.

This is a quilt I wanted very much to make. Even though I'm not a fanatic, I'm very interested in the Bible. I read everything I can get my hands on. I really had no intention of selling this, but "old man Need-More" got the best of me. I don't have the slightest notion how long it will take me, because I have some of the grandest ideas I think I ever had. And, even as I write I have a problem that I will explain to you later.

As I try to work, I find it very hard to do as I would like on this quilt. No, I don't have the slightest idea about the buyer, so it's kind of hard to

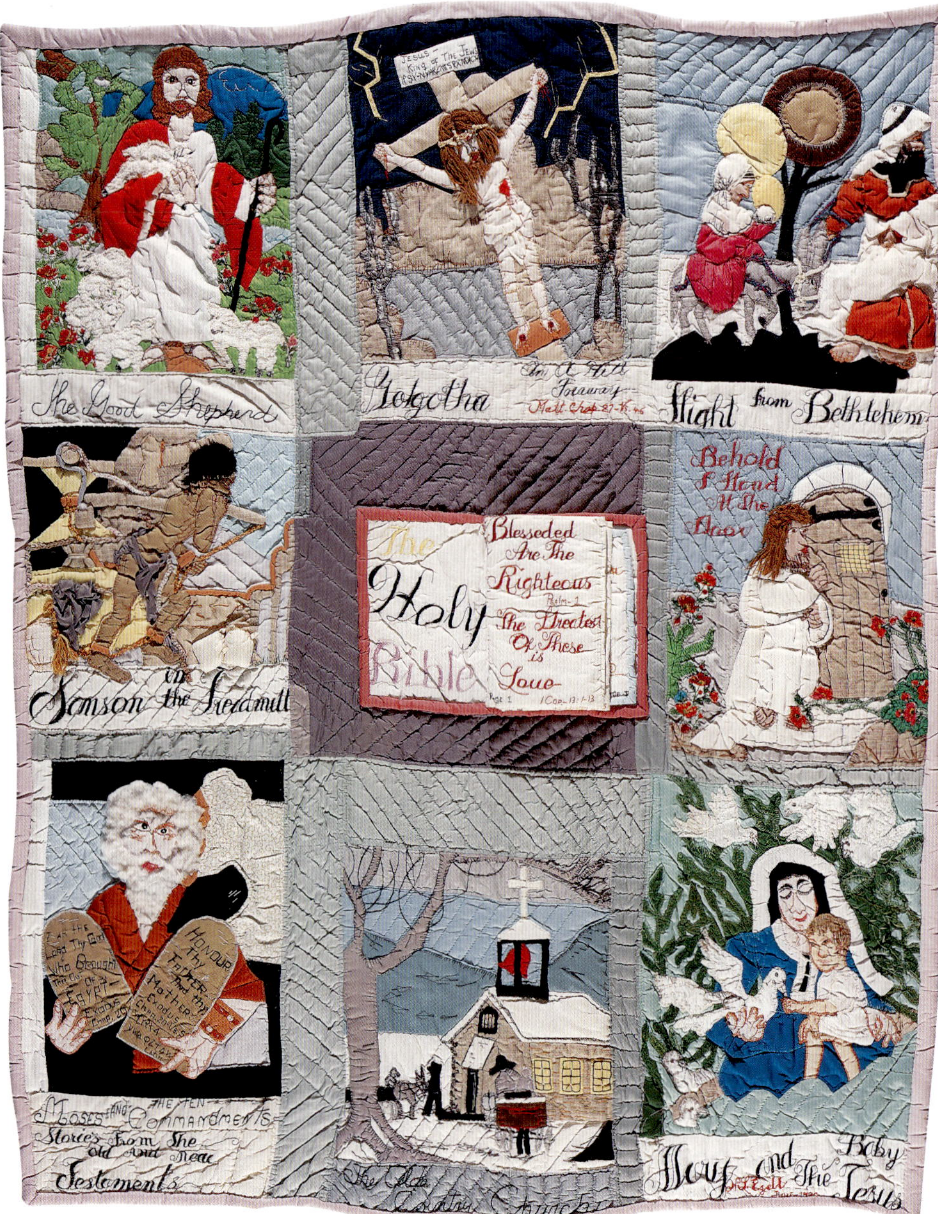

The Bible Story Quilt, Stories from the Old and New Testaments

Signed and dated, "N. L. Ezell June 1990."

Approximately 74 inches by 91 inches, cottons, cotton/polyester blends, cotton terrycloth, polished cotton, wool and cotton yarn, cotton/polyester fleece, cotton tape, ribbon, lace, and embroidery. Collection of Jim Hedges.

get going. I have worked very hard and long this year and I'm very tired, so maybe this is a factor. Now the weather is very hot—kind of gets next to me.

Sunday, August 18, 1991

A long time since I worked on this. I shall certainly finish it, but it is so hard to work. Sometime when I go to church I get consolation. I have been to church and then a church meeting but I feel simply nothing. Sometime I feel like God has forsaken me, yet somewhere in my heart I know this is not so. It's just that I need to make me happy.

I'm trying to work on the block "Moses and the Ten Commandments." I love this very much but I don't seem to be able to do what I want. I have always prided myself on knowing exactly what I wanted to do, but no more. I can't bring things out the way I want to. But maybe I will be able to see you soon, and be able to work better. So what do you think of this? Kind of, sort of, well maybe— yes, I know.

I finally made [up] my mind to go to the doctor yesterday. This morning after starting my medication, I'm much better. A good night's sleep and I feel ready for bear! (smile) Don't these hands say so? I know about my grandson; I saw my granddaughter yesterday and I just generally feel better, so let's go, Nora.

So this "Ten Commandments" block is almost finished. Pretty good work still a little off—I wonder if I'm losing something? Well, I'll try to finish; God help me to carry on.

After a few off days from writing, at least I can add a few words. After

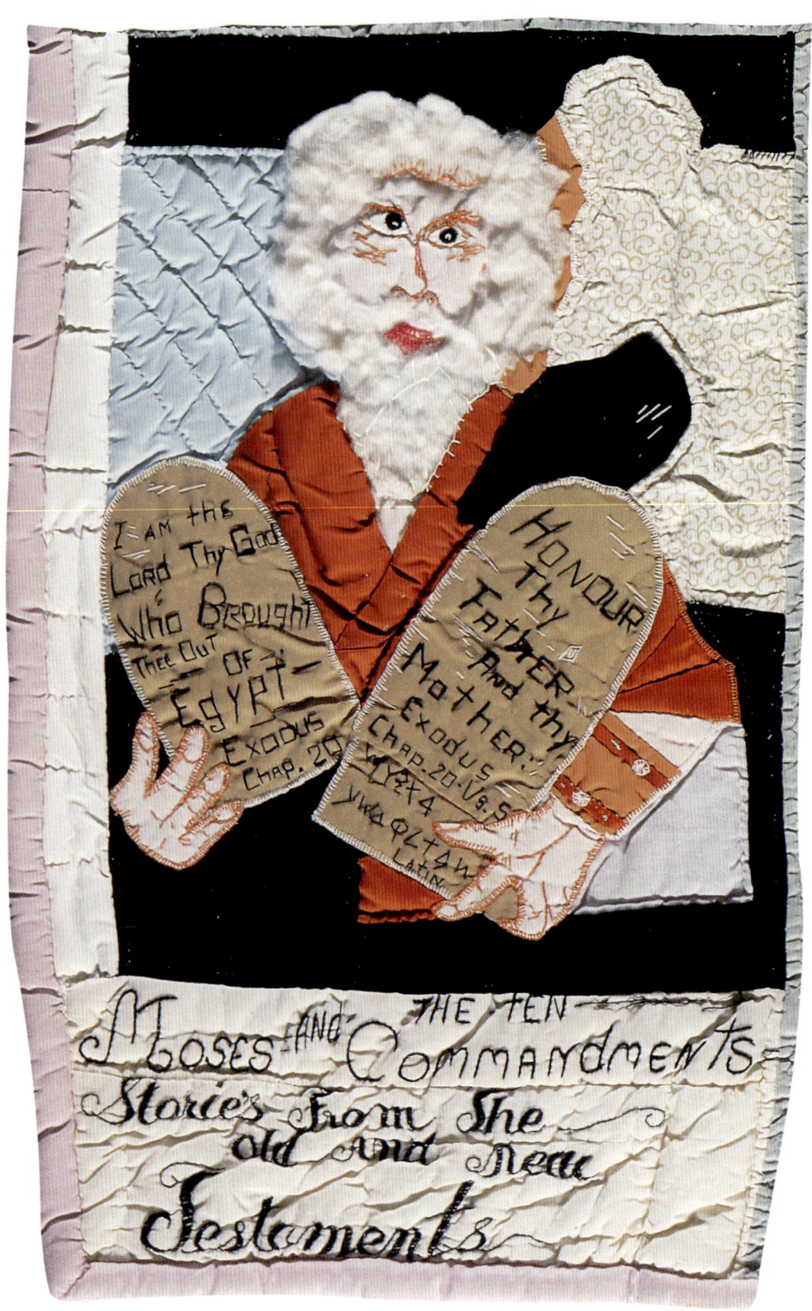

The *Bible Story Quilt* began with this block.

seeing you again and talking to you, I feel better. Usually, I don't care how bad your situation is, somebody else has one more problem than you. Sometimes, repeating this to myself gives me a little hope.

I finally finished "Moses and the Ten Commandments." I started again on "The Good Shepherd" block; some of it came very well and some is a bit more complicated, but with the help of God, I shall do it.

The weather is much cooler and that's good. I have worked very hard in my yard the past two weeks. I have not done a lot of quilting because I have been out of sorts. I have been able to work very well on the Bible story blocks; the work is good, but not like I would like it to be. But I'm getting a little older, so my insights are not as keen as they used to be. Sometimes still my mind takes control.

This week I set up the block "Golgotha" or "Jesus on the Cross." I like it. When I lay down I can't sleep, as my mind is working beautifully now. I got the "Samson" block in my sights. Can you follow me? I can take you on a trip when I design a quilt. (smile)

Today has been one of those days when I tried to rest. I didn't go to church, as sometimes I get to feeling like either something is wrong with me or the church I attend. I realize that sometimes you have to check on yourself. I believe everything in the Bible is true, but sometimes I'm left in doubt.

So I started doing this quilt with the hope that I might get some of my frustration out. I have a special something in each of the blocks. I have thought a great deal and picked out the ones that I think I can identify with; crazy, maybe, but this is how it is. I really had no thought of selling this, but I'm so very happy (and believe me, I don't have much of this in my life), which is not how I started this year.

So our weather has cooled, which is good and bad; as the rains start and it gets cool, my uncle takes over. You don't know him? Oh, he is Uncle Arthur. Still don't know? Well wait a few more years and he will claim you too! (smile)

I'm working hard on the "Golgotha," which is coming along pretty good, really better than I thought. I'm trying not to get too carried away. My thoughts want to do this or that—add on something else.

Friday, September 27, 1991

Tonight I finished the block "Golgotha," or "Jesus on the Cross." Pretty good work. I'm nervous today; I'm getting a lot of that lately, for no good reason, I just get the shakes. I have worked pretty good and the work is [good] too, but somehow I don't seem to be able to relax. It always seems I'm just waiting for something to happen. Oh well, on to the next block, "Samson" or "The Bible." I'll decide tomorrow. Wish me luck.

Mr. Hedges, tell me, do you ever, but ever, find yourself so tense it's pathetic? You haven't? Well good for you.

I've worked good on this "Mary and the Baby Jesus" block, but I'm just waiting. The only thing else that's good is the weather. We are having our best. I'm at my best with this kind of weather, usually that's the case. Some crank who wouldn't give me his name called here for David, is it something with him? I wonder.

After so long a stop, I finally got back to this quilt. I haven't felt really good in quite a while. I've just been hanging on, doing what need to be, and shying away from the rest. My house has promised me that it will definitely clean itself. Everything is so dirty and dusty. Is this the way old age sneaks up on you? If so, shame on me! (smile) So much for the self pity and abuse. On with the quilt.

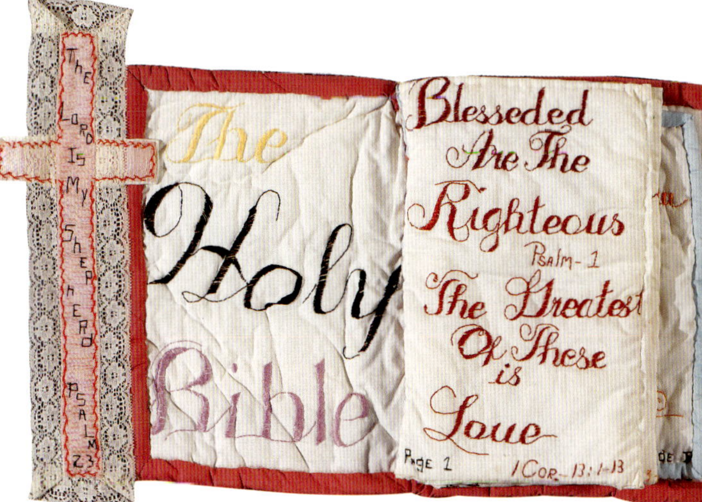

A three-dimensional Bible, complete with special bookmark, centers the quilt.

October 19 and 20

Oh, for the first time I went to Kentuck Park Festival, so many people, so many artists, so many vendors, until I decided never again. I did well as it goes with me. I got orders for two story quilts and one dress, so that is very good, close to $2,500 or a little more. I talked to so many people. I would start with one or two, and end up with 75 or 100. So many people told me they thought I was such a good story teller. Channel 10 also made another part of the commentary. They will air in February. So many people were so tickled to be on television.

October 23

So back to the old grind, the block, "Behold I Stand at the Door and Knock," pretty good work. I got so many compliments. Yes, I carried the unfinished quilt and it really made the show. So on I will go.

When I started work on "The Bible" block, I had so many things in mind, I wanted to do more than I did, but this was a very depressing time with me. We have had some rain which we desperately needed. So I can't think or concentrate at this time. I've had several dreams that disturb me. My grandchildren, especially David and Audrey, have bothered me, but, as always, I try not to intervene. I've had some news concerning the family that wasn't good, but so what? Most of my life they have pushed me out as the dumb one, but God has always taken care of me. To get back to the block, I find that I used verses or chapters that appeal to me at this time. A verse I have always loved and depended on in times of crisis (so please excuse what I need right now).

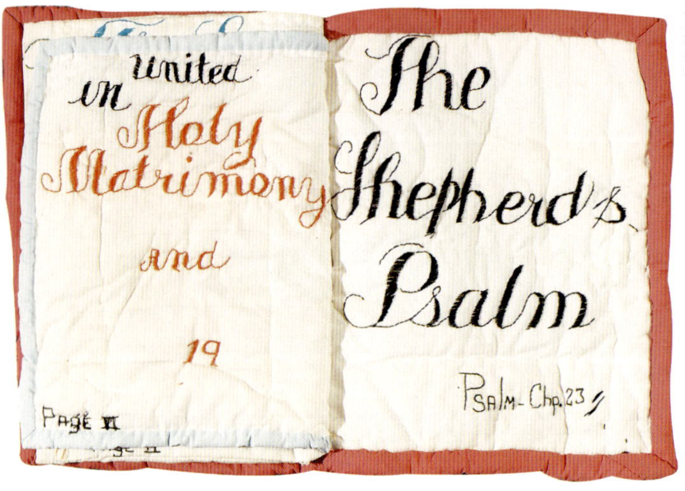

I'm contemplating a move again. Work has been my constant companion for three or more years, but I'm very tired, as I realized one day I would be. Work cannot answer me back, so that gets very tiresome. I want live company. So I'm thinking of moving somewhere else.

Well, it has been Sunday all day, but I've been hard pressed to tell this difference, as this has been one of those kind of weeks, when nothing happens as planned or hoped for. It just does its own thing. Kind of crazy, huh?

I have worked very hard on the "Samson" block. The work and idea is fine but I don't like the color of the man [Samson].

I just couldn't find the color I wanted, even though I bought several pieces. Maybe if I had used more people on the picture it would have been better, but, no matter what, the idea is very good. This was something in the Bible that always amazed me. It was kind of hard to choose between Samson in the treadmill or when he pulled the arena pillars down.

Well, I got to get on, I have finished all the blocks. So I have to set this together and quilt. I would like to have it finished completely by Christmas.

December 1st

It's after Thanksgiving, of course, but every day is Thanksgiving with me. I thank God for keeping me in mind and taking care of me. I have worked long and hard on this quilt and hope it will give you as many happy hours to look at as it gave me to make it.

God bless you and keep you safe for a long time. Buy quilts from me. Hope to see you soon.

Nora Lee Ezell

Winner of the 1990 Heritage Award

Jim Hedges' Perspective on *The Bible Story Quilt* and Its Maker

I first saw Nora Ezell's work in a quilt show at the Brooks Museum in Memphis, but I had little prospect of meeting her, until chance brought us together at an outdoor art festival in Birmingham.

As a result of this first brief meeting, I was fortunate enough to be able to commission Mrs. Ezell to create a Bible Story quilt for me, little knowing what would transpire.

Nora said I must be patient, for it would be over a year before I could see the quilt. Several months later on my way home from Mississippi, I stopped off the freeway in Eutaw, Alabama to say hello by telephone to Mrs. Ezell. This was my second contact with her. To my amazement, Mrs. Ezell stated that she had just been thinking about me and, further, she told me that she wrote to me almost every day.

Flattered and puzzled, I had to find out more about this lady and her quilts, so off I detoured to Nora Ezell's house. What I found was a fiercely independent, self-assured, creative, inspiring, loving lady. Nora always has several projects working at once. She also explained to me that as she makes a story quilt, she maintains a daily diary written to the purchaser, noting the time spent and events of the day.

She wanted to show me the progress she was making on my quilt, and proudly unfolded a large panel of Jesus, Mary, and Joseph. I immediately envisioned this panel as the focal point and centerpiece of the quilt, surrounded by a border of smaller traditional squares. I was elated. It was magnificent.

She then said she wanted to show me the other panel she had completed. It was a scene depicting Samson. This quilt was truly going to be spectacular with two intricate panels, I thought. A couple of hours later, Nora had pulled out the ninth panel. By that time, I was speechless.

The quilt was completed several months later—a true masterpiece accompanied by a the wonderful personal diary of the quilt's progress. The total recorded time was over 1,500 hours. Of course, as Nora explained, she never recorded the time spent working on the quilt on Sunday, since we are not supposed to work for money on the Lord's day.

Jim Hedges

Lookout Mountain, Tennessee

The Second Bible Story Quilt

[During the construction of the first *Bible Story Quilt*, Mrs. Ezell was approached by many other potential buyers. Especially disappointed to learn that the quilt was already sold were the Millers of Louisville, Kentucky, for whom Mrs. Ezell would make the *Kentucky Derby Quilt*. Eventually Mrs. Ezell decided to make another *Bible Story Quilt*, and when they learned of her plans, the Millers immediately made arrangements to purchase the completed top. Because Mrs. Miller is a fiber artist and quilt designer in her own right, she negotiated with Mrs. Ezell for the right to quilt the piece herself. Completely different Bible stories provided the inspiration for the second quilt; blocks are named as follows: Daniel in the Lion's Den, the Song of the Prophetess, Tomb of the Virgin Mary, The Light of the World, The Baptism (spelled Baptistism on the quilt), The Vision of Ezekiel, and The Resurrection.]

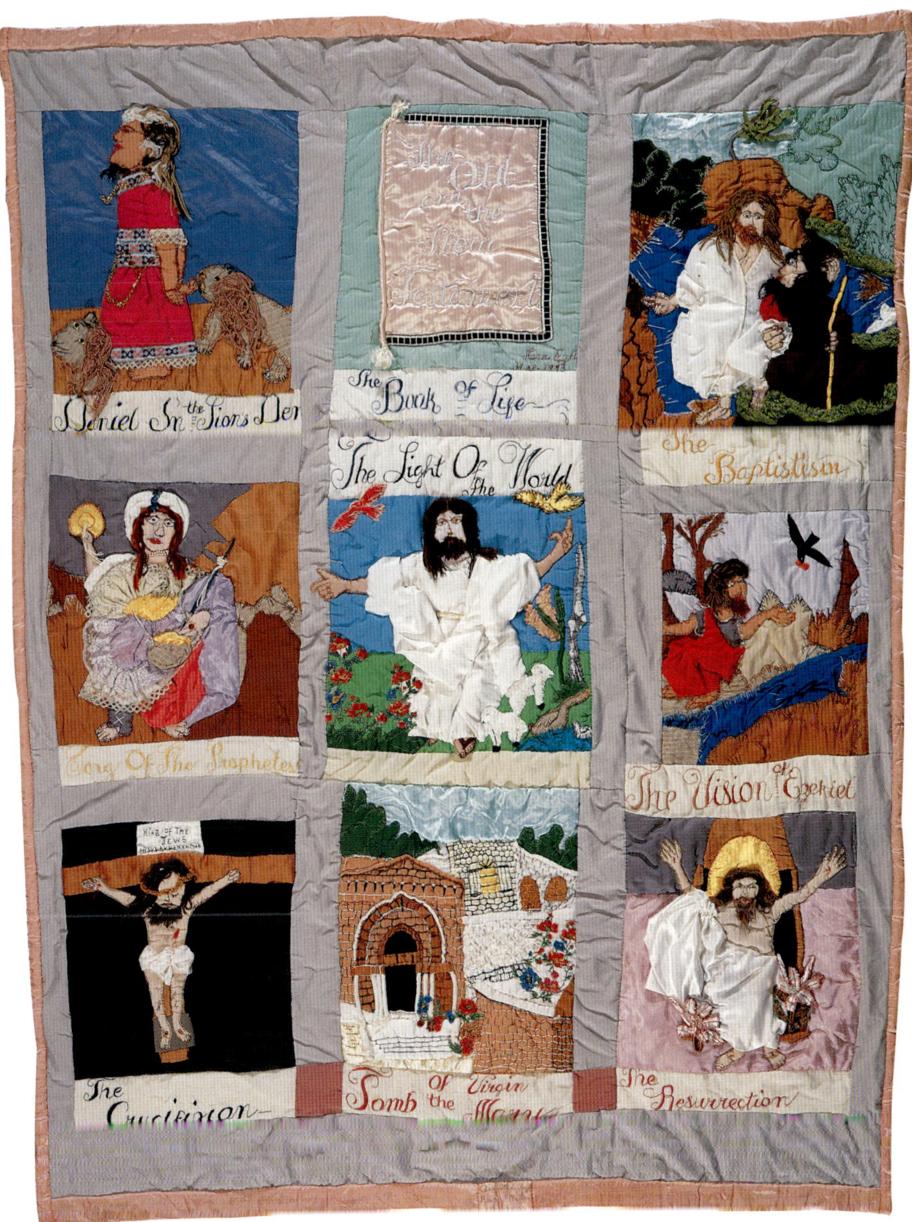

The Second Bible Story Quilt

Signed and dated, "Nora Ezell, Oct. 1993."

71 inches by 92 inches; cotton and cotton polyester fabrics; cotton terrycloth, woven nylon, acrylic yarn, cotton lace, costume jewelry, nylon cord. Quilted by and in the collection of Anne Miller.

Kentucky Derby Quilt

I met Annie T. Miller at the Kentuck Festival of the Arts in 1991. Kentuck is not a festival that I enjoyed—so much dust, too much hot weather, too much tiredness, too much work for one year, too much talking and talking, too much and too many people, just hundreds and hundreds, more, I think, than at City Stages in Birmingham. But I decided I had to make this festival at least once.

I met so many wonderful people. I would start talking with two or three and end up with as many as 150. I saw this man and woman standing around, and eventually they got a chance to talk to me, and what a pair! From Louisville, Kentucky, beautiful horse country. I have never been to the Derby, but one day I shall go. Where will I get the money? I don't know, but I shall certainly go.

I took with me, on this hot, stuffy day, a few quilts from past shows, since I was not able and did not have enough time to make anything new. The exception was one *Bible Story Quilt*, which was not finished, but far enough along to tell what it was all about. She [Mrs. Miller] came right up and said, "I want to buy this."

I had to say, "Sorry, it's already sold."

"Then will you make me one?"

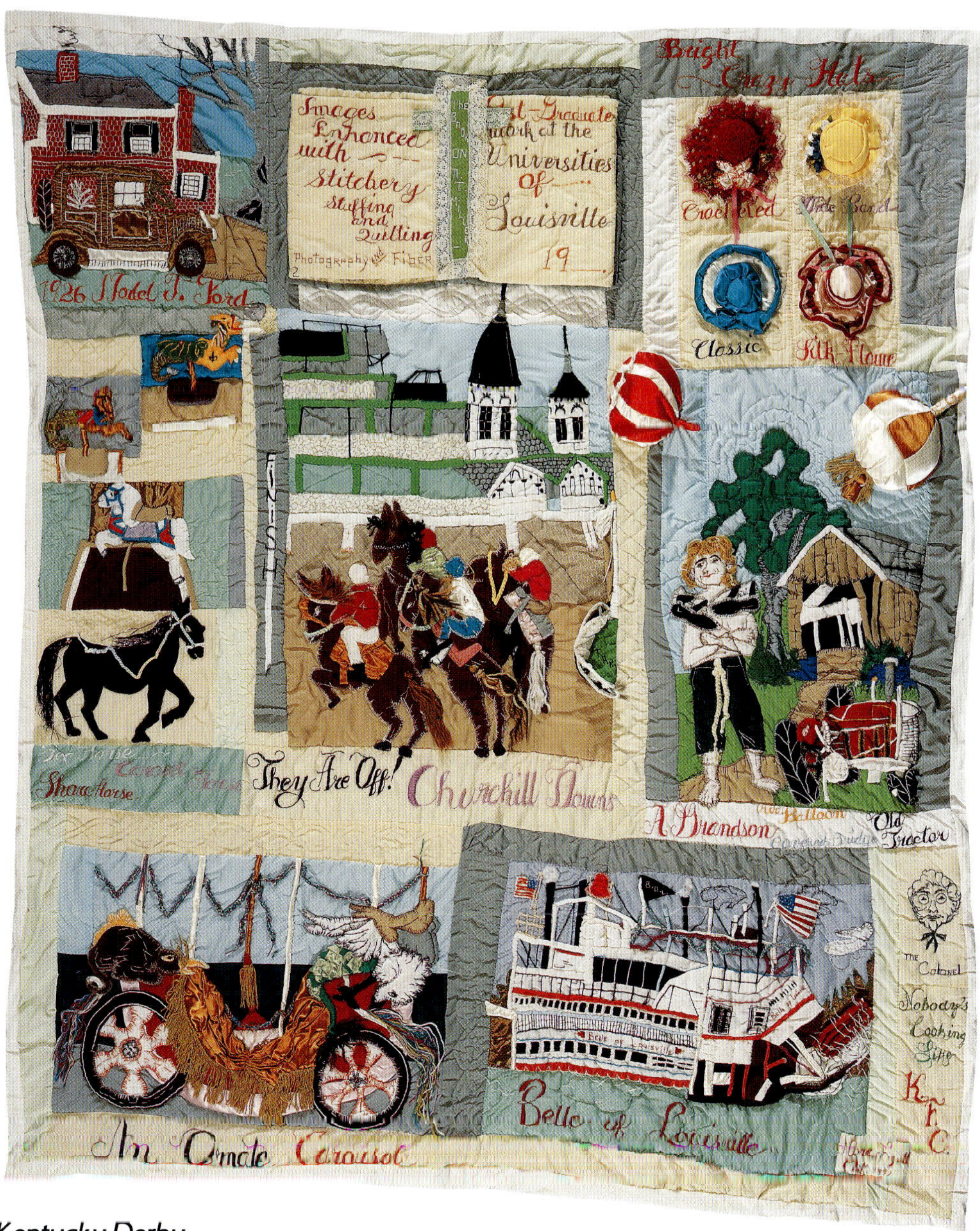

Kentucky Derby

Signed and dated "Nora Ezell, Oct. 1991."

Cottons, cotton/polyester blends, satins, velvets, acetates, ribbons, fringes, acrylic yarn, crochet work, embroidery. Quilted by and collection of Anne T. Miller.

"Sorry, I never make but one quilt of any given subject."

"O.K. Please make me a story quilt."

"Of course I will." After many hugs, I said, "What would you like?"

"You'll do anything?"

"Yes, anything you want, as long as you furnish the material for the pattern." So it was settled.

November 18, 1991

I started this quilt today, on one of those kind of "sorta" days, with my mind on a thousand different things. One [voice] says stay here, another says find you a pleasanter place to live. The main one says go to work on that quilt.

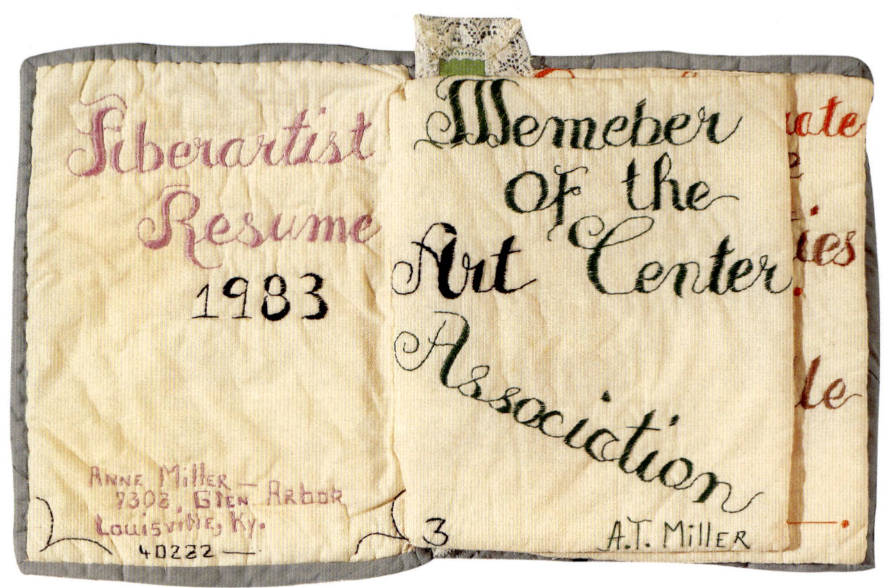

The "Book" on Annie T. Miller contains six pages.

So I got started on the book. About what? About you. This is the "Book on Annie T. Miller." You like that? I hope so. So I work for a few days, and wouldn't you know, my grandchild starts bugging me. Which one? Our family baby, David. Stuck in New Jersey.

So off I go, leaving quilt and all my good ideas, and go after him. When we got in the car, ready to come back to Alabama, wouldn't you know it, I was the sickest I have ever been in my life. Came back and stayed up and down for a month.

I enjoyed doing this and it went pretty good. Not much to it. Just a matter of which thing I would use. Finally got it finished. The book marker. What do you have to say? Amen.

Cloudy and not enough spirit to do anything. After about three sets of prayers and a second nap for the day, I started on "The Gay Hats." Oh, do I love this. Why? Because I never go to morning service at church without a hat. And you know I make them! My husband used to get cute and go out and buy me one, but the ones I made, I loved best. I can just see you with the crochet one, laughing your gay laugh. How I love happy people. Sometimes I don't know which of my grands I love best, because sometimes they make me laugh so. You have to meet them. They are a trip

JANUARY 6TH.

I can look back and wonder, would I ever have thought of this 56 years ago? Oh my, it sounds like a lifetime! When I got married I didn't have a never mind about 1990 . . . much less 92. But here it is, and what do

I have to look back and say? I raised my one child, now dead 7 years and my husband 5 years. I'm alone tonight, "Just me and my quilts." Working on this *Kentucky Derby* quilt, working on this racetrack block. It's doing its best to get the best of me, but no way. I shall finish it, and also the quilt, one day. I have been working, it looks like, forever on it. It is so much to it.

Wednesday, January 8th

A day to remember. I'm talking on the phone to a lady who had sent someone to my house to buy quilts, and who knocks on my door but the guy. So we talked, and he bought one quilt and ordered another; pretty good day.

Well, getting back to this block, he knew in a minute it was going to be Churchill Downs, as he grew up in Kentucky and had been there any number of times. So, back I go to this block that's driving me on. This has not been my best work. Good, but mentally I feel like heck. I laughed when I talked to one of my sisters in California. She said she had been just simply sick and hurting all the Fall, and the same has been said of me. I have worked as faithfully as I could, but that certain something was not there.

January 19, 1992

This has been a weekend to remember; snow when I awoke this morning. I thought maybe I was back in New Jersey or Kentucky. I'm a little sad this morning; so many funerals in the neighborhood. But God is going to do His will. Amen.

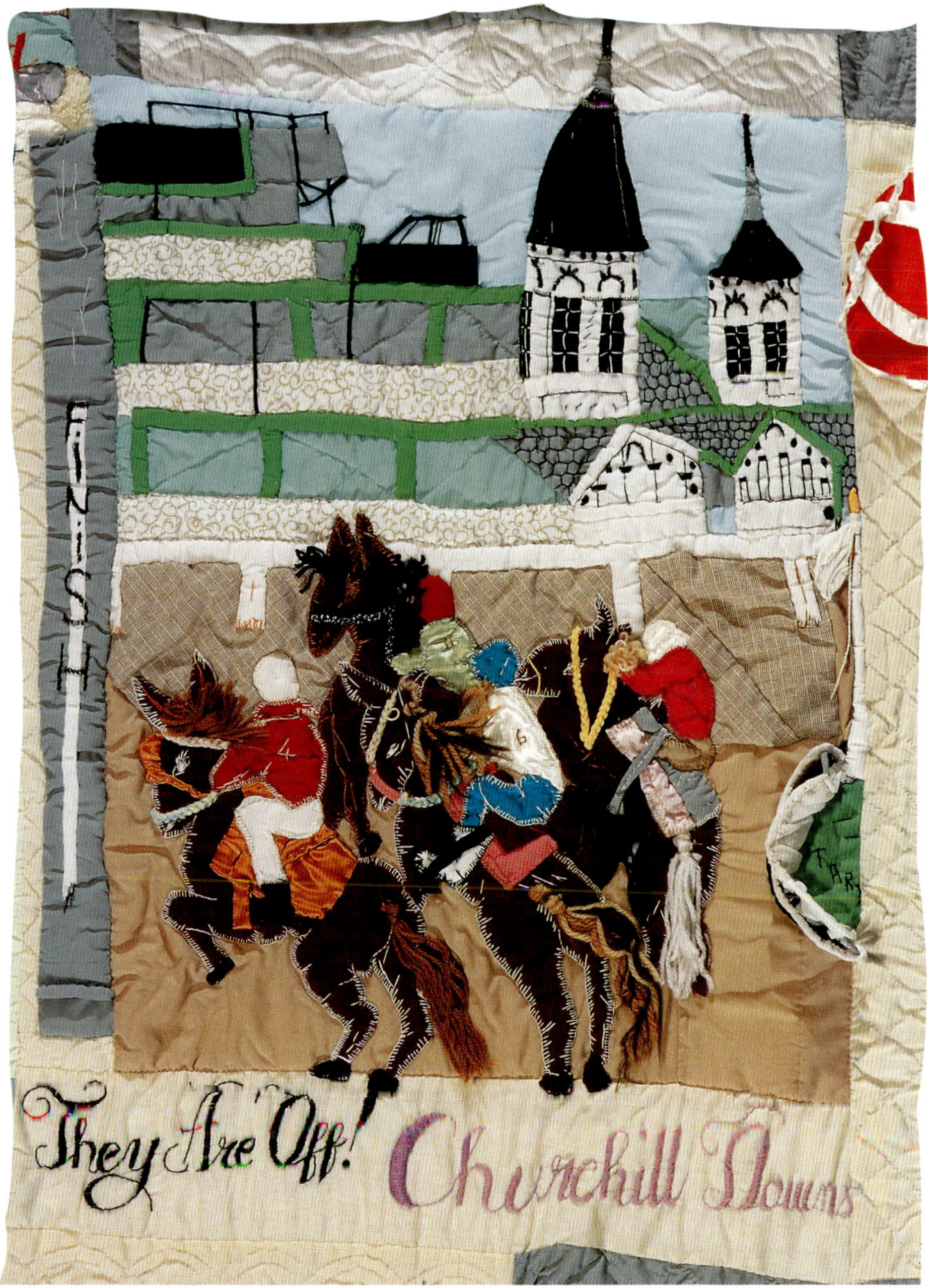

After completing the diary of Anne Miller's achievements, Mrs. Ezell began the picture blocks with this one.

Well, I'm working hard on this "Ornate Carousel Cart." I thought I would sail through it because I had it fixed so good in my mind. But first it was a miss on the wheels, then this drapery-like something. I wish I could be coming instead of going, but at 74 what can you say; be glad you are doing what you are. I see so many of my friends not able to do anything, but God is my rock, my sword and shield, so how can I fail, when nothing is impossible for Him? My mind is running on the next block; what will it be? Black Beauty and your oldest grandson. You like it? Hope he will too. But you know these youngsters, they are so like that. (smile)

Trying to finish this "Carousel Cart." Looks pretty good, but not like I thought it would. I'm still in this melancholy state; don't seem to be able to come out of it. The reason, besides being sick most days, is that I'm still fighting this notion of living somewhere else. Just so tired of this rut I'm in. It is so hard to do this kind of work when you are like that. Worked pretty good for a while this morning; gave me a little lift. So I guess I will run on to the end of this block. The first of May is not too far away, so get going, Nora, so you can see Annie T. very soon.

Spring garden, a "Sampler," "Grandmother's Flower Garden," started a new "Dresden Plate" and a "Crazy Quilt," which is a very old pattern. I have done some beautiful towels, a very few very odd pillows, tried some "fly swatter" hanging decorations, made one granddaughter a winter coat, plus a few outfits for myself. You don't believe it? Come on with me. I have proof there.

Oh yes, I quilted one of the hardest quilts I have ever seen. The lady made it on the sewing machine, but she wanted me to hand-quilt it. I had to stop ever so often and pull and cut off threads. She used a cheap sheet, which was as hard as the callous on my fingers. I almost died trying to quilt it. Some of her seams came open; most of them were not turned right. It was supposed to be a "Double Irish Chain," but please don't ask me what I thought it was. Well, so much for the complaining part of this.

On with the next block. It has still been a triumph for me to get anything done on this quilt. Sometimes I think I must be truly sick. This block came out pretty good. [This is probably the "Belle of Louisville" block.]

Hope you like it. When I started I saw it so clearly, but gradually I lost some of it along the way. Did I ever have to push. But I, and a lot of others that have seen it, find it hard to believe. Do not ask me how I can do it with no training. I never even made a pattern. Well, it's a gift from God, maybe so. But I have a living to make for myself and others and happen not to be (as Mrs. Richards says) "Born with a silver foot in my mouth." (smile) What can you say?

Well, it's getting ready to rain again, but we have had some pretty days. I tried to uncover some leaves and trash. My neighbors' dogs killed some of my chickens, but they paid me, so what can I do but grieve for them. Enough crap. On with the show! The quilt I mean. I have this block, plus "The Car," "J.W. Miller's Carousel Horse," "Hot Air Balloon," and "The Pet Horse" (which I named Black Beauty), so I must get on with it, if I can.

This has been one of those times when I have not been able to do my best. I have been sick and just plain tired. All the hard years have taken their toll, and it has come to the front this past fall and winter. Please don't become confused, I am grateful to God for my life and my living, but I'm merely stating some facts. As soon as I'm finished I must check with my doctor, and later maybe a visit to some hospital. I feel like something is very wrong, besides old age. (Smile)

I have finally finished the 1926 Model T Ford block. It was really a song. I literally flew through it. My mind got very clear; I could see just how I wanted to do every little detail. The picture of the car was overexposed, but I was able to put in all the details, so that a person could tell it was a car. Don't you think so? I can remember when I was in elementary school, the principal, Mrs. Mattie Alexander, had one. I thought it was something; now I have a 78 Thunderbird, the last big car, and do I think it is something!

I have spent an awful lot of time and materials on this quilt. I have tried to do my best, because I may never do another—Story Quilt, I mean.

So tonight, March 15th, I started the last strip or block. I hope by next week I can call and say I have done all I can. I truly hope you will not only like the story, but the quilt also!

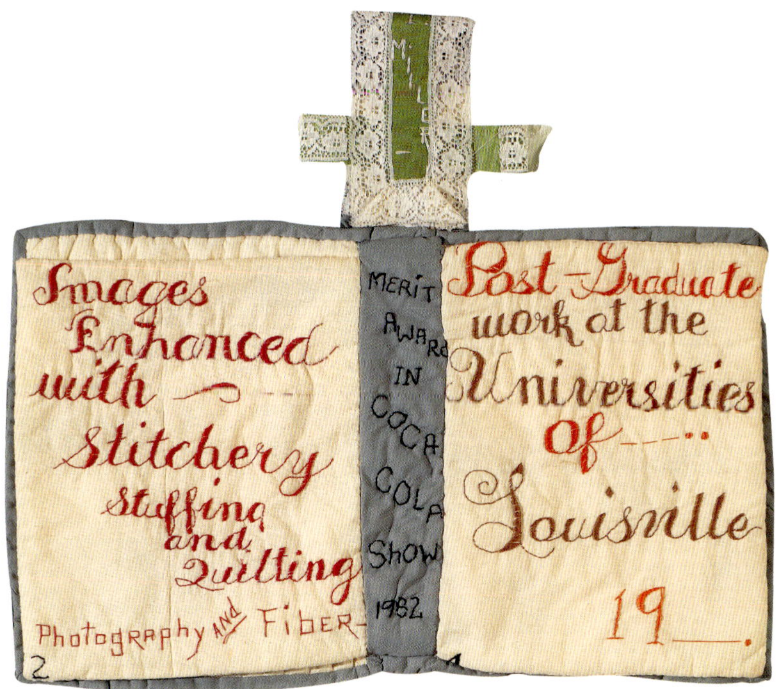

A lace-edged bookmark is folded back to reveal an inscription on the book's spine.

Friday, March 20, 1992

Well, I'm at the end of the *Kentucky Derby* quilt. I started this in October, 1991, so it's been a while. I have enjoyed doing it very much. Some blocks more than others. I had better luck making some. Sometimes I didn't find a good way to do it until afterwards.

So I will have to say goodbye to Annie T. and this quilt, and go on to something else. Right now I shall go to my doctor, and hopefully, get his okay for another year.

I spent a lot of time and money to do this quilt: 845 hours, 22 minutes. I allowed $_an hour. I ended with a price of $_. My price to you is $_.

(No charge for quilting, as she wanted to do it herself. I spent over $122 for materials, embroidery thread, piecing thread and other things I used, and, oh yes, batting.)

I hope you will like this as much as I do.

Wish your husband luck, and maybe I'll see you this year.

Love ya!

Nora Ezell

HERITAGE AWARD WINNER—1990

A Note from The Kentucky Derby Quilt's Owner

My husband, John, "discovered" Nora at the well-known Kentuck Festival and insisted that I go back to meet her. I had passed her booth, thinking she was just another quilter, but then she unwrapped a fabulous Bible story quilt! Alas, it was already sold, even though it was not finished. My heart sank, but she readily agreed to do a commission quilt.

We decided upon a more personal theme, which would include our family, our hobbies, and the famous Kentucky Derby. John's hobbies include photographing covered bridges, driving a model-T Ford, and carving (at that time, he was doing carousel horses). My hobbies are fiber-art related. Nora had always wanted to attend the Kentucky Derby, so we included that, and I sent her lots of clippings for inspiration.

Nora agreed to a collaboration after I sent her my résumé, which includes a first prize in stitchery in an international show. She would do the piecing, and I would add the quilting. She worked at her own pace, keeping her famous log on whatever paper was handy, and she kept stitching through health and sickness.

Everyone we show her work to is amazed at her talent, as are we, but we have a special feeling for it because we know Nora and consider her a very good friend. Like peanuts, one Ezell quilt is not enough. I say that, and I also design quilts. When she said she was starting another Bible quilt, I quickly spoke for it.

We feel so honored to add her work to our collection of folk art. I have enjoyed every hour spent quilting these quilts. It has allowed me to more fully appreciate the imagination, talent, and beautiful embroidery this wonderful woman puts into her work.

Anne Miller
Louisville, Kentucky
July 5, 1995

Time Log for the Musical Instrument Quilt

[Because this was a commissioned piece for an institution, not an individual, Mrs. Ezell did not keep the usual personal log.]

Date	A.M.	P.M.
BLOCK NO. 1: GLORIA CURRY BLOCK		
June 5th, 1992	8:00 to 11:00	6:30 to 9:00
6th	5:30 to 10:00	
7th, Sunday	no work	
8th 92	8:45 to 10:00	6:00 to 9:00
9th	9:30 to 11:30	7:00 to 9:00
10th	shopping	5:30 to 8:00
11th	7:30 to 10:00	8:00 to 10:00
12th 92		12:00 to 4:30
13th	6:15 to 9:30	
14th 92	No work	
15th	8:15 to 10:00	5:40 to 8:30
16th	7:40 to 9:50	6:30 to 9:30
17th	6:00 to 10:00	
18th	8:30 to 10:30	5:15 to 9:00
Fri., 19	City Stages [festival in Birmingham]	
Sat. , 20	"	
Sun., 21	"	
22	No work	
23	"	
24, Wed	6:00 to 9:00	
25	Dr's appointment	8:15 to 9:15
26 Fri	8:15 to 11:00	
27 Sat	7:00 to 9:00	
28 Sun	No work	
6/30 Mon	6:00 to 9:00	

Finished: Hrs. 61, Mins 51 Price $183.75

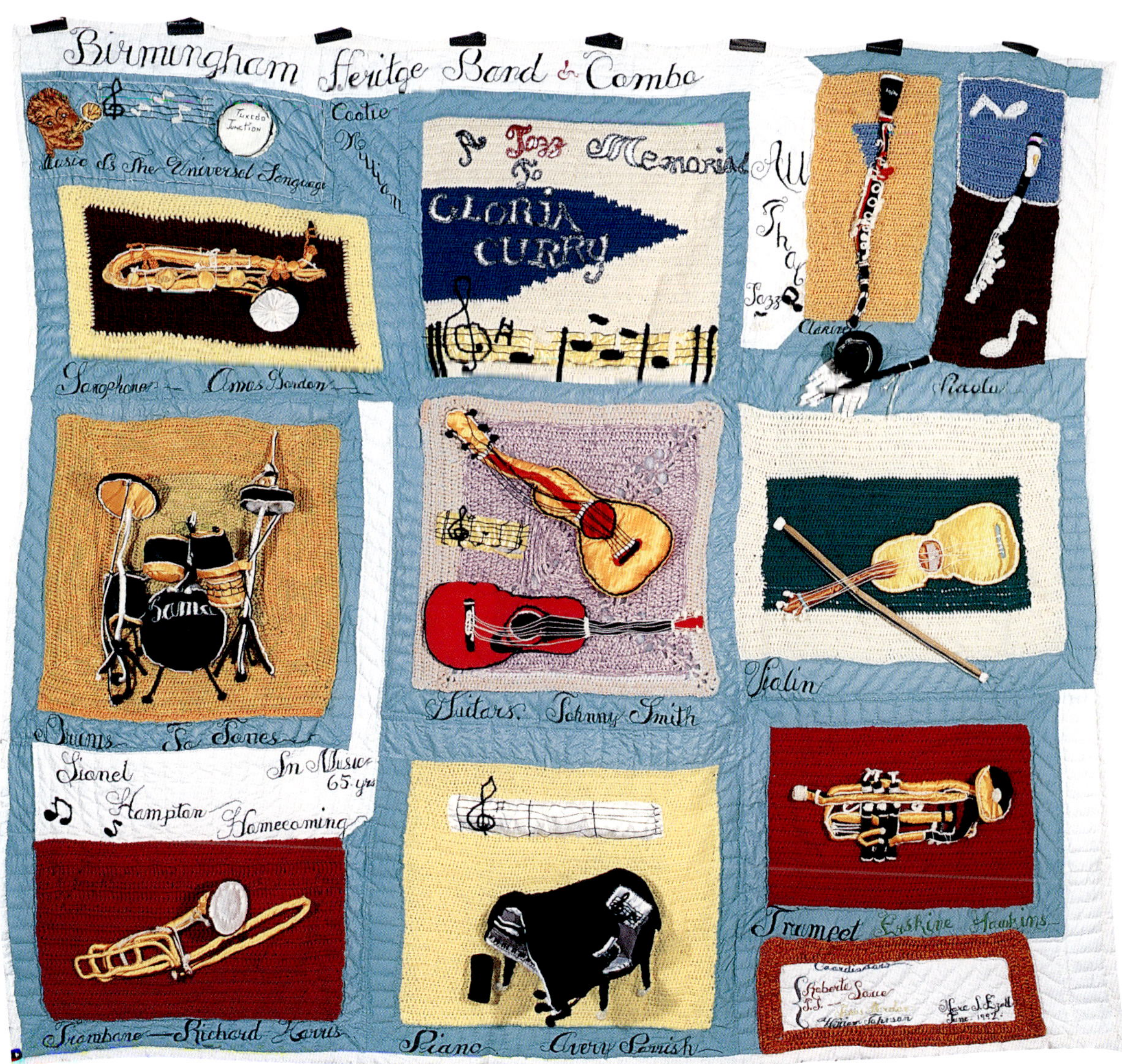

Music is the Universal Language

Signed "Nora L. Ezell, June 1992."

75 inches by 84 inches. Collection of the Alabama Jazz Hall of Fame, Birmingham, gift of Roberta Lowe. Photo courtesy of Crane Hill Publishers and Keith Boyer.

Block No. 2: Piano (Kimball Classic)

Tues 30th	7:15 to 10:00	
July 1st '92	8:00 to 9:15	6:00 to 9:00
2nd '92	6:30 to 9:30	
3 '92	4:30 to 9:30	
July 4th '92: Piano keys		6:30 to 9:30
5:00 to 9:15		
5th Sun.	No work	
6th Mon.	7:30 to 10:00	6:00 to 8:30
7th	8:00 to 9:00	5:30 to 9:00
8th	7:15 to 10:00	6:00 to 10:00
July	9th Thurs.	5:30 to 9:00
10th Fri.	7:40 to 10:00	6:30 to 9:00
11th Sat.	1:30 to 4:00	
July 12th Sun.	No work	
13th	7:30 to 10:00	7:00 to 9:00
14th (allstar game)	6:30 to 10:40	
15th	Shopping	
16th	7:15 to 10:15	

Finished the piano block: Hrs. 62, Mins. 35 Price $187.50

Started the Clarinet Block

16th Thurs.	5:15 to 8:30	
July 17th Fri.	7:40 to 10:00	5:30 to 9:00
18 Sat.	1:00 to 5:15	
19 Sun.	No work	
July 20th Mon.	7:30 to 10:00	5:40 to 9:15
21th Tues.	6:00 to 10:00	
22nd Wed.	8:15 to 10:30	5:00 to 8:30
23rd Thurs.	No work—shopping	
24th Fri.	6:30 to 8:15	

Finished the clarinet block: Hrs. 28, Mins. 30 Price $85.50

Above: The musical scale took 3 hours and 26 minutes to make. Opposite page: The drums are three-dimensional, and like the other blocks, are mounted on a crocheted background.

STARTED THE TRUMPET BLOCK

Sat. July 25th	1:00 to 4:30	7:40 to 9:00
Sun. " 26th	No work	
Mon " 27th	7:40 to 11:00	6:00 to 9:00
Tues " 28th	8:15 to 10:15	No work
Wed. " 29th	7:30 to 9:30	5:30 to 8:30
Thurs. " 30th	9:10 to 10:30	
Fri. " 31st	7:40 to 11:00	6:00 to 8:30
Sat. Aug. 1st	1:00 to 5:00	
Sunday	8:00 to 2:00	No work
Monday 8-3rd	9:00 to 11:00	5:30 to 9:00
Tues. 8-4th	7:30 to 11:00	
Wed. 8-5th	7:50 to 12:00	

Finished: Hrs. 44, Min. 45 Price: $137.25

STARTED THE DRUM BLOCK

Thurs. 8-6th	6:10 to 9:30	
Fri. 8-7th	6:30 to 8:00	6:15 to 10:30
Sat. 8-8th	No work	
Sun. 8-9th	No work	
Mon. 8-10th	Sick	
Tues. 8-11th	Sick	
Wed. 8-12th	Shopping	
Thurs. 8-13th	6:30 to 11:00	6:00 to 8:00
Sept. Tues. 1st '92	7:00 to 11:00	7:30 to 9:00
Wed. 2nd '92	9:00 to 11:00	
Thurs. 3rd.	7:30 to 9:00	
Fri. 4th	6:30 to 11:00	
Sat. 5th '92	11:00 to 4:00	7:30 to 9:30
Sun. 6th	No work.	
Mon. 7th	6:30 to 10:00	5:30 to 8:10
Tues. 8th	7:00 to 9:30	
Wed. 9th	No work	
Thurs. 10th	6:30 to 8:30	5:30 to 9:00
Fri. 11th	6:35 to 9:00	6:00 to 9:30
Sat. 12th	12:30 to 5:00	
Sun. 13th	No work: In Montgomery for the reception	

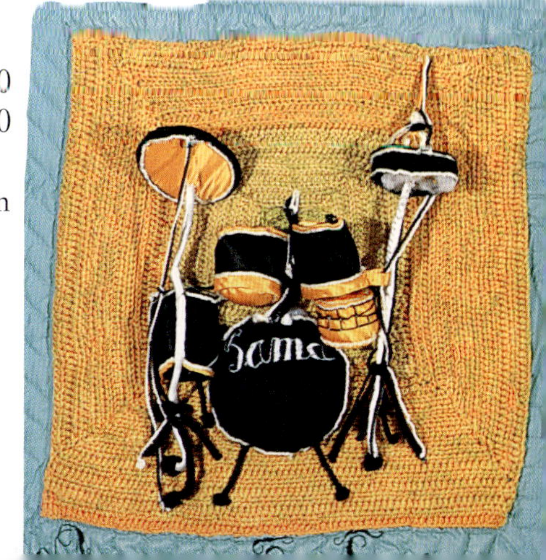

[for "Signs and Symbols: African Images in African-American Quilts"]

Mon. 14th	Sick	
Tues. 15th	Sick	

(In making the drum block I watched the time on the musical scale. It took 3 hrs. 26 mins.)

Wed. 16th	6:45 to 8:45	6:30 to 9:30
Thurs. 17th	6:30 to 8:30	5:15 to 9:00
Fri. 18th	shopping	6:00 to 9:00
Sat. 19th	No work: resting	
Sun. 20th	No work: resting	
Mon. 21st	In Washington	
Fri. 25th		
Sat. 26th	No work	
Sun. 27th	No work	
Mon. 28th	Shopping	6:30 to 10:00
Tues. 29th	6:30 to 11:00	6:00 to 9:30
Wed. 30th	6:15 to 10:00	6:45 to 9:40
Thurs. 10-1st' 92	5:30 to 11:00	
Fri. 10-2nd' 92	6:30 to 10:00	5:45 to 9:50
Sat. 10-3rd' 92	No work	
Sun. 10-4th	No work	
Monday 10-5th	6:30 to 10:00	5:00 to 9:00
Tues. 10-6th	6:15 to 11:00	6:00 to 9:00
Wed. 10-7	7:00 to 10:15	
Thurs. 10-8th	7:30 to 10:30	
Fri. 10-9th	6:00 to 10:30	7:00 to 10:40
Sat. 10-10th	4:00 to 6:30	6:30 to 11:00
Sun. 10-11th	No work	
Finished Drum Block:	Hrs. 163, Min. 31	Price: $490.50

Started Trombone Block

Mon. 12th	1:00 to 4:30	6:30 to 9:00
Tues. 10-13	6:30 to 10:30	
Wed. 10-14th	6:00 to 11:00	6:30 to 11:00
Thurs.10-15th	6:30 to 11:30	
Fri. 10-16th	6:00 to 11:00	
Sat. 10-17	7:30 to 9:40 1st game World Series	
Sun. 10-18	Kentuck Park Festival—yesterday too	

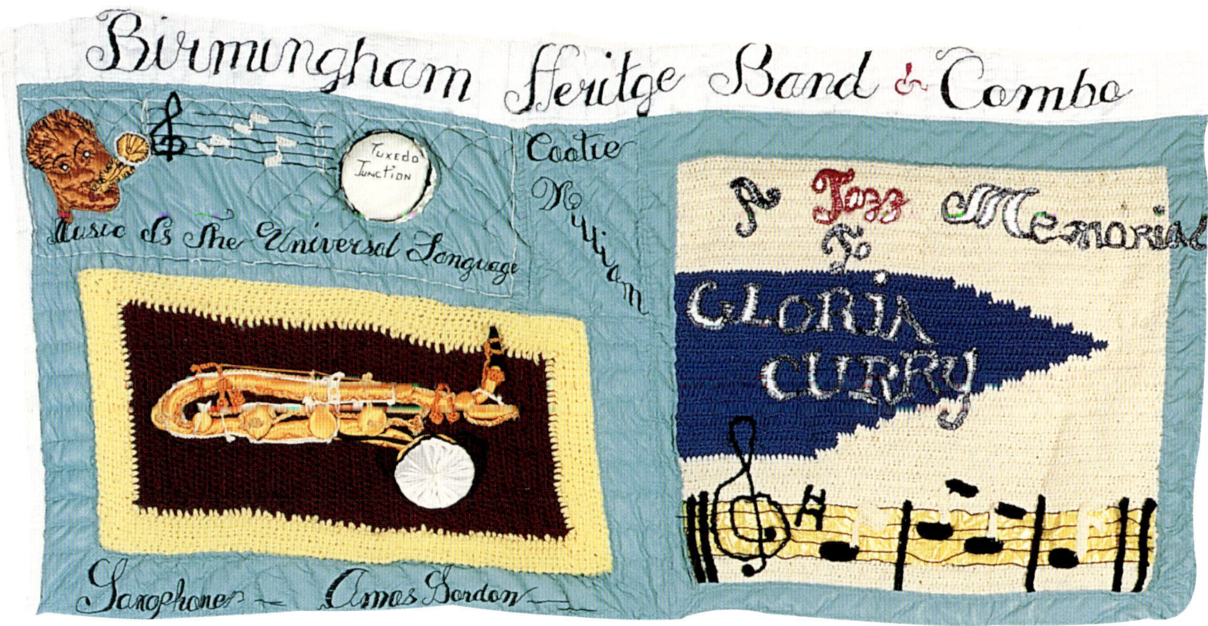

When asked about the reason for the crocheted background of each block, Mrs Ezell explained that Gloria Curry had been an avid needlewoman. Substantial quantities of yarn were among her possessions, and part of Mrs. Ezell's directive when the quilt was commissioned was that she somehow incorporate the yarn.

Mon. 10-19th	8:40 to 11:00	
Tues. 10-20th	Shopping & washing	
Wed. 10-21th	7:30 to 11:00	6:30 to 10:30
Thurs. 10-22nd	7:00 to 10:00	6:00 to 9:00
Fri. 10-23rd	8:30 to 11:00	7:00 to 10:00
Sat. 10-24th	1:00 to 4:30, 7:30 to 10:30	
Sun. 10-26th	No work.	
Monday 10-26th	9:00 to 11:00	7:00 to 10:00
Tues. 10-27th	6:40 to 12:00	
Finished trombone:	Hrs. 62, Min. 40	Price $188.20

Story of the Silk Necktie Quilt

November 1992

Late on Saturday afternoon, my phone rang just when I was about to go on top of the little bathroom I was adding onto my house. Was I adding or building?—of course I was. I do whatever there is to do, as I have lived alone since my husband died seven years ago. Well, let's not get ahead of the story.

There was a man on the telephone; at first I though it was somebody trying to give me a hard time, but I finally decided it was somebody trying to ask me if I was the quilt lady. This stumped me, as there are quite a few women around here that quilt. But he kept trying to tell me he had read an article about me in *The Atlanta Journal*, then I realized he must be looking for me. He said he was from Atlanta, but he was in Eutaw. He had no address, but had looked in the directory and got the number of the only Ezell he saw. He wanted to come to my house, but I lived about 21 or so miles from Eutaw. I hated to stop my work, but I agreed to come and get him.

When we got back to my house, he asked me several questions about my work. For instance, he wanted to know who taught me to quilt. I tried to explain to him that no one taught me. He didn't seem to understand or didn't want to. He kept saying somebody had to! He wanted to know then

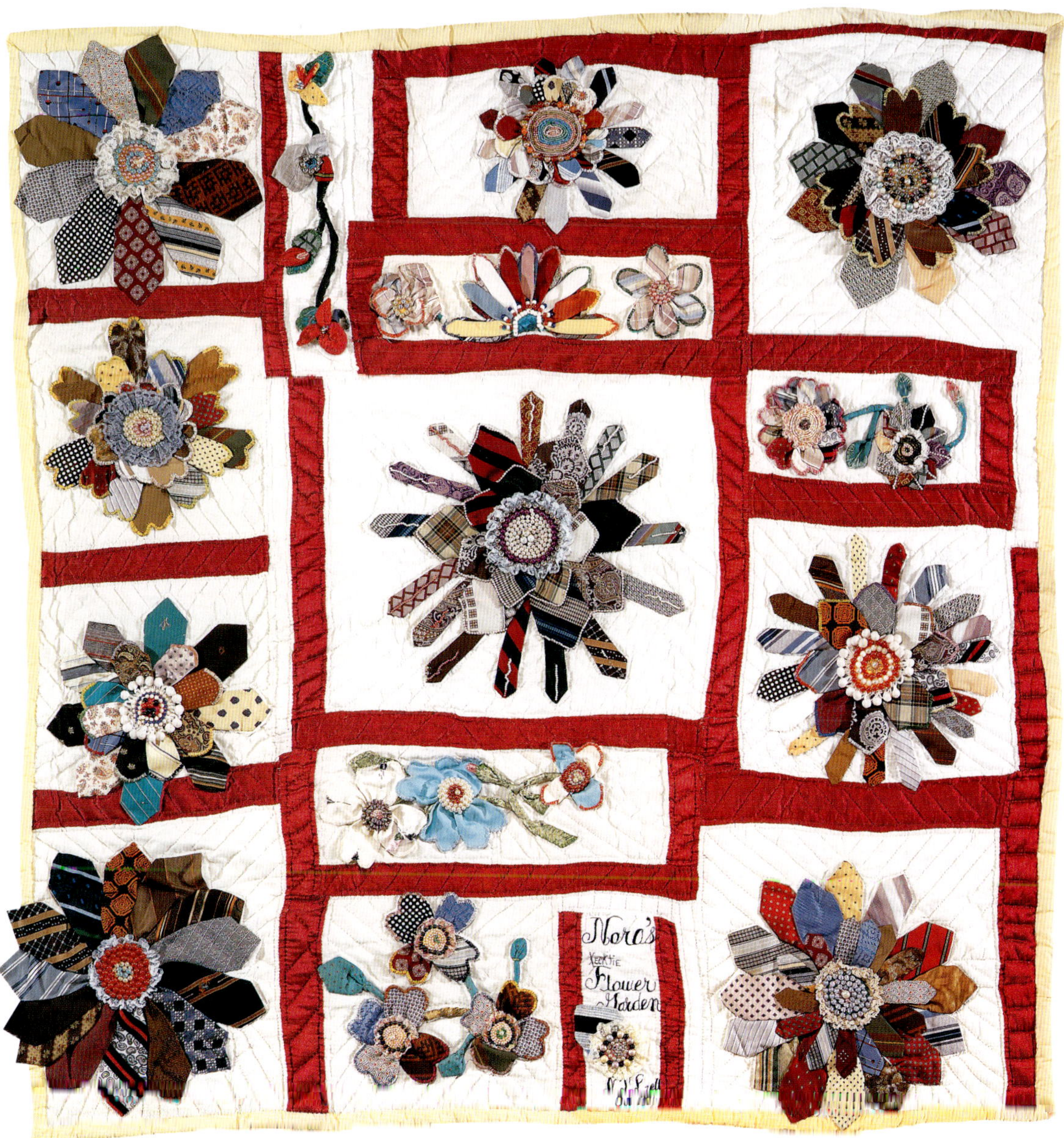

Nora's Necktie Garden

Signed and dated, " N.L. Ezell, Oct. 1994."

80 inches by 86 inches; assorted silk, cotton, polyester neckties; laces; costume jewelry, ball fringe, beads, white cotton background fabric, red satin sashing. Collection of the artist.

did I use patterns. I told him I did for traditional quilts, but for my pictorial quilts, it was all free-handed. I told him I didn't even make a pattern to use while working, because I only do one of a kind, so I don't need a pattern.

I talked a long time to him. He had a box in which he had a roll of silk neckties. He tried to tell me how to make the quilt. That is one thing I don't like. My mother used to tell me "I looked better than I listened." All my life I have been the type that could do anything I could see anyone else do. I'm still that way. I can reproduce anything I can see.

What I'm saying is that I work from pictures, ideas I have in my head, and anything anybody can tell me about.

He finally left and his ideas I hoped he took with him. There was no way I could do what he was talking about. The day at last ended. When Monday came, I tried to do what he suggested, but what a mess I made! Finally, I called him and told him, so he said to just please make him a quilt.

So I started to work that quilt along with one I was quilting for Mr. Willett. I was also working on a musical story quilt for the Birmingham Heritage Band, a Bible story quilt for Mrs. Annie T. Miller, a Children of the World quilt for Mr. Roland Freeman, and a Good Shepherd wall hanging for Mrs. Kathy Hutchison in Fayette. But no one quilt ever interferes with the others. I work only as long as the ideas hold. Then I go on to something else.

Sometime I ask myself why I can't get anyone to work with me. It doesn't bother me as much as it used to. I just go on, but it does make me

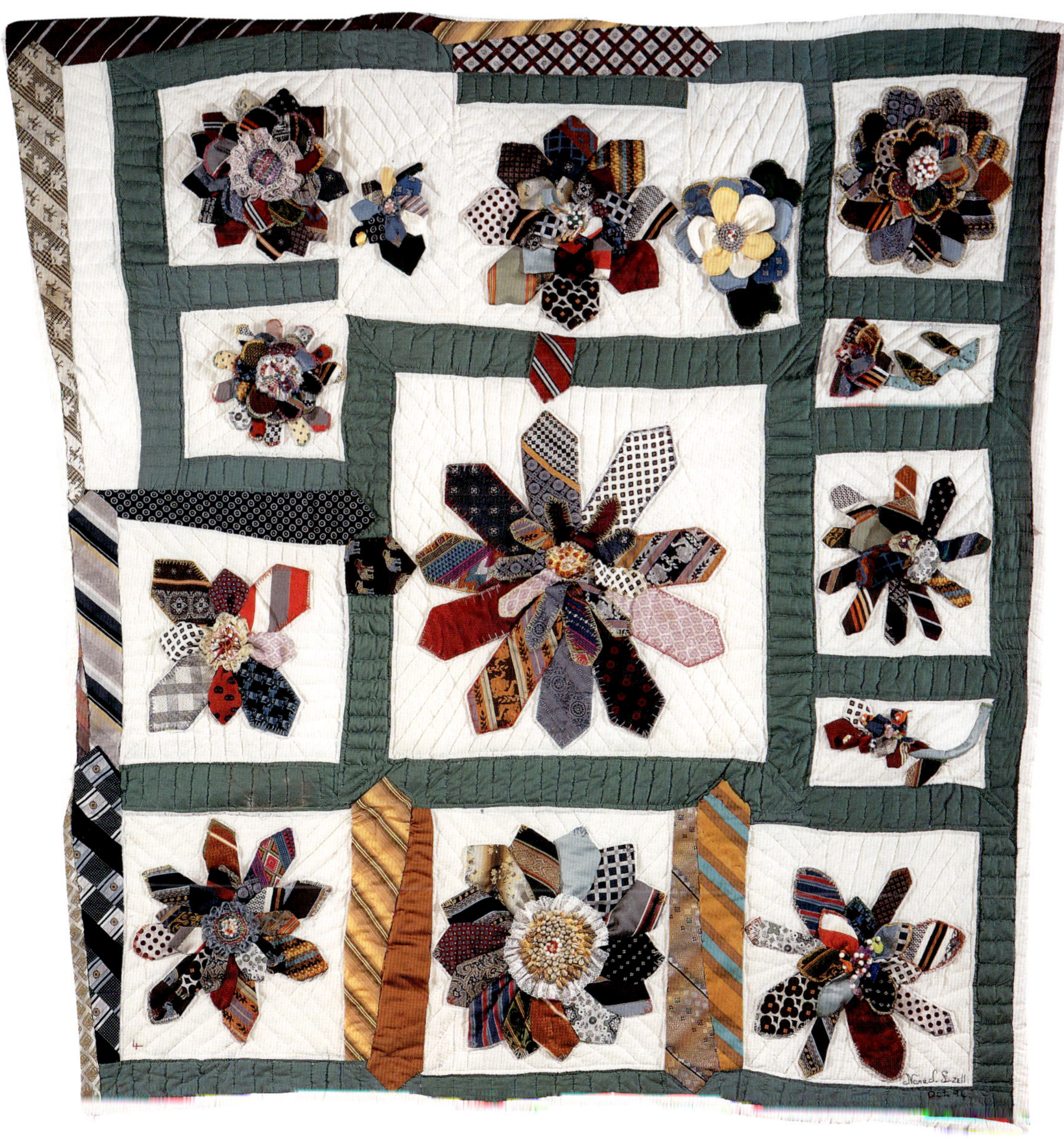

Flower Garden #1

Signed and dated "Nora L. Ezell, Oct. '94."

Approximately 86 inches by 79 inches. Ties are primarily of synthetic fabrics of the 1940s and 1950s; cotton background and green sashing fabric; ribbon, lace, Mardi Gras beads, costume jewelry, embroidery floss, pipe cleaners, cowrie and other shells. Collection of Georgine and Jack Clarke.

wonder. I'm glad I have a Saviour I can tell all my bothers and no-good things to.

I had a friend whose husband told me one day, to be exact, the day he died, "Don't be weary in well-doing," and one thing I know is that I do the best I can at all times. My quilts are a good and true expression of my inner self. In fact, I try to put a little bit of me in every quilt I make. Some more than others.

Do I sell all of my quilts? No. Ever so often I give one away, and not all to my grandchildren. Sometimes I get a little carried away, so let me get on with this quilt story.

To begin with, my uncle (Arthur Ritis) was determined to stay with me at this time of the year. My hands, especially my fingers and wrists, hurt so bad and were so stiff. When I do some

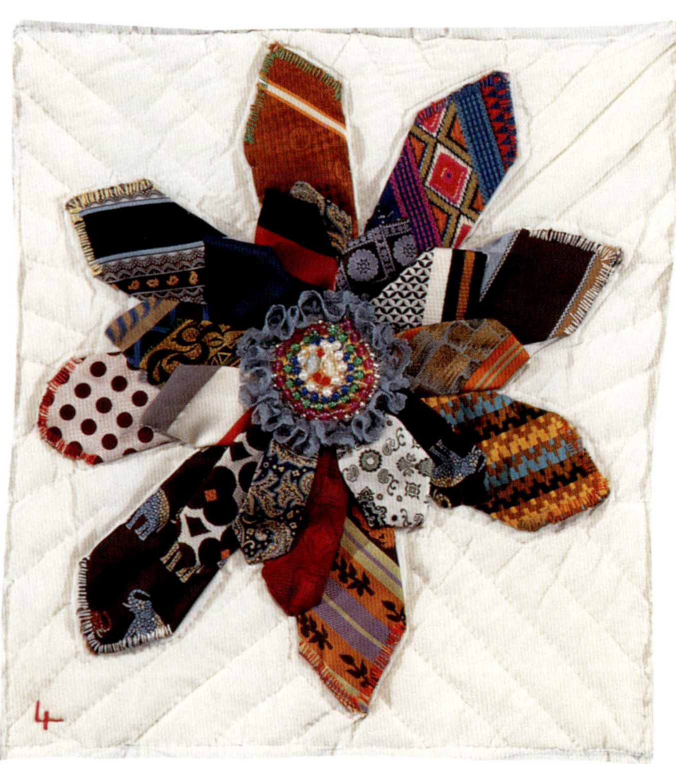

A small "4" is embroidered in red in the corner of a block. The beads in the center of the flower are of the type thrown from Mardi Gras floats in Mobile and New Orleans.

things, I look back over my work and wonder if it was really me who did it. But I tell myself to do my best, and if somebody wants it, so be it.

I found that most of the time I had to use a number 5 or 7 needle, where I can usually piece and quilt with a size 3. These silk neckties asked for that, so I finally ended up with a size 5. I had so much trouble holding the material, as silk is thin and light. Well, most of them were. Raw silk is thick and heavy, so I had a problem trying to put the two together.

I tried a pattern I had in my head called "Peter's Cross." If you recall, Peter was crucified head down on an "X"-shaped cross. So with this in mind, I proceeded. This wasn't easy, as some of the ties were one size, and others another size. It took me a little over 160 hours to do this top. When I got it finished, I had to go back and do an old-fashioned brier stitch on each seam, which took me another 37 hours.

He had told me he couldn't afford an expensive quilt, so I had to keep that in mind.

I have made three necktie quilts including this one. I made one in '84 when my daughter first got sick. Two of my sisters had come from California to see her. One of them went past a flea market and bought the ties for me. I carried the quilt I made from them to a seminar in Epes [Alabama] and sold it on the first showing.

My grandson bought the next ties for me. I went with him to look for filming equipment, and I saw a plastic bag full of ties for 75 cents, so he bought them for me. I made a quilt and took it to Washington, D.C.,

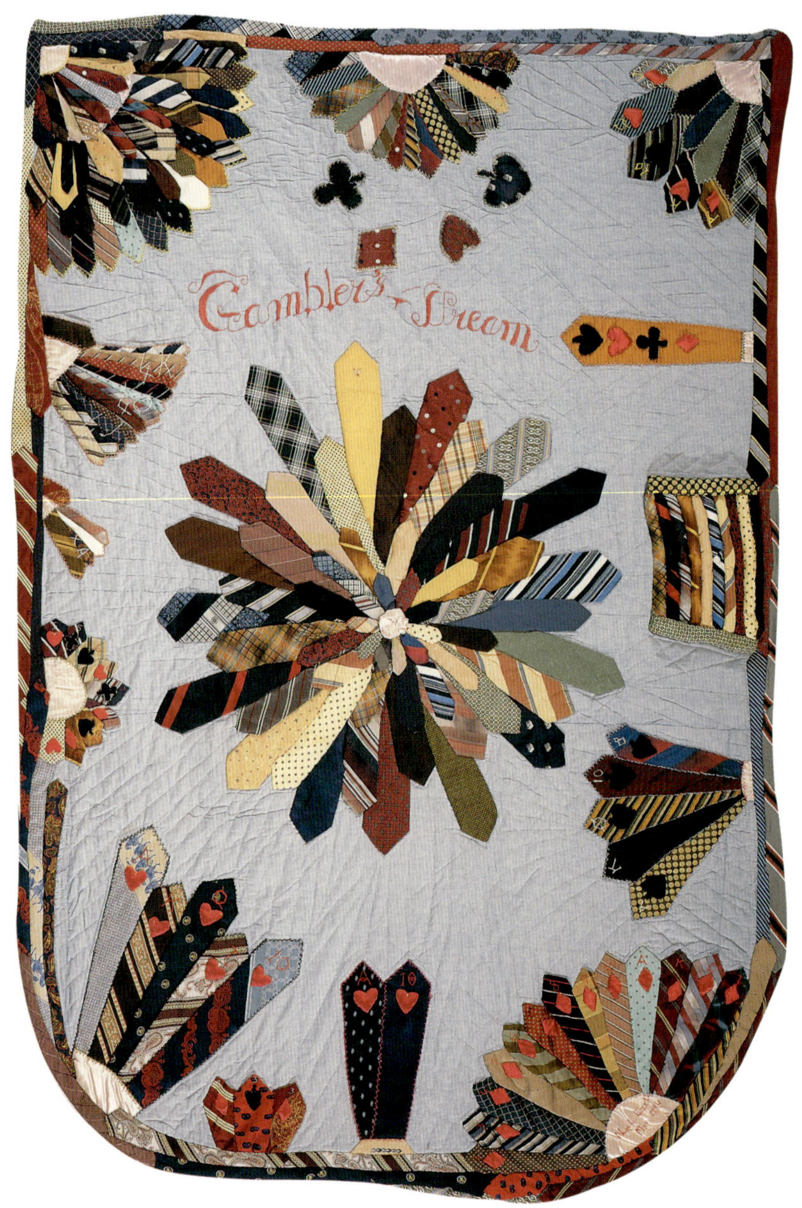

Gambler's Dream

Signed and dated, "Nora L. Ezell, May 1994."

69.5 inches by 101.5 inches. Background fabric is cotton chambray; ties are silk, acetate, and polyester; other materials include satin and cotton embroidery floss. Collection of Robert and Helen Cargo.

with me when I went to receive the NEA award. Then I took it to Kentuck Park in Northport, where I could have sold it, but I decided to keep it for a while. I don't like to show the same quilts at every show I go to, but it is kind of hard to get a lot of quilts done. As I've said, I work alone and sometimes put so much work into them.

Well, this has come out very well, so I guess it will pass. It was quite a job. The lining fabric was so hard to sew. That's one reason why I like to choose my own fabric.

I've been asked so many times, how many ties will it take to make a quilt? I don't know. I used as many as I wanted to for these quilts.

Well, I must get on with something else. Getting ready to start moving, thank God and the devil too.

Hope to see you sometime soon, Mr. Ray Milland.

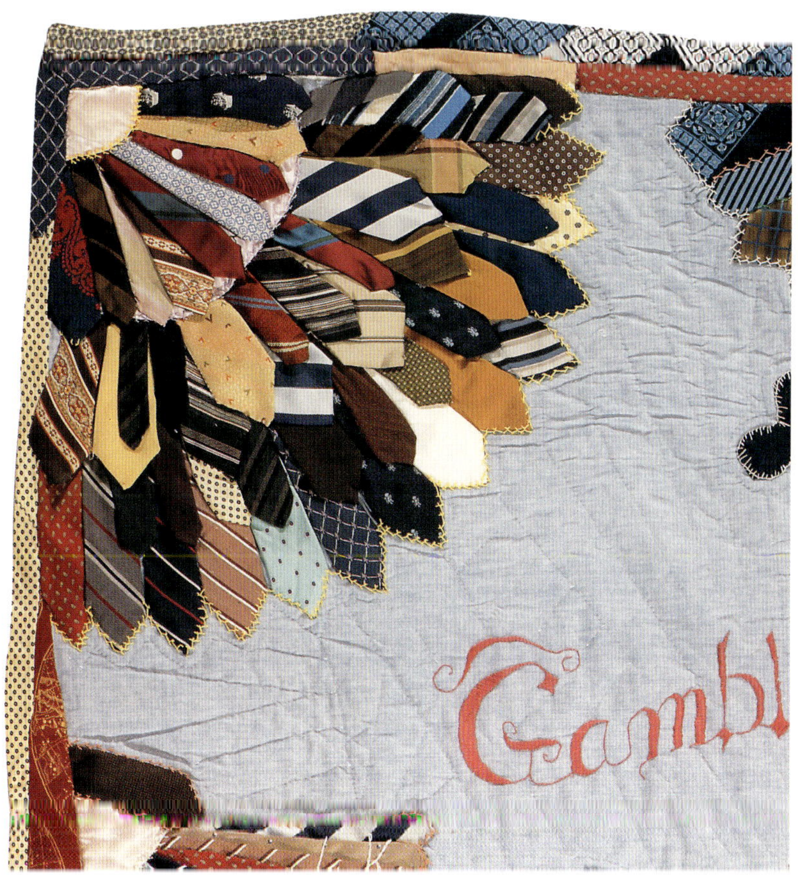

The quilt depicts "dream" hands for different card games—whist, poker, blackjack, etc. Fifty-one ties were used for the design in the upper left corner.

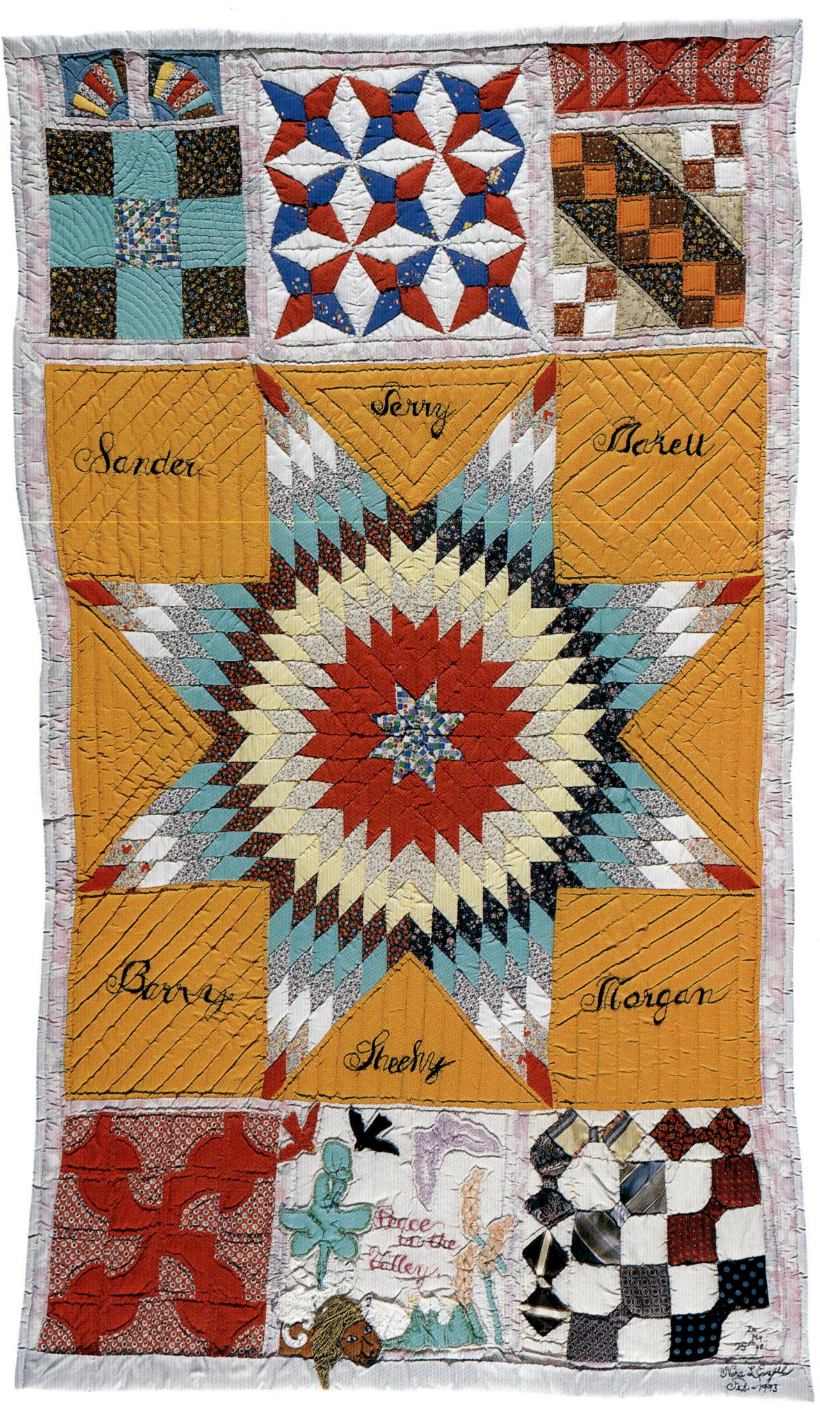
Sander
Sheehy
Morgan
Peace in the Valley

Sheehy Family Wall Hanging

Assisted by Jashaan Smith, age 13 at the time

March 12, 1993

On a rainy, snowy day in March I started this little wall hanging sampler for one of my best friends, Mr. Dan Sheehy, who came all the way from Washington, D.C., to visit me in my home. I met him in September of '92 in Washington when I went to the Heritage Fellowship Awards [from the National Endowment for the Arts]. He is a very wonderful person, and I consider him one of my special friends.

Oh, it's cold today. Our last winter days. In fact, our worst day. But thanks to God, I feel very good today. Even though both my uncles are visiting me. Of course, they may be your uncles too. I mean Uncle "Arthur" and Uncle "Itis." You don't know them? Well, good for you—they really boss my days and sometimes my nights. But I'm determined to keep on going as long as I can, so I tell them, "Get thee behind me."

I have a good idea in mind to make a quilt, and I want to get going as

Sheehy Family Wall Hanging

Signed and dated, " In my 75th year Nora L. Ezell, Feb, 1993."

50 inches by 88 inches; cottons, cotton/polyester blends; synthetic fabric neckties; fringe, nylon trim, lace, cotton terrycloth; embroidery floss. Collection of Dan Sheehy. The blocks are, from left to right, top row: "Fans" over a "Nine-Patch;" "End of the Earth" (also known as "World Without End"), "Wild Goose Chase" over an "Underground Railroad." The central block is the "Star of Hope." "Drunkard's Path," "Peace in the Valley," and "Bowties"make up the bottom row. Collection of Daniel Sheehy.

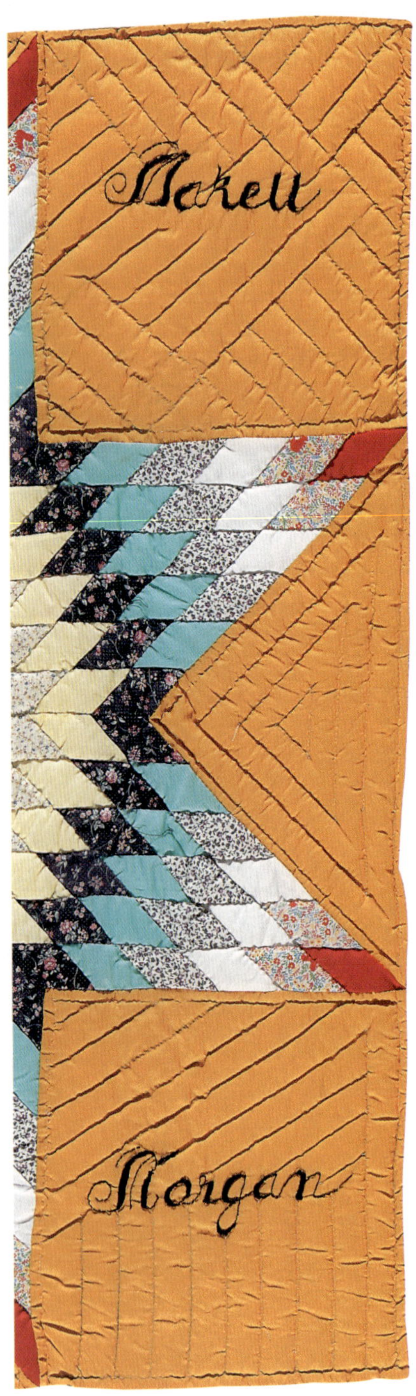

hard and fast as she can. One of my sisters said once that she could do anything I ever did, it just took her a little longer [now, with age.]

Well, would you believe it, we have about three inches of snow! I not only have my grandchildren, who were supposed to be in Tuscaloosa, but I have a friend I just met who came in from Atlanta to do an interview and got caught in the snowstorm. She is very nice, but she is a vegetarian, which means meals are hard to prepare. Since I come from the Deep South, I can't imagine planning a meal without meat.

God told me He would not put any more on me than I can bear, so this, I guess, is another one of my tasks, so I shall do the best I can, and thank God for it!

Well, it is 4:30 a.m., and I have been tossing and turning all night, so I decided to get up. I pieced a block called "The Underground Railroad." It came out all right, even though I

The names of the Sheehy family members are embroidered around the central star. Mrs. Ezell's skill at quilting is clearly visible in the background.

had a sick feeling in the pit of my stomach. I have a book on the life of Harriet Tubman, the black woman who led so many slaves to freedom. It tells how she worked this amazing thing.

Our snow is about gone. Now it's raining. I have company as usual today, but I'll play with this and that until I find something I can work with. What's better than a cup of Red Diamond coffee? My dad would say, "If I could get a cupful, I could match and double with the best."

Getting on with this little wall hanging quilt. I want to do a "Star of Hope" block today. (It's sometimes known as the "Texas Star.") It's very pretty when done right.

My little great-granddaughter has just asked if she could get up. When she is 13 instead of three, I'll have to give her a spanking to get her up. My great-grandson has the flu again. This is one of those weeks when I got out of bed, I should have crawled under it. Well, let me get started with this little wall hanging. The work on the blocks are coming along very well. I'm using as many bright colors as I can. I hope to finish it next week.

I don't know what happened, but I have the children again. Last week the snow and flu, this week I can't even decide. Oh, God said He wouldn't put more on me than I could bear. Sometimes I have to turn my eyes from the hills and look toward Heaven and say, "My God, how much more?" My mind is not staying with this work. I just simply have too many distractions. I have made six blocks. I just have about three more.

It's Sunday morning, and I'm not going to church. It seems as if that is the story now. When I feel like going, the weather is bad. When the weather is good, then I'm bad. I guess that is the story with growing old. I'm trying to decide what I will do for the next block. I finished the "Star of Hope" block but have to fill in the corners.

I was wondering as I read my Scriptures this morning on "standing strong" what holds me up when the strong winds of evil and torment press me down. What keeps me looking up when my head is bowed down and all I can do is lift up my eyes, when there is such a heavy load on my back, and my shoulders ache so with things I'm trying to do? Something whispers in my ear, "Nora, don't be weary in well-doing, because I am with you always. I will not put more on you than you can bear, just keep on trusting, right on praying, right on believing that I am God and beside me there is no other."

I thought about my friends Joey Brackner, Hank Willett, Shirl Johnson, Dan Sheehy, Robert Cargo, Jessica Bernstein, Michael Tucson, Gail Trechsel, Amy Kilpatrick, Randall Williams, Tom Cork, Ray Gilliland, Roland Freeman, Anne Miller, Kathy Hutchison, Roberta and J. L. Lowe, James Hedges, Ramona Lampell, Vanessa Greene, Mary Nelson, Nancy Gonce, Polly Smith, Georgine Clarke, Jane Cauthen, and my wonderful sweet granddaughters, Beverly J. Smith and Audrey Phillips, my one child, Annie R. Phillips, and so many more too numerous to mention that have been my crutch, and I feel like going on with my life and all my quilts.

March 23rd

I wonder where does the time go? Seems like yesterday was the beginning of the year. So it's raining again, which is always a bad time for me. My "uncles" stay with me night and day. My grands and great-grands feel like I should have had more children, so they just pile more and more on me.

Trying hard to get back to Mr. Sheehy's wall hanging. Going slowly, but I'm happy with the work. All the blocks have something in common. Most of them are a ray of sunshine for me. As I choose the blocks, I think on all the things, good and bad, that have happened in my long life. I'm so grateful to God, and so glad I have met the people who have helped to make it better for me. Before I finish this little quilt, I will tell you about each block and how it applies to me. I can do this easily, as quilts (my patterns) really are a part of me. The only other thing is God and my prayers.

The "End of the Earth" stretches both ways, with no end to it.

On with this little quilt! I'm trying to set my blocks. It is quite colorful. He said he likes bright colors. He is a wonderful person, so I'm doing my best to say "Thanks" to him in this quilt. Seems as if I have known him forever.

I think he said put a block of my story quilts, so I think I will do one from the Bible, as I believe that God is part of my life.

Thursday morning

Trying to get going. Did a little work in the yard yesterday. Guess the old girl is not what she used to be. I feel so tired, but thank God the mind and hand are going on. I want to do this block for all the gentlemen that can go for the "Bowtie," an old-time favorite in the quilting bee. I'm using men's neckties to make the squares and triangles that are put together to form the bowtie.

Just when I started to go to bed, I thought of doing a picture story block in this quilt. I planned several things, then decided on something that would represent peace. I thought of all the pretty things God has made—trees, water, birds, animals, and flowers. I came on the song "Peace in the Valley." I thought of the verse in the Bible about the lamb laying down with the lion, and how a little child would lead them. I made a block called "Peace in the Valley."

Monday, March 29

This day starts another week. I've finished piecing this little quilt. I have done a pretty good job. I like my work. I hope I can quilt it as good.

I'm very restless and worrying a lot about getting moved and about the outlook of this place. Sell it? I have thought on that. I know that I will be able to take care of it, but it requires a lot of work. I know something will work out. Like my quilts, sometimes they don't turn out like what I had in mind, but they are always good. God is so good to me. He always has to teach me tolerance, but learn it I shall. Well, I have the day planned, so I guess I better get started.

The blocks I have put in this little quilt simply say I always try to do the best I can, regardless of how it looks to the other person.

The "Star of Hope" says "Look to God for all things, take your burden to him and leave it there. He can and will fix it for you." I worked and prayed for years before something good came my way. In other words, I took a little and made the best I could from it. I'm so glad it happened just the way it did. Now I can appreciate it better—I know what it means both ways.

The "Bowtie" block says, "Think of your heavenly and earthly fathers and your husband who you miss when you do a quilt." He would always rip whatever I did wrong. I think of my pastor and all the men that have helped me along the way.

"The Underground Railroad" says, "There have been forever Black women who are strong enough to take care of family and reach out to someone else." Often I think of the cook in the country kitchen who, instead of killing two chickens, killed three, and then forgot one wing. When her mistress found an extra wing, the cook said, "I forgot to tell you—one of those chickens had three wings!" You call that making a meal for her family.

The "End of the Earth" block says there is no end to God's love and the good things we can do. Any way you turn or look, you can find them. What better way to say I love you than to make a quilt that stretches both ways, no end to it.

"Drunkard's Path" says that it is so easy to do nothing and go astray for anyone who wants to do that. I have always wanted to do something worthwhile. It does my heart good to make a quilt. I have the best thoughts of my life while I'm quilting.

"Nine Patch" says, "Anyone can do this if they will." It is usually the first block a quilter learns to do. I think, too, it says that women are the center of the family, but the man is the keeper, the one who makes it possible for all to live.

The little "Fans" and the "Wild Goose Chase" say, "It's the little things in life that count—like a smile, a kiss, a good word of praise. They can mean so much." Did you ever have a little child put his or her arms around your neck and give you a hug? Did you ever see the light on someone's face when they see a special quilt you have made just for them? If you haven't, you don't know what a pleasant thing you have missed.

I think I have said enough for you to understand me, for I find the worst thing I know is to be misunderstood.

Have a good day, Mr. Sheehy.

A Tribute to the Civil Righters of Alabama, No. 2

Tuesday, December 29, 1993

I'm trying hard to get started on another *Civil Rights Quilt.* It's a few days after Christmas 1993.

I must repeat, I have seen days and nights this Fall when I didn't think I would make it. Since God is wise and knows all things, He knew He had other things for me to do—namely, make this *Civil Rights Quilt* for you. I have been thinking from day one what I would put on it. Some of the things you want are on the other quilt [belonging to the Birmingham Civil Rights Institute]. I never make two quilts the same, because I do not use a pattern, only pictures. But, having just finished two other story quilts, here goes.

I want to do the DeForest Baptist Church in Talladega, Rosa Parks and the bus, Martin in jail, the 16th Street Baptist Church in Birmingham, the University of Alabama at Tuscaloosa, the Pettus Bridge at Selma, and something from the Freedom Riders.

January 25, 1994

Tuesday, very cloudy and looking like rain. Very nice over the weekend, for which I was very glad, as I was taking part in the show at the Montgomery Museum of Art, "Signs and Symbols [African Images in

African-American Quilts]." Pretty good, not too many people, but enough to make a lively and worthwhile show. As usual, I gave the show, as I do my work, everything I've got.

I got very upset by an article written by the guest speaker. I do not mind being interviewed, and I try very hard to give a good interview, but I do not like for a reporter to write what they want and say I said it. Some may think they are stories, but I try hard to tell them as I heard them. I never say a lot about Africa or about the quilts that represent it. That is because I don't know. My mother made beautiful quilts and embroidery, but she did not teach me. My style and my patterns are my own (except "The Little Donkey"). I do not copy anyone's work. My style of presenting work is my own, with a little help from Gail Trechsel.

As I always say, it is hard for me to try and remember this civil rights stuff. I took no part except to pray, because I always leave whatever will be to the good Lord. I don't mean I'm not concerned, because I am, but what I mean is that I don't like to force my ideas or notions on anyone. I guess that is why I work so well by myself. Of course, most think my ideas are too complicated. I have finally finished the DeForest Baptist Church from Talladega; this was a church visited during the Pilgrimage.

Well, it has been another long three weeks, with lots of bad feeling and sometimes sick enough to go back to bed. I'm not a religious fanatic, but I do believe in God—or better still, in right and wrong. I have worked very hard on this block, the 16th Street Baptist Church. I tried a different

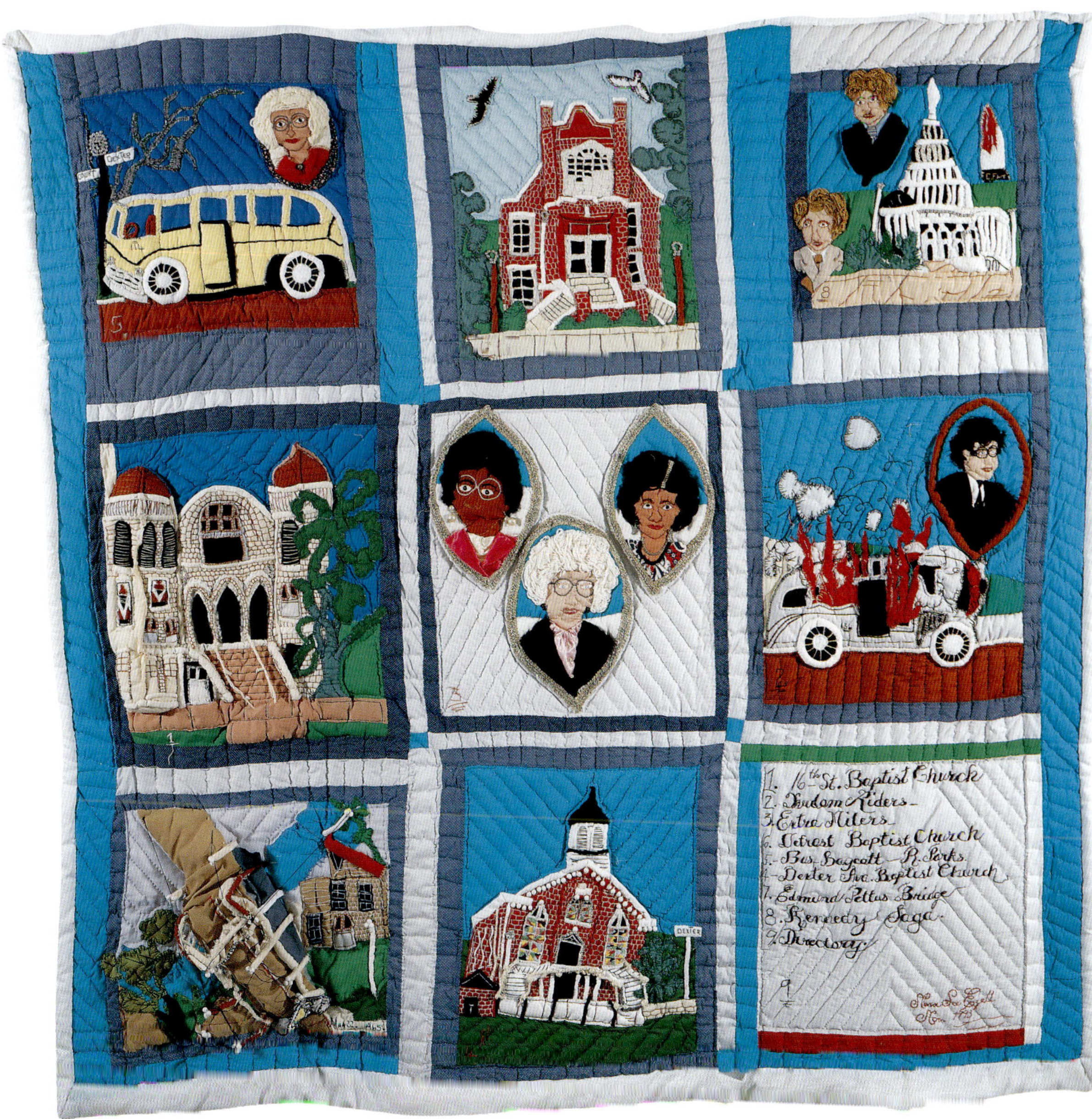

A Tribute to the Civil Righters of Alabama, No. 2

Signed "Nora Lee Ezell, Nov. 1993."

80 inches by 78 inches.

Collection of the Bimingham Museum of Art; bequest of Rena Hill Selfe.

approach and a new version, and it's pretty good. As I often say, I am my own best critic. This is as I like it. I wonder where this comes from—from God, maybe.

After 267¾ hours, I finished this block. Hope you will like it too. Well, stop lollygagging and get on with the next block, which will be number 3, Rosa Parks and the bus. Here I go again with this oppressed feeling—my family, my children, but I guess it is best that I don't interfere. Maybe they will work their problems out. Damon, I think, is sick and is under a lot of stress. I would love to do something, but I don't know what, and I just simply don't want my feelings hurt. I'm trying very hard to come back, and I have come very close to going off the lower edge. Thank God for His mercy. I prayed the best I knew how and He turned me around and once more put my feet back on solid ground. My mind is back together and back on my work, which I love very much. So I better get on with this quilt.

It has been so very hard for me to keep going forward. So many things have happened that have left me with an open mouth. I just finished this Freedom Riders block along with Judge Johnson, who was both a fair and honest judge. When I go back to that time, it helps me to see just how great God is.

When I started this block, I didn't know just how I would come up with something to go with the block title. This bus is really burning (smile), just as it did that May morning so long ago. I do hope you can see what I have in mind.

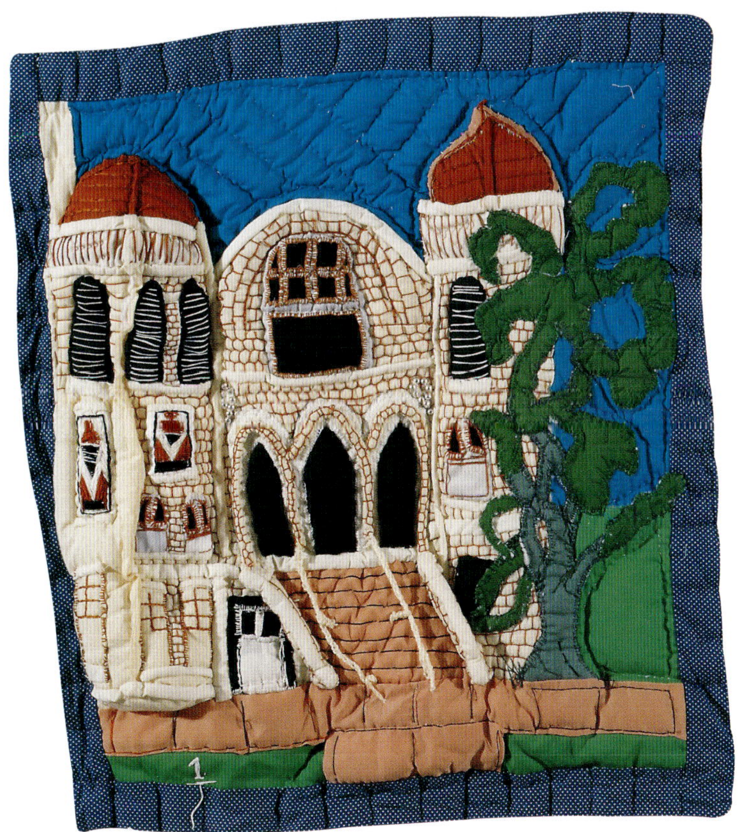

Mrs. Ezell admits to a special fondness for churches. This is one of three on the second *Civil Rights Quilt.*

On I must go. Just a little bit more will see the end of Number 15. I mean story or picture quilt. Very good work, but hard for me to keep going. I'm trying to keep on, as I wonder where the world is headed. I pray the best I can for God to do His will. I am truly sorry for the shortcomings of man. Especially for me, who always feels like I must solve all the problems. Tonight I'm working hard on the Edmund Pettus Bridge, which was one of the most forward points of interest in the Civil Rights Movement. When I think of this, I'm lost, because I truly believe that God will solve all the unjust problems. We stand and look on both black and white, and each thinks he is right. One thing I truly know is you nor me can hurry God, he will fix it on his own time. Maybe the march did [bring] justice, I just don't know. I have spent about 235½ hours trying to show how I feel about the Bridge. When I go across it on my way to and from Montgomery, I try to decide what it was all about. I also try to decide whether it has helped civil righters or the black Americans.

After many, too many, hours, I have finally finished this *Civil Rights Quilt.* More hours than I ever put into a quilt: 1,568, to be exact. I used $98.00 work of materials, $14.08 worth of batting and padding, $12.60 for lining (sheeting @ $4.49 per yard), six spools of quilting thread, $26.00 worth of embroidery floss, knitting, crochet, and candlewicking thread, and one box of toothpicks. So you would like one—OK what? You would like another *Civil Rights Quilt?* I'll be glad to do my best. As one of my sisters says, she can do anything she ever did, it just takes her so damn much longer, and I say, "Me too."

Really I have enjoyed doing this. I think it is my best work.

Love ya all!

Nora Ezell

P. S. I haven't quilted this yet, so add at least another 100 or so hours. (smile)

The American Indian's Saga (as I see them)

April 13, 1993

Hello! It's such a beautiful day—so good to be alive—I'll just simply throw it out to whoever can grasp it. I feel pretty good today. Was up at 5:30, began quilting at 6:15. Brother A.'s program was very inspirational and laughable. I feel like it's going to be a great day.

Got started on this quilt at 11:15. I hope it turns out as well as I think it might. I have saved stuff for this for a long, long, time. So many things I identify with in the telling of this story. My great-grandfather on my father's side was a Black Creek Indian. I love their life story (Indians, I mean).

April 15th

Friday already, my how the time goes when I decide to get going. A tomahawk caught my attention, and I have played around for 25 hours until I have finally made one that looks like I wanted. Now that I have come up with the arm and the hand to hold the tomahawk, I like it. I want to have something to show.

This morning is a stormy one. This is tornado time. I've finally gotten started on making a beautiful robe. I love my work now, but I'm sorry I have slowed up so. But my work is good—don't you think?

April 17th, Sunday

I didn't go to church, decided I would rest for my trip tomorrow. I have decided to go by myself. I'm in a very, very deep blue melancholy depression. I heard some very distressing news—yes, you guessed it, it's about one of the grands. I just stand and say, "My God, how much more?" I still don't know the details. Maybe that is what bothers me. I wish I could fix all the things that they need. How can I when I can't fix my own? But I pray as honestly as I know how. My Bible tells me prayer is the key to the Kingdom.

Well, I'll try to start on this quilt again. Working on Keokuk, a very fine Indian chief. Made one arm and the tomahawk. Working the robe and other arm. Wish me luck!

May 3

I have not done too much. There's a simple reason, though; every other day I'm down and out. Can't seem to concentrate—just kind of stupid, to use my favorite word. I've finished all my orders and just finished a quilt show and contest in Florence [Alabama]. Won a merit award, which is another star in my crown. Didn't enjoy the event too much, had

The American Indian's Saga (as I See Them)

Signed and dated, "Nora L. Ezell, Dec. 1993."

Approximately 72 inches by 102 inches. Velvet, cotton, satin and metallic fabrics; egret, guinea, and chicken feathers; silk and velvet cords and ribbons; acrylic and wool yarns; bits of crochet; embroidery floss; lace; fringe; beaded tape; synthetic fur; beads; plastic cleaning bags; plastic and metal safety pins; wooden sticks and twigs; paper and ribbon flowers; cardboard; and a cotton dish towel. Collection of the artist.

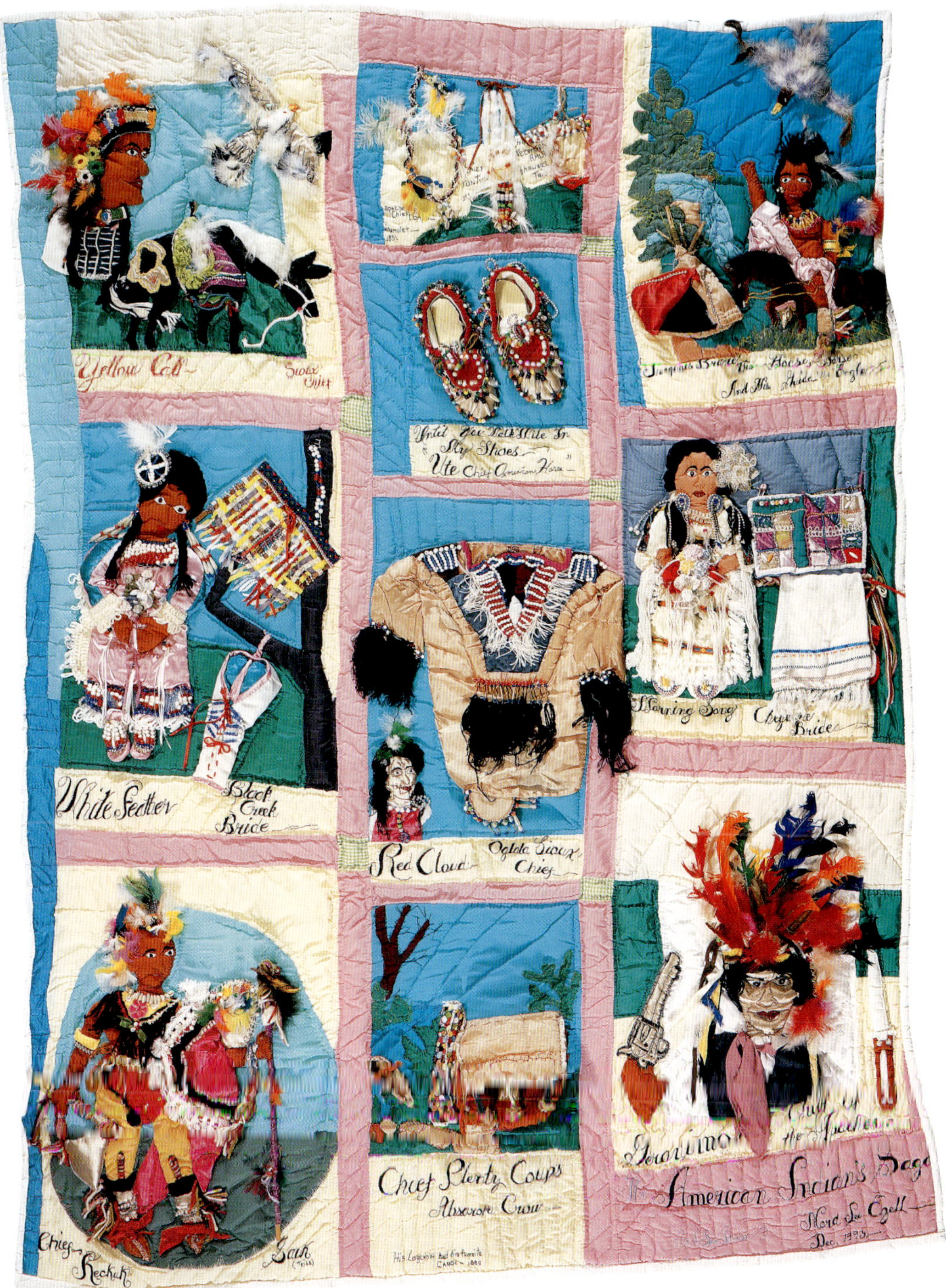
Yellow Calf
White Feather
Red Cloud
Oglala Sioux Chief
Chief Plenty Coups
Geronimo

too many other troubles. I would love to do all I can this year, because, who knows, it may not come this way next year. Sometime I feel so tired. Well, let's try to get on with this block.

Still on the Keokuk block. He must have been a great guy to have this costly wardrobe! Well, get on girl, you have a long way to go.

Last weekend I did the Arts Alive show in Florence. Nice, clean, friendly city. But not the best show. I have to go back a few years to find a really great one. Won two awards—one on crafts and one on Fine Arts. Sold one quilt, no orders though. I just sold one for $3,355.80—the second civil rights quilt. I'm sitting in B'ham at the Sloss Furnace Museum and had a little time to write a little something. Nice setup.

Doing a little work on this Indian quilt. Still on the same block. I will be for a while, because, as I have repeated so often here lately, I am so slow. But what can you say? I'm really doing my best.

[No date]

Can't believe it. I finally, after so many hours and days, finished this Keokuk block. Really, I spent about one month or 300 hours.

[No date]

Well, it's Sunday again. Fixed my clothes for church, but I'm so sore—head, eyes, neck and feet. Can you imagine that? Started taking Benedryl this morning—hope it helps some. A little lonely around the edges, kind of silly I guess. Worked in both yards again this week. Wish I could sell that place.

[Mrs. Ezell has moved by this time to Tuscaloosa from her former home in Greene County, outside of Eutaw. She is referring to the upkeep on both of her homes and wishing she could sell the Greene County place.]

Guess I'll move on to the next block on this quilt, which is "Nightshadow" —a great horse and his master, the great Sioux warrior and chief, Yellow Calf, who revered the eagle.

[No date]

It's another week and I am tireder than I was last week. Do you suppose time is catching up? I wonder. I have not worked since the 18th—not on this. It seems as if I am waiting for something. I've done a little work on my house—nothing I can say grace over. You know, nothing about which I can say, this is good; I can just say I'm doing something. I've gotten my Chief about like I want, and the work on his horse will pass. Got to get on, as I have a long ways to go. Got a nice check in the mail—$1,542. What do you think of that? Maybe I pleased somebody.

May 26

Work is gradually coming. My strength is beyond me. I say I don't feel like nothing, but what I do, I'm pleased with. So here goes another idea.

May 30

Here's Memorial Day, a day to remember your mother, your aunt, your grandmother, or whoever. I must have gotten a little something from each one. I'm home alone this holiday, which is alright with me. Still working on this Yellow Calf block, trying to do the eagle, which is their God.

June 12th

It's twelve days away from my 77th birthday. Almost every day I try to see what I have done. Did I or did I not leave my mark? I have always tried to. If I did no one any good, I pray I did not do them harm. As I ponder these things this morning, I stand in awe of God, who has brought me this far. So many dangers, both seen and unseen, through the shadow of death, death of my closest loved one; but still He has left me here for some reason. To take care of my grandchildren and great-grands. To try to make my house pretty for others to see.

That is why I keep a log or timetable with these quilts, so I can also keep a timetable on me. One thing I know: God did not have to make this beautiful morning, but He did, and I'm so glad and I thank Him for it.

Well, so much for me. Let me get on with this block. The Creek brave and his house, horse, and guide—the Great Eagle. I have a wonderful friend at a certain store who is saving stuff for me. The work has come on pretty good.

[No date]

I spent a little better than 208½ hours on this block. I'm trying to point out what was important. In most tribes the squaw did some things, and the braves did other things. The squaws did the decorating—made the bowls, cups, and the mats to sleep on. This reminds of women of days gone by. Some of us had the opportunity to live and work with them.

[No date]

My next blocks are about the brides. Sometimes they will be identified as to whose bride or whose daughter they are. If a Cheyenne chief's daughter married, her dress was usually made by the blessed women of the tribe. She had to make her bridal blanket, but all the women in the tribe combined to make the "bride's mat," which consisted of the best work. The beads they used were sometimes traded for; others they dyed themselves. They dyed all the grasses, reeds, and leaves they used with berries and roots, bark and leaves. They knew nothing about buying it.

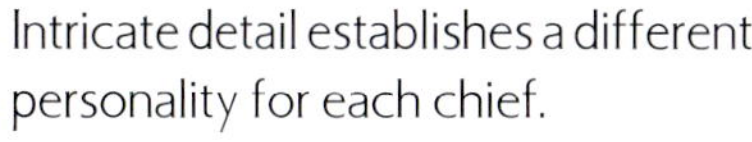

Intricate detail establishes a different personality for each chief.

[No date]

If I keep working with the Council, I will ask if one summer I can go to the reservation and work, or watch some of the Indians work. They are the only people that really fascinate me (if there is such a word).

I have never made a quilt I have enjoyed more. Well, enough of the sentimental stuff. So after 327½ hours I finally finished "Geronimo," his 45 Colt and Bowie knife.

Getting on with Chief American Horse, "Try to walk a mile in my moccasins." For the last few days I had a different feeling—like I was very happy. Do you suppose I am destined to live alone? As soon as I get around people, I become very depressed—like the whole world is on my shoulders. It is a strange omen.

One thing I know is that I'm at peace with the world. I don't bother nobody, I don't ask no one for help but the Lord, and I'm so glad He has never failed me yet. With a feeling that maybe I would be able to finish this quilt, as I have put in so many hours already, I'm first on a high, and now on a depression so deep it don't look as if I can get out. But with the help of God, I keep pressing on—on to the end of these moccasins. After 110 miserable hours, I'm done!

So no baseball, the players are out on a strike. So what's new? I'll start tonight—8-12th 94—on this block with Plenty Coups as chief, with his proud Crow warrior.

[Although Mrs. Ezell dated the finished quilt Dec. 1993, she continued to work on it into early 1995.]

Baseball Quilt

Made for Jessica Bernstein, September-December 1993

September 28, 1993

Dear Jessica,

This afternoon I started your *Baseball Quilt.* I have some good ideas and thoughts along with the information you sent me. I have gotten together some materials that I thought would bring out our ideas. I'm not 100 per cent, but much better. I have lost so much weight until I was weak, but, many thanks to God, I'm still going. It is a beautiful Fall day, cool but not too much. I'm doing the work I like best, and I'm satisfied with it. As I often say, I'm my own best critic. Well, here goes . . . Wish me well. "Block IV, Riverfront Stadium, Cincinnati Reds . . ."

October 29

It is 11:17 on a rainy Friday morning. I have been a while getting back to work on this. I have in the meantime done one festival and one pilgrimage (a Eutaw thing). I've only done one Eutaw festival since I've lived here [in Tuscaloosa]. I guess my works and me didn't measure up to their standards. But I really enjoyed it—and it was not too hot or cool.

I would really like some better pictures to work from. But, through the years I have prided myself on doing what I'm asked, so I'll start without the pictures.

November 6, 1993 (Saturday)

I started the Johnny Bench block. I think I can do bigger pieces better, but I'm going to give it my best shot.

Saturday 11/6/93	9:30 a.m-12:30 p.m	
Sunday 11/7/93	No work.	
Monday 11/8/93	6:50 a.m-10:00 a.m	1:15 p.m-4:30 p.m
Tuesday 11/9/93	No work	
Wednesday 11/10/93	No work	
Thursday 11/11/93	No work	
Friday 11/12/93	10:00 a.m-1:00 p.m	6:00 p.m-8:30 p.m
Saturday 11/13/93	10:00 a.m-1:00 p.m	6:00 p.m-9:30 p.m
Sunday 11/14/93	No work	
Monday 11/15/93	12:30 p.m-4:15 p.m	6:00 p.m-8:30 p.m
Tuesday 11/16/93	2:00 p.m-4:30 p.m	6:30 p.m-10:15 p.m
Wednesday 11/17/93	9:30 a.m-11:00 a.m	6:30 p.m-8:30 p.m

If I had to give my opinion, this would not win it, but it looks kind of good. (smile) Today is rainy and my two old uncles are trying to take over. Sometimes I'm so achey, but I go on.

Another gloomy day. I guess this is old age. I have often wondered when it would catch up with me. I raked a few leaves for exercise. So now I'll sit down and do a few stitches on this next block

I finally finished the Johnny Bench block, so much for that. So this is the Clemente, the #2 block.

After 31½ hours, I finally finished the Clemente block. It came out much better than I thought.

I'm really getting to feel my age and all my work. I really thank God that he has been so good to me. When I look back on all the years and all the work, I see that I have done so very many things. Sometimes I try to see what keeps me going on.

It's 5:30, the Wednesday before Thanksgiving Day.

Every day is Thanksgiving Day for me. I think this is what God wants. Oh, well, let the old girl get going on the Alan Trammel block, #3.

This is Saturday, the next day after Thanksgiving.

In fact, this is the day after everybody but me shopped until they dropped. Not feeling too good, but trying to do a little on this block. So very tired of baby-sitting. The time has come when I don't want nothing to do toward raising kids!

Another beautiful November day.

Sometimes I wonder, what did I do to get this? I washed a couple of loads of clothes and swept the yard. Really raked leaves. Finished the Alan Trammel block. It came out pretty good, only I don't like the helmet so well. I finally decided I could do no better. I don't suppose he will ever see it. (smile) So on with the Reds and Riverfront Stadium.

After a few days, which is something like 42 hours, I finally finished this block. I ran into a lot of difficulties. My poor mind just sometimes doesn't want to concentrate.

I have finally decided that whatever I wanted to do, it was not go back to child raising. I don't understand the workings of their minds. My ideas of right and wrong—politeness, respect, love, and honor—is nowhere in their categories. Really, besides taking so much of my time, I couldn't keep my mind on my work. As the young folks say, "I can't handle it."

I hope this looks a little like Riverfront Stadium. On December 9, I'll try to do Lou Whitaker and McCovey, Willie that is.

It's beginning another week, and it looks like the same on seven and six. Yesterday was pretty, but very cold, so I stayed in, not going anywhere. Now I understand why God said, "Serve the Lord while it is day, because in the dark no man can see." In other words, serve him while you are young, because when you get old, you can not. If anybody had told me four months ago that I would be in this shape today, I would not have believed it. But, thanks be to God, I can go and do a little something, so I will try to get on with the block. It is not as good as I would like, but I hope you will be like God and take the will for the deed.

After 22½ hours, I finished the overhead look of Riverfront Stadium. I don't have a picture that is clear. It was kind of hard to do, but I hope that somehow the idea comes through. I laugh making this hanging, as his [?] favorite team is the Orioles, but he didn't choose one person from that organization, but so what? I think I could have done this justice if it had been more National League players. I hope the names will say something.

Here goes the Hank Aaron block. The copy I am using is simply too dark to give many details. But, being a National Leaguer, I remember a few things—like his team, his state and city, and some other things about him. This is why I say just tell me your subject and let me do the rest. I hope you will like this.

Kind of hurrying now, as the holidays approach. Not that I like to do what everybody else is in such a hurry to do. Here goes the Willie Mays block and the end. I could have done much with this block. We lived in the same community, the one where he was born— Westfield, a suburb of Birmingham. We attended the same school. I knew his family—went to school and played basketball and volleyball with his aunt that raised him after his mother passed—knew his father, too. This came pretty good.

On December 24, Christmas Eve, I finished the Willy Mays block after 38½ hours. It took 165½ hours to make the blocks, 25 hours to quilt the wall hanging, and 4½ hours to hem it, for a total of 294¾ hours.

Thanks.

Nora Ezell

The Star Puzzle Quilt

[Although she never duplicates a story quilt, Mrs. Ezell will make copies, on request, of her patchwork quilts. A favorite with her audience has been the design shown on these pages, named "Star Puzzle" by Mrs. Ezell and "Fractured Star" by various of her fans. Although she has made at least two more quilts by this design, there are distinct differences among the pieces.]

Top left: **"Star Puzzle Quilt"**
Signed and dated "Nora Ezell, June 1991."
Approximately 72 inches by 78 inches. Cotton and cotton/polyester blend fabrics. Collection of Bess Lomax Hawes.

Bottom left: **"Star Quilt"**
by Nora Ezell, Eutaw, Alabama.
Collection of the Museum of American Folk Art, New York; Museum of American Folk Art purchase made possible in part by a grant from the National Endowment for the Arts, with matching funds from the Great American Festival.
Dated August, 1977 in embroidery. Machine and hand-pieced, hand quilted cotton, synthetics. 79 inches by 94 inches.

Top right: **"Star Puzzle Quilt"**
Signed and dated "Nora Ezell, Aug. 1994."
71 inches by 84 inches. Cotton and cotton/polyester fabrics. Collection of Henry Willett.

Bottom right: **"Star Puzzle Quilt"**
Signed and dated "Nora Ezell, Oct. 1995."
76 inches by 89 inches. Cotton and cotton/polyester blend fabrics. Collection of Mary Elizabeth Johnson and John Huff.

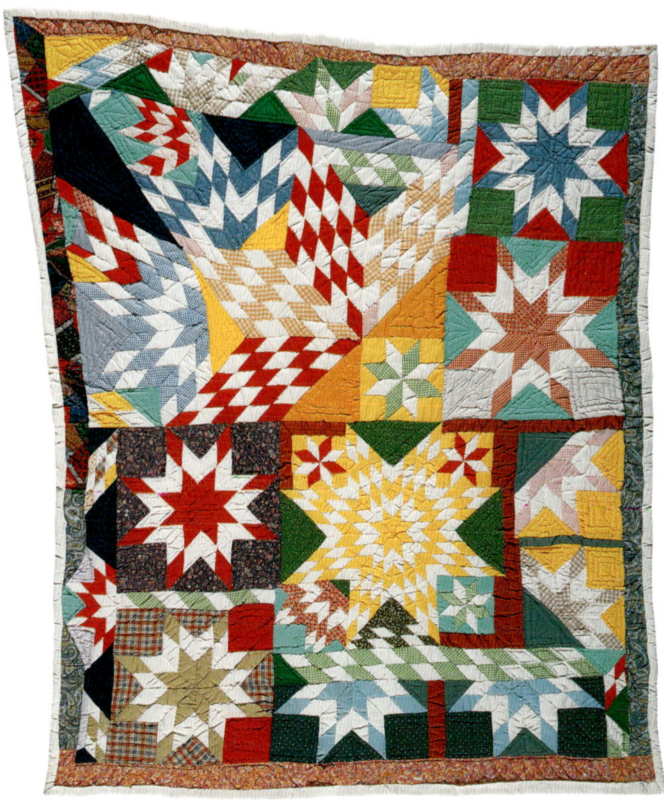
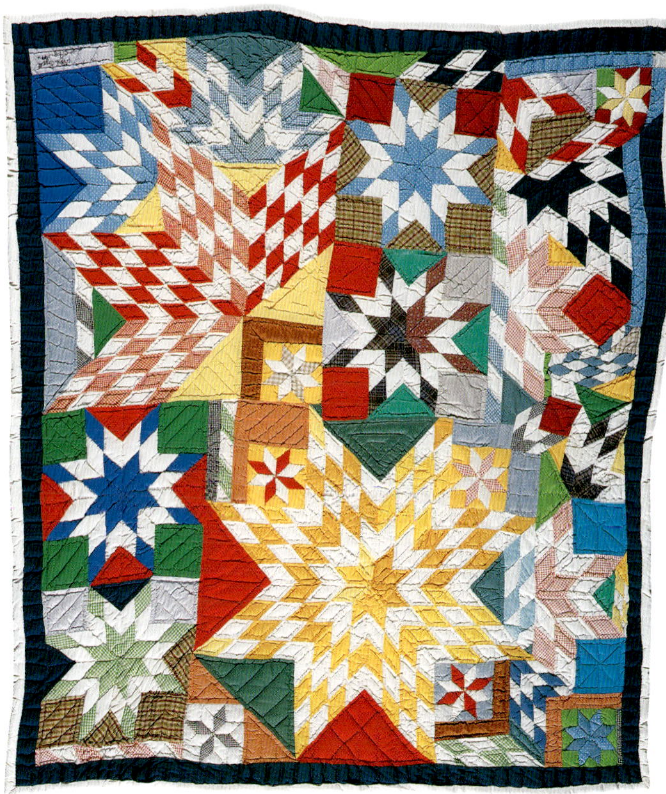
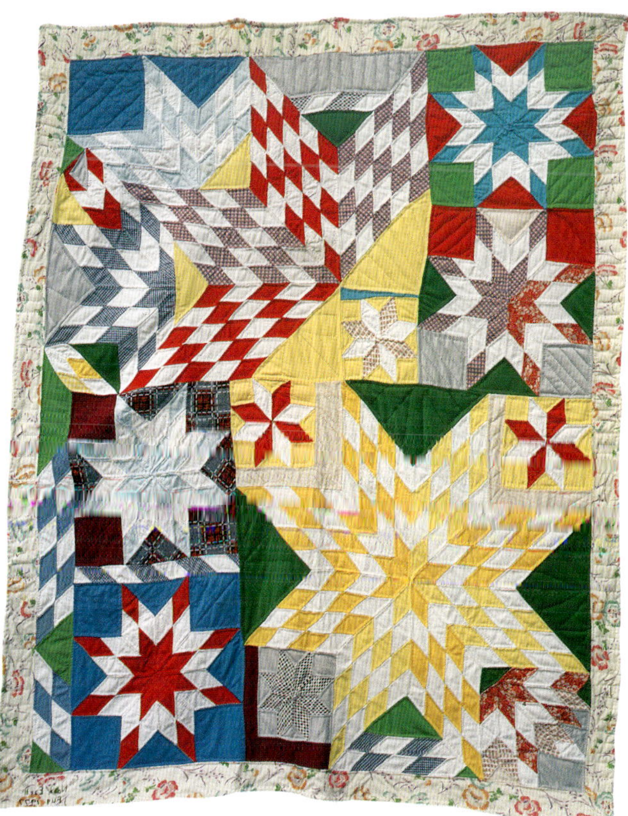
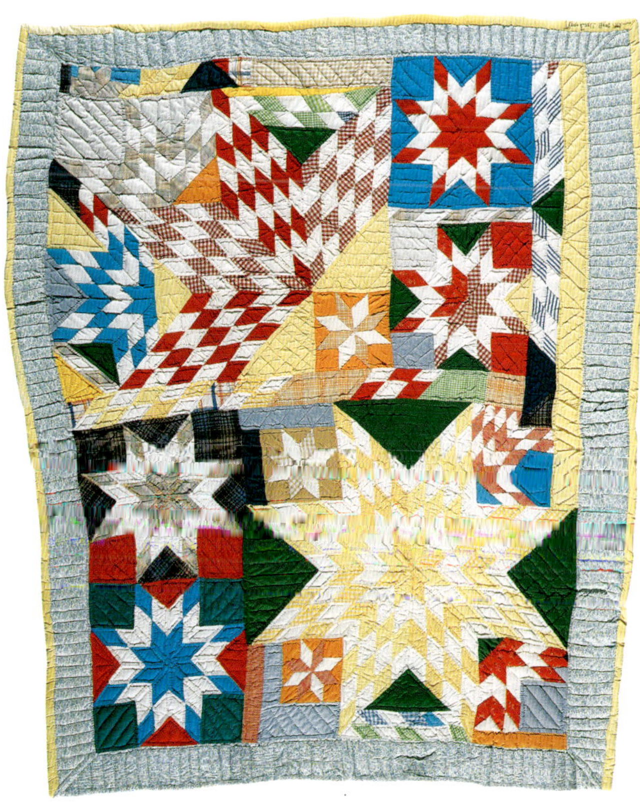

Part Three

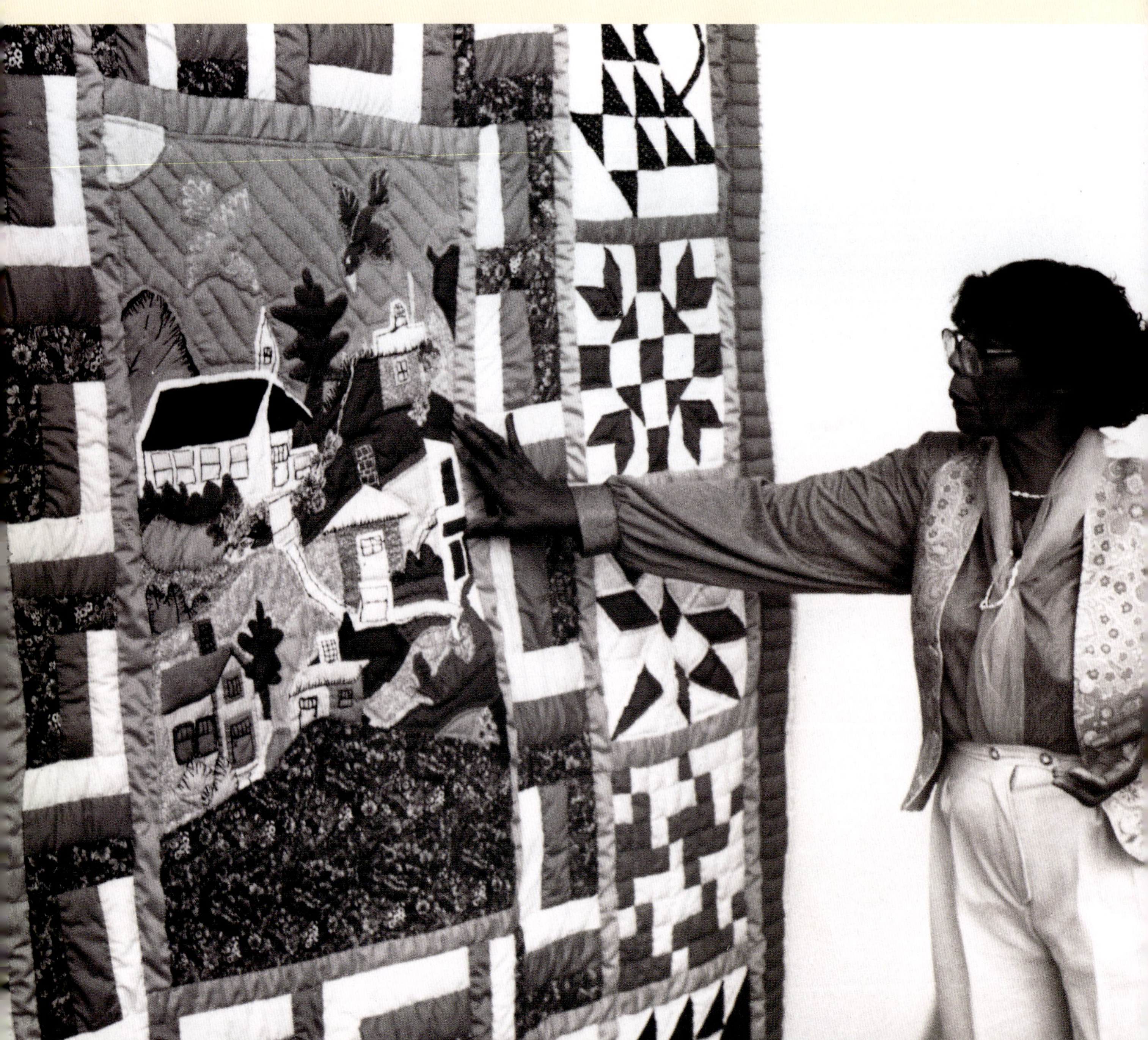

In the Public Eye

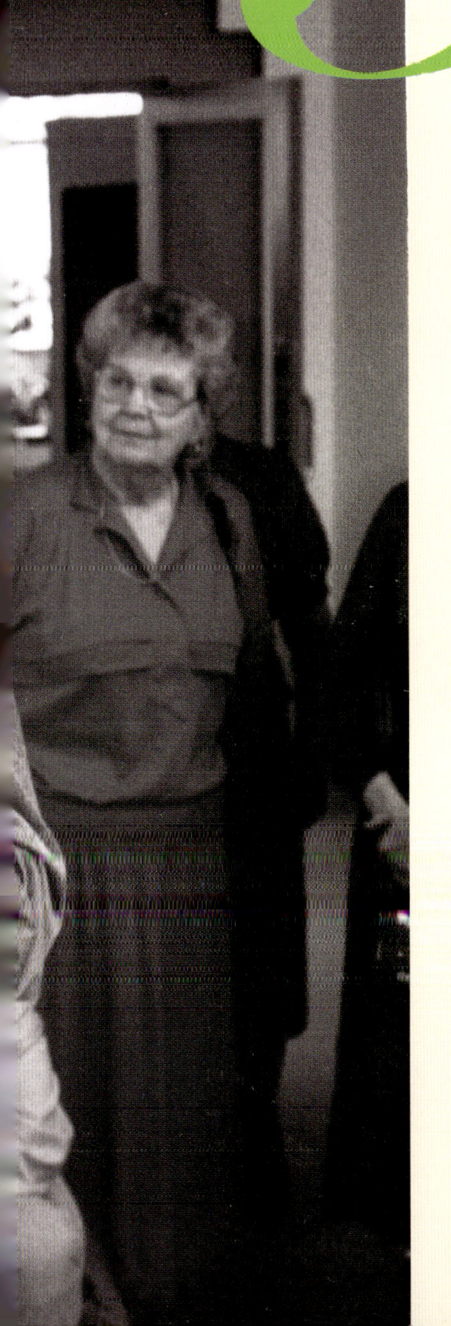

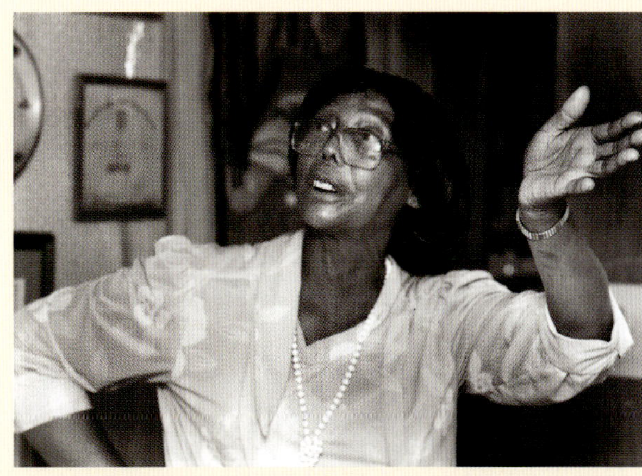

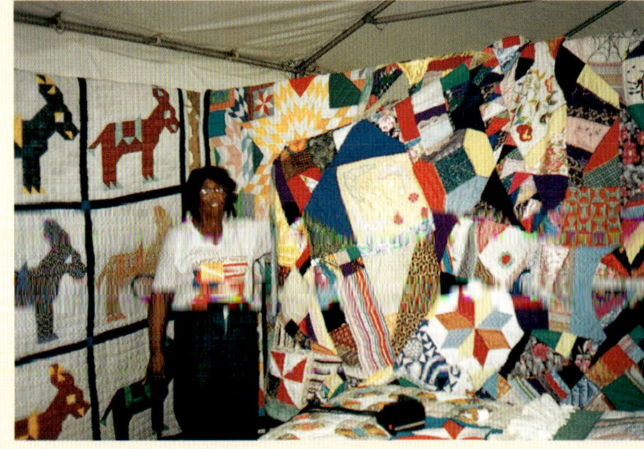

At A Show

[Although her work had been part of other shows, such as "Stitching Memories: African-American Story Quilts," sponsored by Williams College in Massachusetts, in the fall of 1986 Mrs. Ezell was looking forward to her first one-woman show. It opened October 5, 1986, at Stillman College in Tuscaloosa in the Art Gallery, perhaps as a response to the story quilt she made to celebrate the college's centennial. Her comments on that piece, her third story quilt, begin this section.

Her second one-woman show opened at the University of Alabama on June 13, 1987. Her original diary contains the printed program from that event, but no commentary from her.

She showed at the Coker Methodist Church in Coker, Alabama on October 7, 1987. She helped produce the show, and also took second place in the non-traditional patterns category. The red second-place ribbon is affixed to a page in the original diary, again without comment.

The Birmingham Public Library show, "From the Top of My Head," featured only Mrs. Ezell's quilts. It was curated by Mrs. Ezell's friend and mentor, Gail Trechsel, and opened on March 24, 1990. Passages written by Mrs. Ezell in her diary before and after the show are included in the text that follows.

In May 1990, she was part of a showing of Alabama crafts at the Alabama State Council on the Arts Gallery in Montgomery. In December of that year, she participated in the Christmas Quilt Show and Sale, also sponsored by the Council. A newspaper article about the show appeared in *The Montgomery Advertiser* and is excerpted in the pages that follow.

The Folklife Festival in Birmingham's Linn Park, a permanent part of the annual City Stages extravaganza, was June 15th and 16th in 1990. In addition to having a booth in which she exhibited and demonstrated her work, she was featured in the "Talking Tent"; her subject was "The Narrative Quilts of Nora Ezell." An instant snapshot in the original manuscript of this diary shows her in the booth, surrounded by her quilts, which she identifies as: "On the table, 'Old Fashion Star,' in back, 'Grandmother's Flower Basket,' 'Arkansas Tulip,' 'Dogwood,' and 'different blocks.'" She has been a regular at City Stages ever since.

Northport, Alabama, near Tuscaloosa, is home to one of the premier folk art festivals in the country, the Kentuck Festival of the Arts, founded in 1976. Mrs. Ezell began actively participating in the show in 1990. Her booth, filled with quilts, is now located each year on a special avenue of Alabama's heritage artists.

These were the events she had included in her diary prior to 1992, the point at which she decided to begin looking for a publisher for her book. Since that time, she has participated in any number of gallery and museum shows as well as continuing with state, regional, and national folk festivals.]

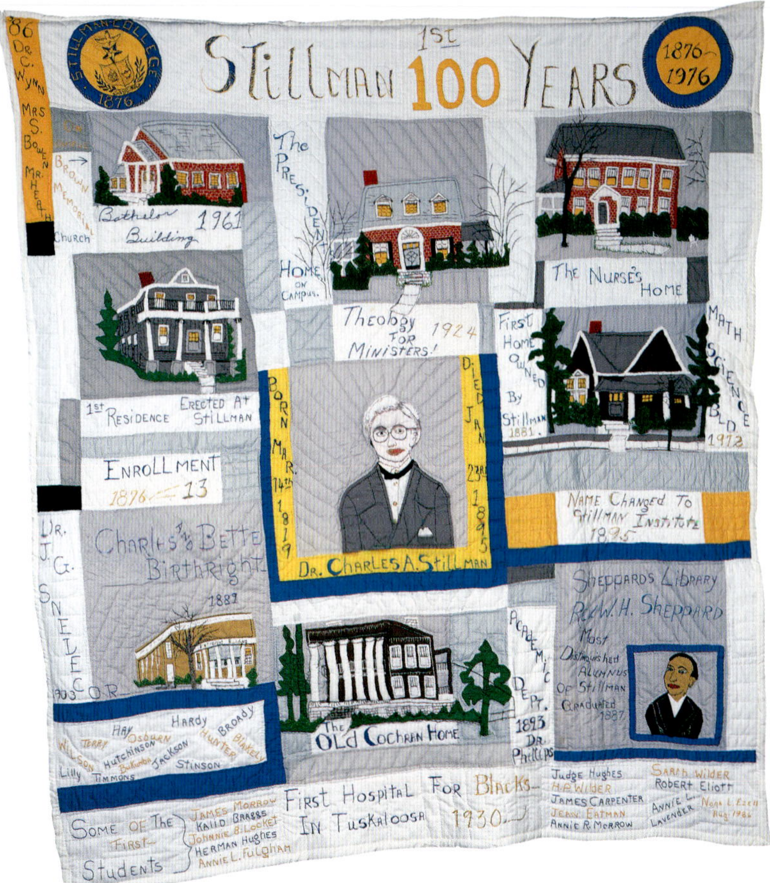

"Stillman: First 100 Years"
Signed "Nora L. Ezell, Aug 1986."
Collection of Robert and Helen Cargo. Photograph courtesy of Robert Cargo.

The Stillman College Show

Stitching Memories: African American Story Quilts

[From the program accompanying the Williams College Show, Stitching Memories: African-American Story Quilts, mounted in 1986:]

> Nora Ezell has no official connection to Stillman College in Tuscaloosa, Alabama. But when she learned that the school, one of the oldest traditionally all-black colleges in the country, was celebrating its 100th anniversary, she offered to create this quilt for them in commemoration of the occasion. She worked closely with the school's librarian, gathering pictures of places and people to be included, such as the central portrait of Dr. Stillman, the school's founder.

[Mrs. Ezell remarks:]

"I thought I did a very good job on this quilt. I was very disappointed that this quilt was not bought by Stillman College, but I did eventually sell it. The show was a good show."

[In the comments she wrote alongside the commentary in the Williams College program, she said that she considers this and the Martin Luther King, Jr. Quilt to be her best work.]

The Birmingham Public Library Show

Opened March 24, 1990

[Before the Show:]

The reasons I have come to do public shows are many.

First, I love to make pretty things;

Second, I love to be useful or make something that is useful;

Third, I love to see the joy on a person's face when they look at something I do or have done;

Fourth, I love to take nothing and make something out of it; really, that's what quilts are all about;

Fifth, I love to help someone do these things (even though I have few takers). One reason I have found most people have not been successful in quilts is that you have to be creative! You have to know or learn how to blend your colors, know what colors are best for your subject: birds, flowers, houses or whatever. I know what you are thinking, but in the beginning this was not the case.

Sixth, I would love to see this art craft taught in schools. How many of you know adults that can't sew or do anything constructive? Time is too important to waste.

Seventh, I love to talk about quilts. Quilts have always told a story, not like what I do, but some women saved scraps from all the children's dresses, men's shirts, wedding dresses, baptisms, graduations, special birthdays, and births of grandchildren, and then they made a quilt. It became a story of a family growing up. In the beginning, we made and used our quilts only for bed covers: now we use them for so many other things. There was a time when the quilting bees were the biggest thing in the community. You couldn't get your chores done fast enough to get there.

I have to say that even if I had never met the [Alabama State] Council [on the Arts] and had the opportunity to go all over Alabama and teach my craft, I would have just worked with what I could get and enjoyed it in my home. There is joy in quilt making.

Now I'm working hard getting ready for another show in Birmingham. Thank God for Gail Trechsel, who has helped me so much. I've tried to do my best. I truly hope I've said or done one thing that has helped someone. My quilts are my way of saying "If you will only give me a chance, I can and will do."

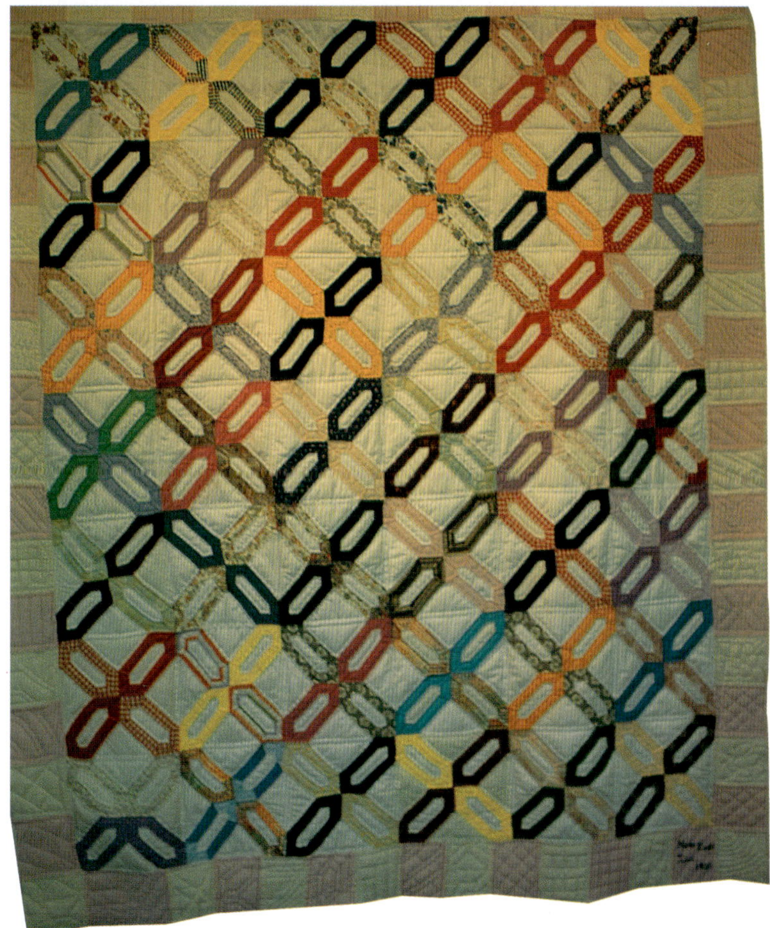

"Mary's Friendship Chain"
Shown hanging in the Birmingham Public Library show, March 24, 1990.
Photograph by Gail Trechsel.

I've enjoyed these shows so much. I have gained some insight into my line of work from other artists. I heard someone say, or maybe I read it, that "I believe in tolerance," and one of the requirements of tolerance is that not only do you listen to the other fellow's viewpoint, but you don't try to cram yours down his throat. I'll say what I think to anyone that will listen, but I won't force anyone to do like I do. My quilts are my expression of what I think. I might try it your way, but in the end, I will do it just like I want to. You can, if you try, tell a story in a quilt, and the good part about it is you don't have to argue with no one about it.

I truly hope everyone will enjoy the show as much as I have doing it.

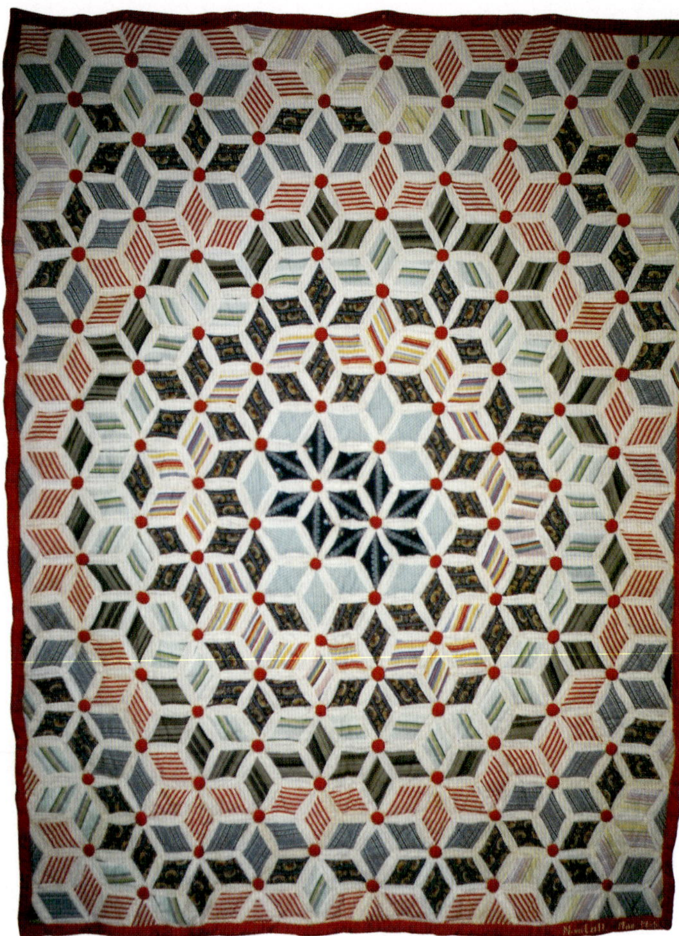

"Cathedral Window"

This quilt, which Mrs. Ezell says she made from a pillow pattern called "Suncatcher," was a part of the Birmingham Public Library show.

71 inches by 89 inches. Photograph courtesy of Robert Cargo.

[After the Show:]

The Birmingham Public Library was one of the best shows that I have ever done—I made more money than ever at a show. I sold $2,440 in finished quilts and got orders for $1,300 more. I have really worked this year, which is only five months old. I hope God will keep me and give me the strength to go on.

Now tonight, almost two weeks later, I'm trying to put my house back together and also continue with my work . . . Sometimes I wonder what I am looking or hoping for. I have never been nobody's special something, but I would have liked to be. To begin with, not one of my grands [grandchildren] or great-grands even mentioned going with me [to the show at the Birmingham Public Library]. Not only did they not go, but they didn't even call to ask me how the show went or if I had a safe trip. I was so hurt. But I learned a long time ago that, when planned, the show must go on. Everybody [at the show] told me that I was good. But my heart was aching because they [my family] didn't care enough about me [to come]. When I looked out over the good crowd, I saw only my sister-in-law—on a cane, bless her heart.

But thank God my show was very good. I must get to work on my orders. I do not allow anyone to limit my time, like asking for a quilt by a certain time.

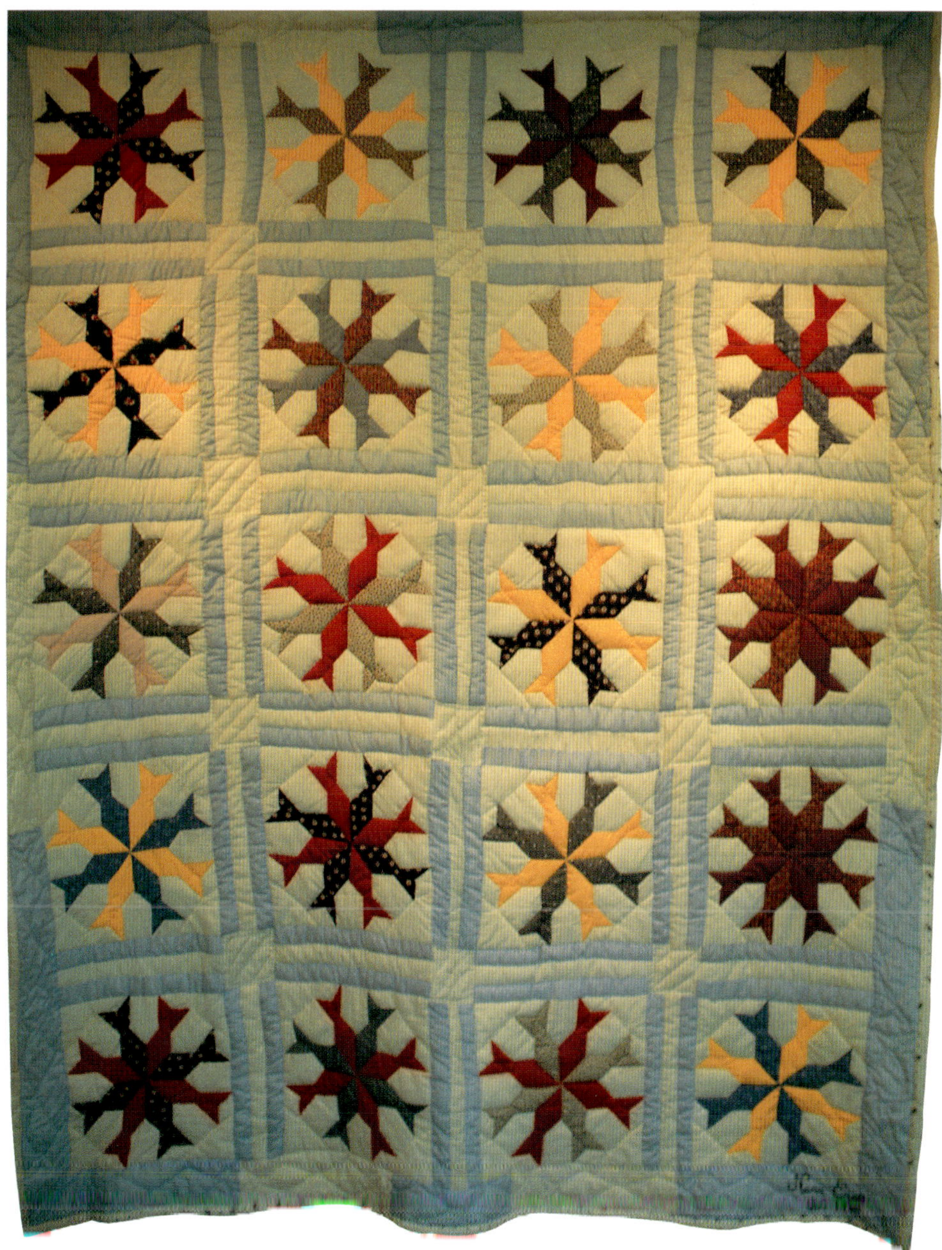

"Fish Quilt"

Many of Mrs. Ezell's story quilts were also in the Birmingham Library show.

Photograph by Gail Trechsel.

[*Birmingham News* art critic James Nelson was enthusiastic in his review of Mrs. Ezell's show, portions of which are quoted below. The significance of being reviewed by the art critic will not be lost on those readers following the same path as Mrs. Ezell.]

By JAMES NELSON

To say that quilting is only a craft is to say that painting is merely a skill. "The art of quilting is not in the mechanics that can be learned as a craft, that is, the ability to sew small, even and neat stitches. The art of quilting lies in the selecting, the cutting and arranging of fabric pieces into a design or ornamental abstraction, reflecting traditional patterns or contemporary events of note.

Nora Ezell is a recognized treasure in the state of Alabama. Selected by the Alabama State Council on the Arts to serve with a Folk Arts Apprentice Program and by the Folk Artists Program of the National Endowment for the Arts, Ms. Ezell has taught and exhibited the art of quilting for much of her adult life.

This exhibition offers a sampler of the kind of work she does and how she does it. Here we see traditional patterns and variations on those traditional patterns that strike the chord of familiarity while showing a freshness and charm that delights both memory and eye. There are contemporary narrative quilts that tell of times, places and events considered by the artist to be worth the work . . .

In the "Jones Valley Sampler, " Ms. Ezell recalls her Fairfield (a Birmingham suburb) past with home, church, school, and mill nestled in a picture-pretty site, framed by various abstract designs . . .

If one can refer to a quilt as "gussied up," as in highly elaborate, Ms. Ezell's pine burr design, which she prefers to call a "Once in a Lifetime Quilt," consists of fancy dress fabrics folded into small triangles and stitched into a circular pattern. The traditional name comes from the view of looking down on the tip-end of a pine cone. For Ms. Ezell, it is a one-time quilt, because it takes a lifetime to acquire enough fancy rayon, satin, and silk scraps for such a quilt . . .

The most beautiful quilt in the show is the "Broken Star Quilt." Beginning with a dark blue eight-point star in the center, diamonds of fabric radiate out to large square patches of peach-colored fabric which form a transitional square on the quilt. Beyond these patches, triangle-tipped bits of fabric repeat the radiating design of the center star to the outer border of the quilt. The colors go from a navy blue to lighter blues, grays, paisley print and peach, each enhancing the sense of radiating energy from the center . . .

One of the most charming works is the "Donkey Quilt." Ms. Ezell's grandson drew a picture of a donkey and asked if she could make it into a quilt. She took the picture, worked it out on graph paper, and developed with one-inch squares a pattern that describes the animal filled with the wit and innocence of childhood.

These quilts are delightful examples of a tradition that places ingenuity alongside practicality, which values imagination along with the work ethic, and which reflects the human capacity for seeing beauty in every task well done.

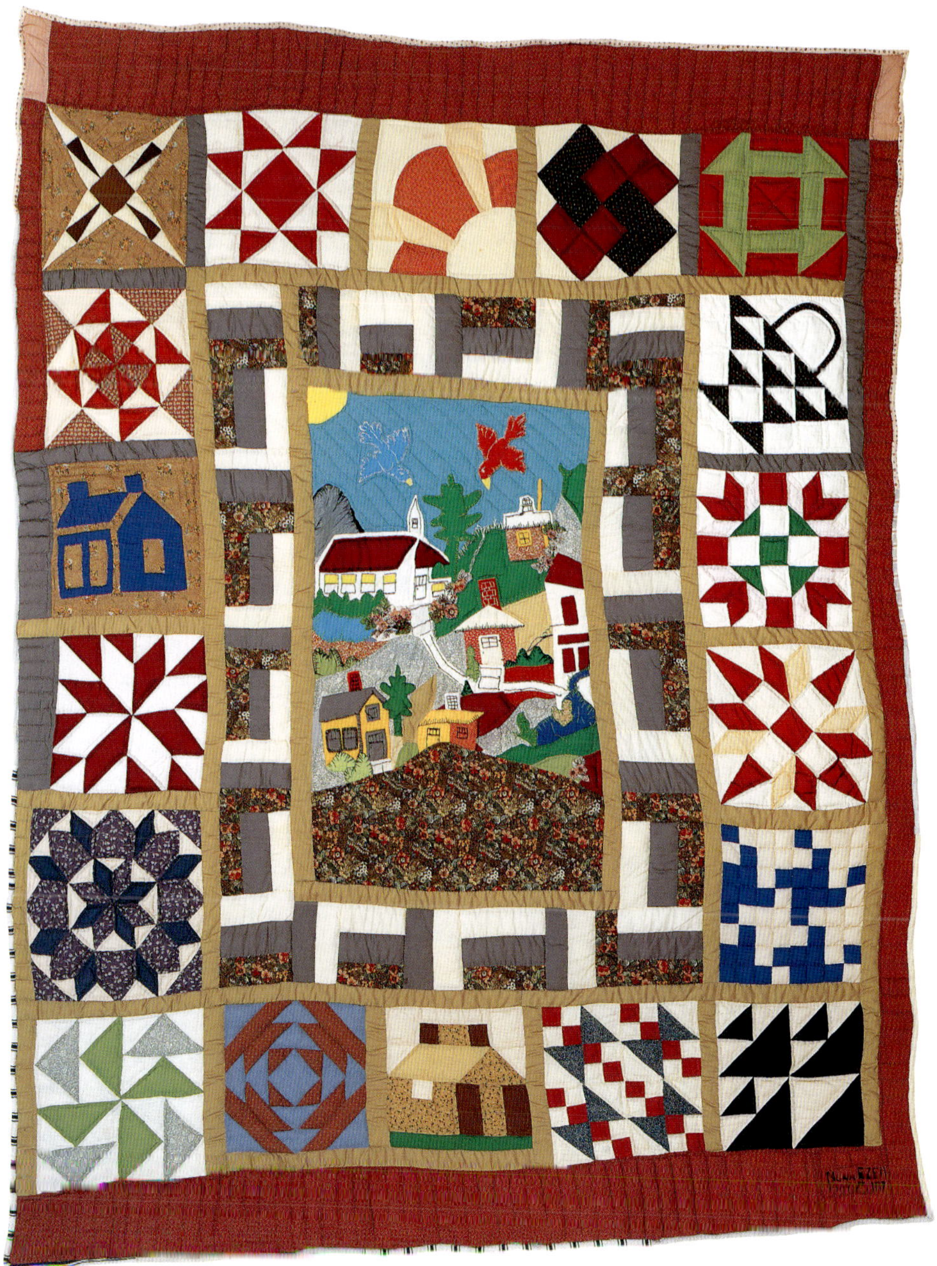

Jones Valley Sampler
signed "Nora Ezell, May 11, 1987."
Collection of Robert and Helen Cargo. Photograph courtesy of Robert Cargo.

The Alabama State Council on the Arts Christmas Quilt Show and Sale

[*The Montgomery Advertiser* featured an interview with Mrs. Ezell to accompany the Christmas Quilt Show and Sale sponsored by the Alabama State Council on the Arts in December of 1990.]

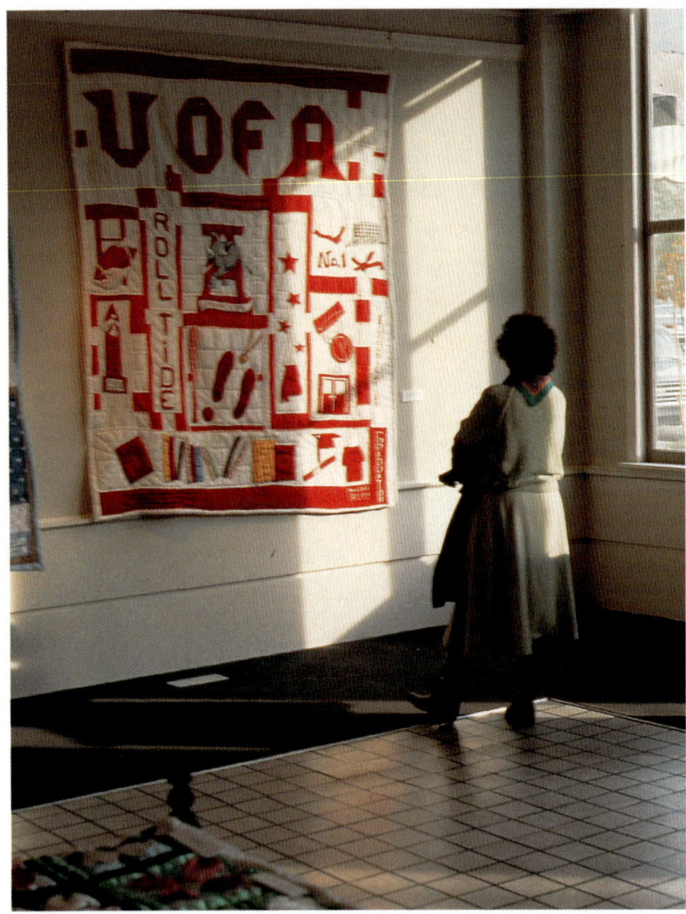

Mrs. Ezell spends a reflective moment alone with her quilts at the Alabama State Council on the Arts' Christmas Quilt Show and Sale in December of 1990.

Photo by Joey Brackner; courtesy of the Alabama State Council on the Arts

By JAMIE CREAMER

. . . Just inside the [gallery's] front door hangs the original quilt—labeled as The Martin Luther King Life Story— which, through quilted designs, depicts such historic sites and scenes as the Selma Bridge, the Greene County Courthouse, the Dexter Avenue King Memorial Baptist Church, the Rosa Parks incident leading to the Montgomery bus boycott, and a picture of King, complete with reference to his "I have a dream" speech and his Nobel peace prize.

Nora Ezell . . . is right proud of the quilt, which took her 586 hours and a lot of creative effort to design.

"I had no pattern of no kind," Ezell said in a phone interview from her . . . home. "Everything is just my perception of how things looked. I just came up with it all as I went along. You know I had plenty of information and events to work with, though," she said. "I could have made a quilt that would've been as long as Dexter Avenue, just telling that story."

. . . It was Ezell's daughter who, several years ago, saw a chronicle of King's life in their local newspaper and got the idea that her mother should make a quilt based on his life.

Ezell started on the project in 1983, then "laid it aside" for a while after her daughter died.

"Working on it brought back memories, and I couldn't deal with it," she said.

The Alabama Folk Heritage Award, 1990

[The Alabama State Council on the Arts circulated the following press release, which was reprinted in many of the newspapers in the state, clippings of which are in the original diary. Across one she has written: *12-16th-1990—A Day to Remember*.]

Nora Ezell Named Alabama Folk Heritage Award Recipient

Congratulations to Nora Ezell of Mantua, Alabama, who was recently chosen as the 1990 recipient of the Alabama Folk Heritage Award, the state's highest honor for achievement in the traditional arts.

The annual award was established in 1987 by the Alabama State Council on the Arts to recognize master folk artists who have made significant lifetime contributions to their artistic traditions.

Nora Ezell is a quiltmaker of extraordinary talent and commitment, as well as an articulate spokeswoman for an art form that is deeply rooted in Alabama culture. She has become recognized by quilt scholars for her 'storytelling' or narrative quilts depicting images of the University of Alabama, the life of Martin Luther King, a history of Stillman College, and life in Jones Valley.

Her latest masterpiece, *A Tribute to the Civil Righters of Alabama*, was commissioned by the Birmingham Civil Rights Institute and illustrates events and individuals involved with the Movement in Alabama.

In addition to her selection for the 1990 Folk Heritage Award, Nora Ezell has participated as a master artist in the ASCA Folk Arts Apprenticeship Program. An exhibition of her quilts is scheduled for the Alabama Artists' Gallery in November.

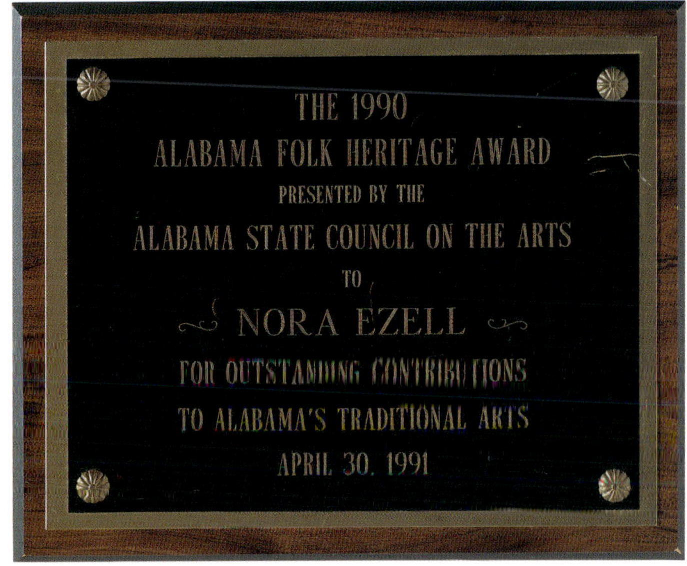

The National Heritage Fellowship, 1992

[Mrs. Ezell's original manuscript contains a clipping of the following story from *The Washington Post*, dated Monday, May 11, 1992. She does not say how she first learned of the NEA Fellowship.]

Agency Honors 13 With Fellowships

Thirteen folk art masters have been named National Heritage Fellows in the National Endowment for the Arts program to recognize individuals who carry on folk traditions in the United States. The winners, who also each get a $5,000 grant, will be honored at a three-day gathering in Washington beginning Sept. 22.

The fellowships are the most visible part of the NEA's Folk Arts Program, which began them 11 years ago under the direction of the recently retired Bess Lomax Hawes. Her successor, Dan Sheehy, called the 1992 winners "vivid testimony to the creative genius of our nation's many peoples and to their determination to carry their traditions into the future."

The 1992 fellows are: Francisco Aguabella, an Afro-Cuban drummer from Glendale, Calif.; Jerry Brown, a Southern stoneware potter from Hamilton, Ala.; Walker Calhoun, a Cherokee musician, dancer and teacher from Cherokee, N.C.; Clyde Davenport, an Appalachian fiddler from Monticello, Ky.; Belle Deacon, an Athabascan basket maker from Grayling, Alaska; Nora Ezell, an African American quilter from Eutaw, Ala.; Gerald Hawpetoss, a Menominee-Potowatomi regalia-maker from Milwaukee, Wis.; Fatima Kuinova, of Rego Park, N.Y., a singer in the Bukharan Jewish tradition from Central Asia; John Naka, a Bonsai sculptor from Los Angeles, Calif.; Ng Sheung-Chi, a Chinese *Toissan muk'yu* folk singer from New York; Marc Savoy, a Cajun accordion maker and musician from Eunice, La.; Othar Turner, an African American fife player from Senatobia, Miss.; T. Viswanathan, a South Indian flute master from Middletown, Conn.

[The Sunday, May 10, 1992, *Tuscaloosa News* carried the following story:]

By BOB MCNEIL

Two Alabamians are among the 13 folk artists slected by the National Endowment for the Arts to be this year's National Heritage Fellows.

The NEA's $5,000 fellowship will go to Nora Ezell, a 74-year-old African-American quilter from Eutaw in Greene County, and 50-year-old Jerry Brown . . .

Ezell, a multi-talented needleworker and master of quilt appliqué and embroidery, and Brown . . . were chosen from among 229 traditional artists who were nominated by their peers, the NEA said.

Ezell, winner of the 1990 Alabama Folk Heritage Award, was featured in a one-woman show at Stillman College . . . and in several exhibitions at the state Arts Council in Montgomery. Her Martin Luther King Quilt . . . was included in the national touring exhibit, "Stitching Memories: African-American Story Quilts" . . .

"These fellowships are a celebration of America, pure and simple," said Anne-Imelda Radice, acting Arts Endowment chairman. "The fellowships not only pay tribute to a range of artistic tradition that spans the diverse cultures among us, but they also honor talented and selfless people like Jerry Brown and Nora Ezell . . . who help to preserve and pass on valuable artistic legacies for generations to come," says Radice.

The endowment has been handing out the one-time awards since 1982 to master practitioners of traditional arts.

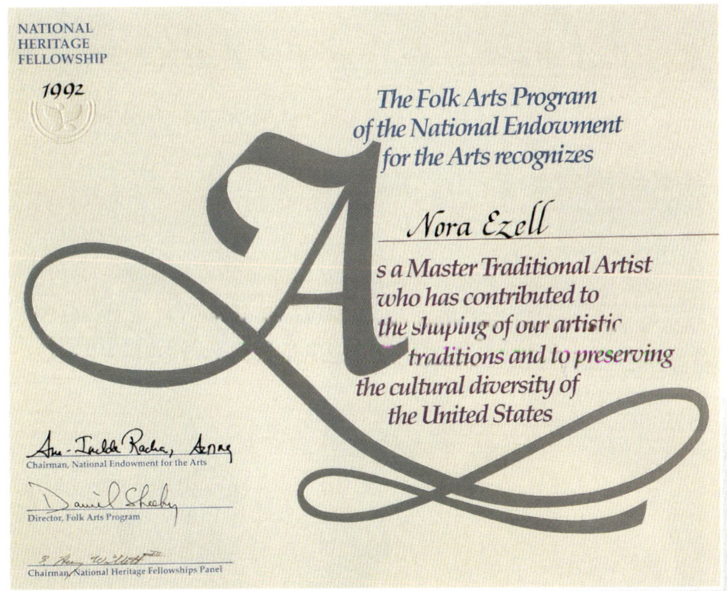

NATIONAL
HERITAGE
FELLOWSHIP

1992

The Folk Arts Program of the National Endowment for the Arts recognizes

Nora Ezell

As a Master Traditional Artist who has contributed to the shaping of our artistic traditions and to preserving the cultural diversity of the United States

Chairman, National Endowment for the Arts

Director, Folk Arts Program

Chairman, National Heritage Fellowships Panel

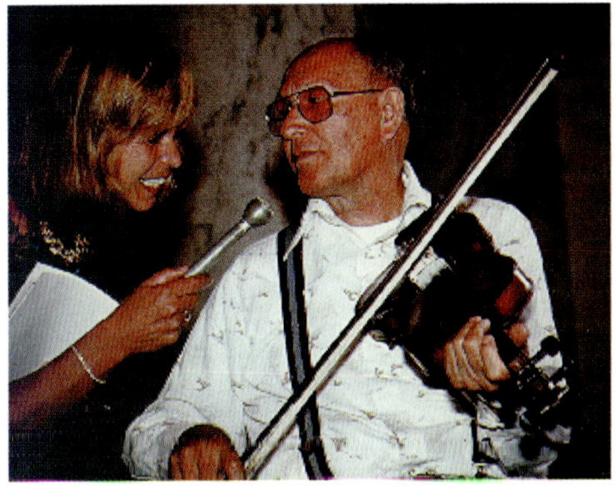

The award from the NEA has a place of honor in Mrs. Ezell's living room.

A letter from the President of the United States hangs nearby.

Above right: Fiddler Clyde Davenport is interviewed by a reporter from National Public Radio. Below: Fife player Othar Turner makes music at the NEA Fellows awards ceremonies in Washington, D.C., on May 11, 1992.

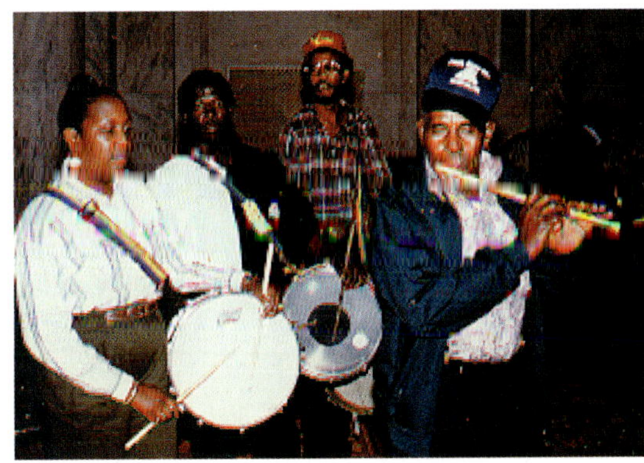

THE WHITE HOUSE

WASHINGTON

September 16, 1992

Dear Mrs. Ezell:

I am delighted to congratulate you on your recent recognition by the National Endowment for the Arts. The National Heritage Fellowship is awarded to a select number of traditional American artists, and you can be justifiably proud of this high honor.

Our Nation boasts a rich cultural heritage, and through your fine work, you have not only helped to preserve time-honored artistic traditions but also added to the wealth of American folk art. The United States is doubly enriched, as your talent, skill, and dedication will undoubtedly inspire other artists to follow in your quest for excellence, thereby affirming the best in American art, history, and culture.

Barbara joins me in sending best wishes to you for continuing success.

Sincerely,

Mrs. Nora Ezell
Route 1, Box 211
Eutaw, Alabama 35462

Caught by the Camera

Right: A fond reunion between Mrs. Ezell and the little Chinese boy on her quilt, ***Children of the World***, takes place at a show in Chattanooga in 1994.

Below right: Nina Brock shares a laugh with Mrs. Ezell while visiting in her booth during the 1993 National Folk Festival.

Lower left: Mrs. Ezell discusses the making of the three-dimensional Bible in the center of ***The Bible Story Quilt***.

Photographs this page by Jimmy Hedges. Courtesy Rising Fawn Folk Art Gallery.

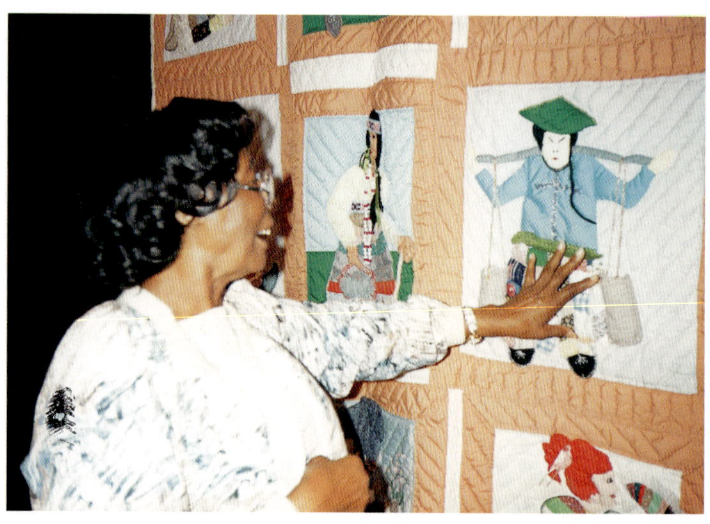

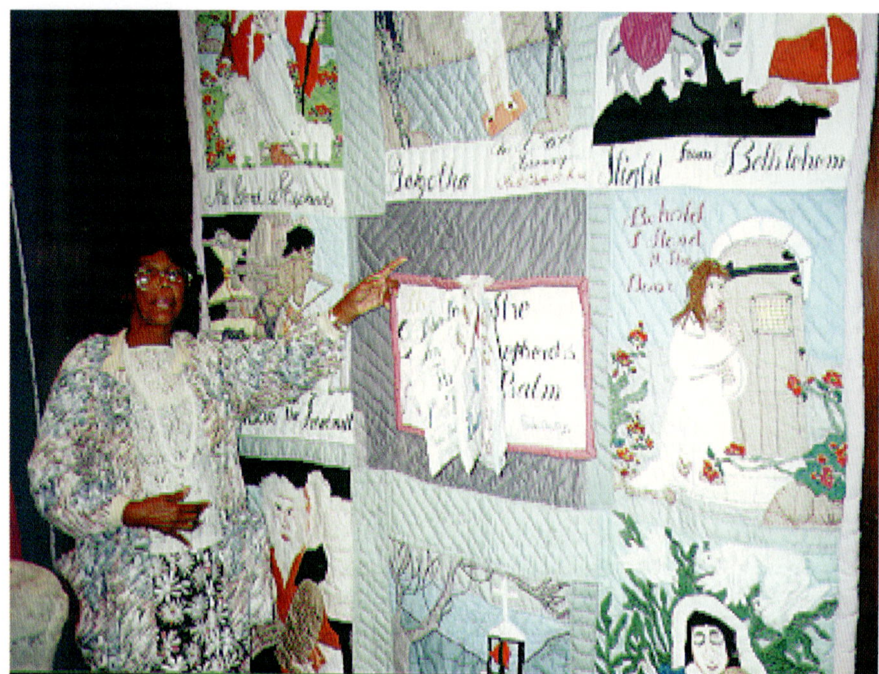

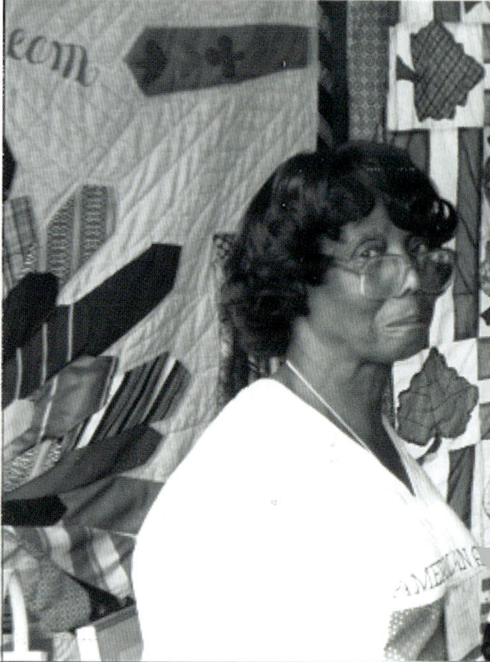

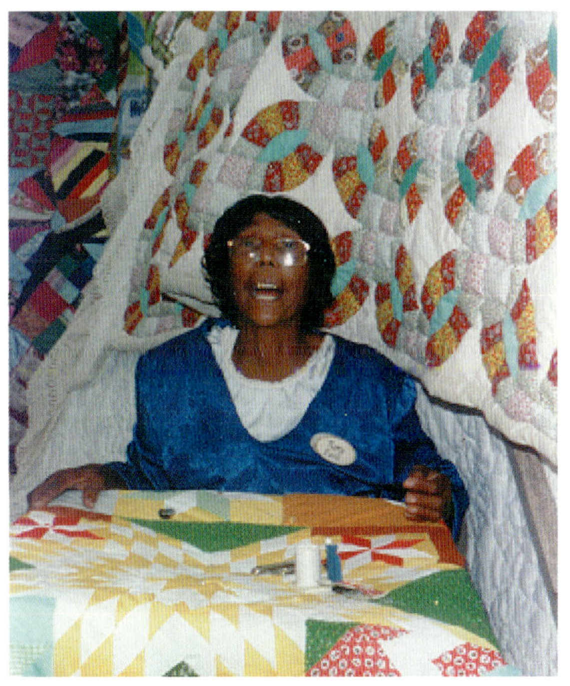

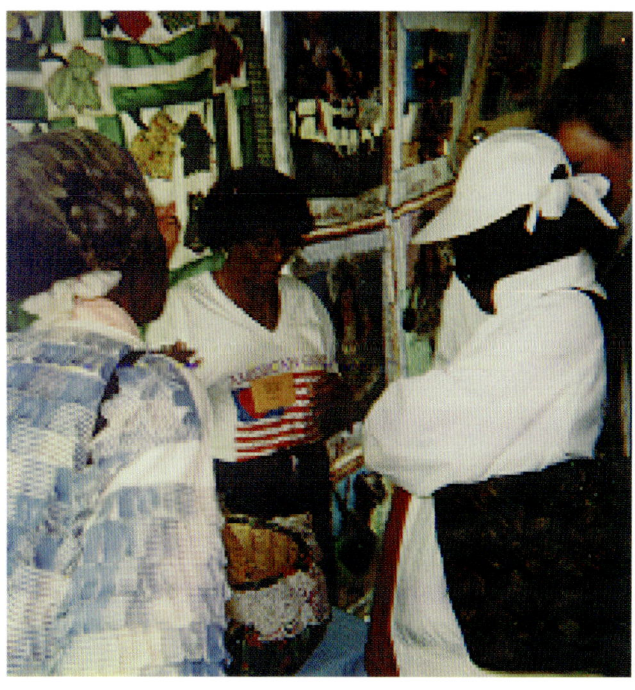

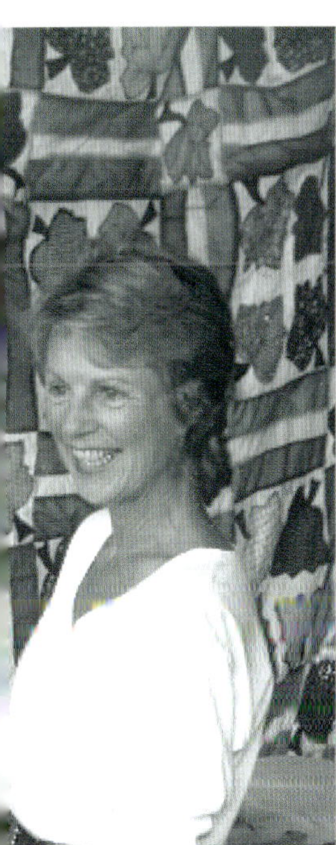

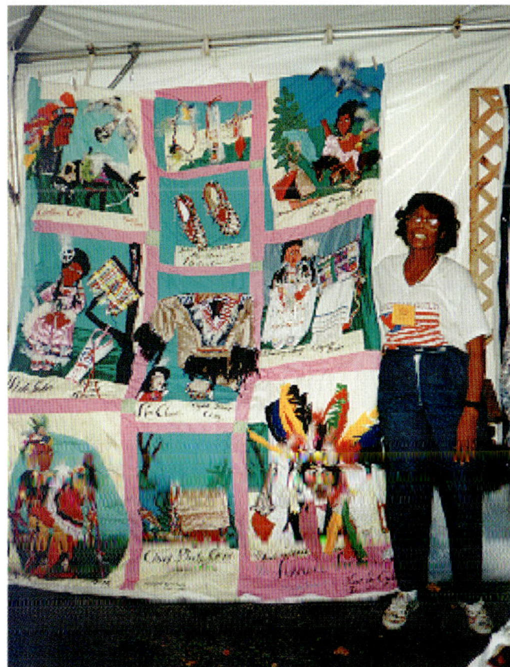

Top left: Not one to waste time, Mrs. Ezell quilts on a "Star Puzzle" while talking to visitors during a festival.
Photograph from the collection of the author.

Top right: Two of Mrs. Ezell's admirers, Ella McCoy and Helen L. Kelly, visit at a festival. Ms. McCoy is a collector of Mrs. Ezell's work.
Photograph from the collection of the author.

Left: A happy smile lights Mrs. Ezell's face as she stands beside her masterpiece, *The American Indian's Saga (As I See Them)*, at the National Folk Festival 1994.
Photograph by Jimmy Hedges. Photograph from the collection of the author.

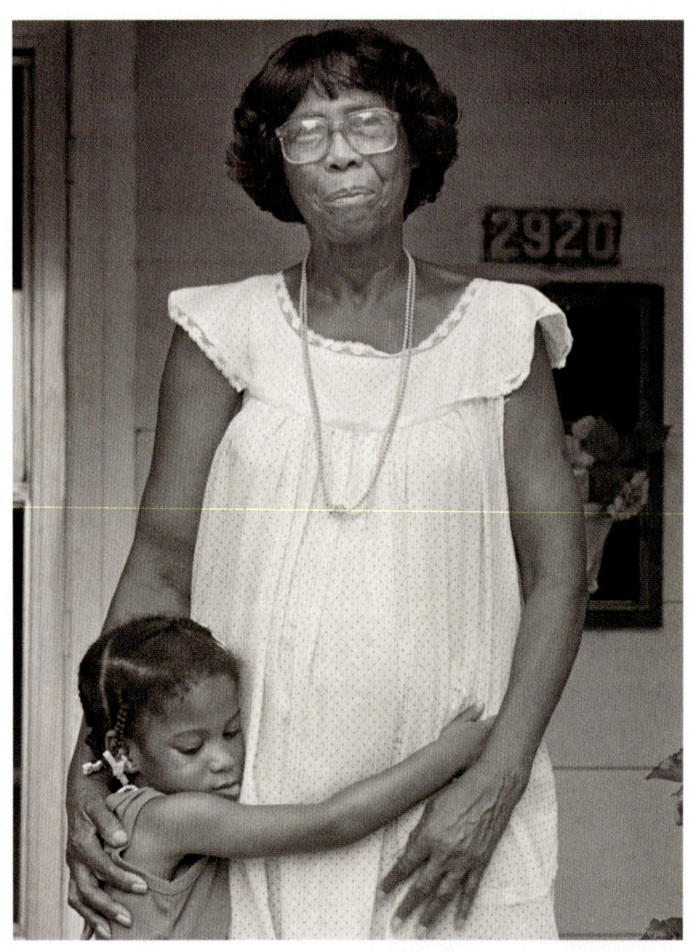

Mrs. Ezell and a favorite "grand" pose on the steps of her home in Tuscaloosa.

Photograph by Keith Boyer. Collection of the author.

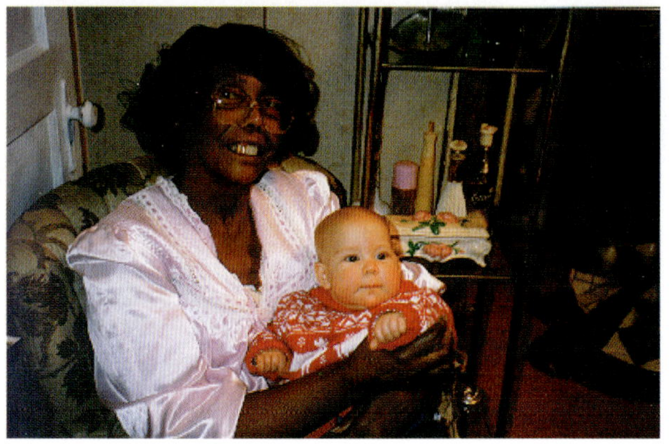

The beginning of new friendship—Mrs. Ezell holds Celia Carnes, November 1994.

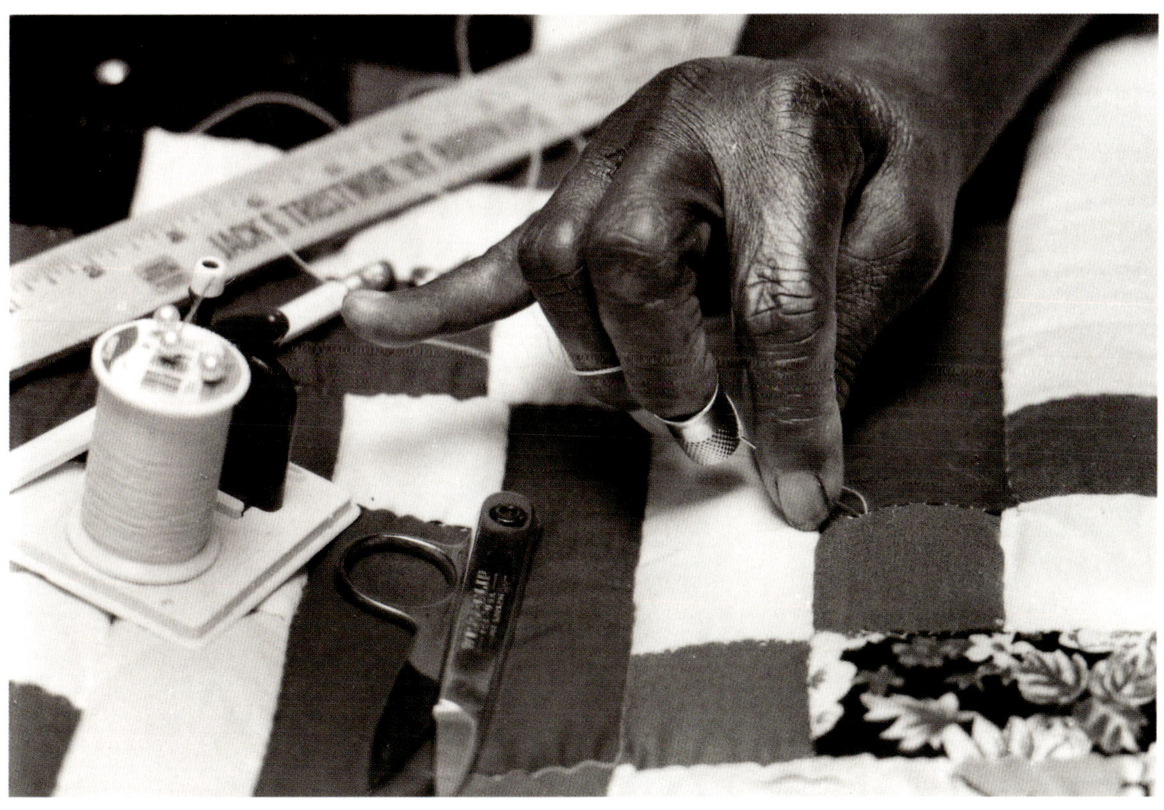

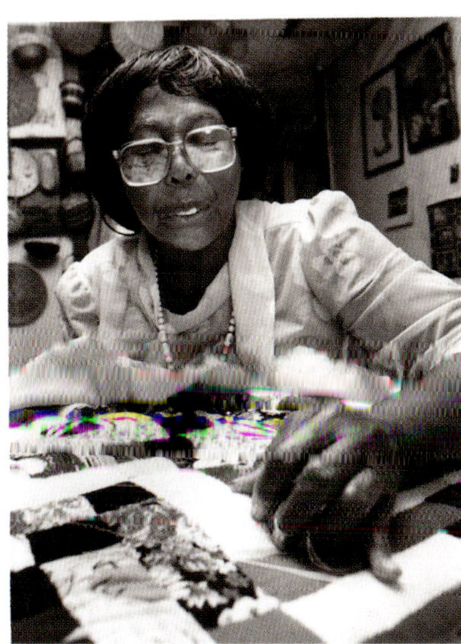

Some of Mrs. Ezell's favorite tools and supplies rest close by her hand as she carefully stitches "in the ditch," the seam holding two pieces together.

Photograph by Patricia Miklik, Courtesy of *The Montgomery Advertiser.*

Quilting is a time to relax. The tough decisions about pattern choice and color selection have been made.

Photograph by Patricia Miklik, courtesy of *The Montgomery Advertiser.*

Epilogue

As she passed her eightieth birthday, Mrs. Ezell was comfortably settled in a house in Tuscaloosa. She continued to quilt, taking commissions and working on pieces for her own pleasure. She impatiently awaited the publication of this book.

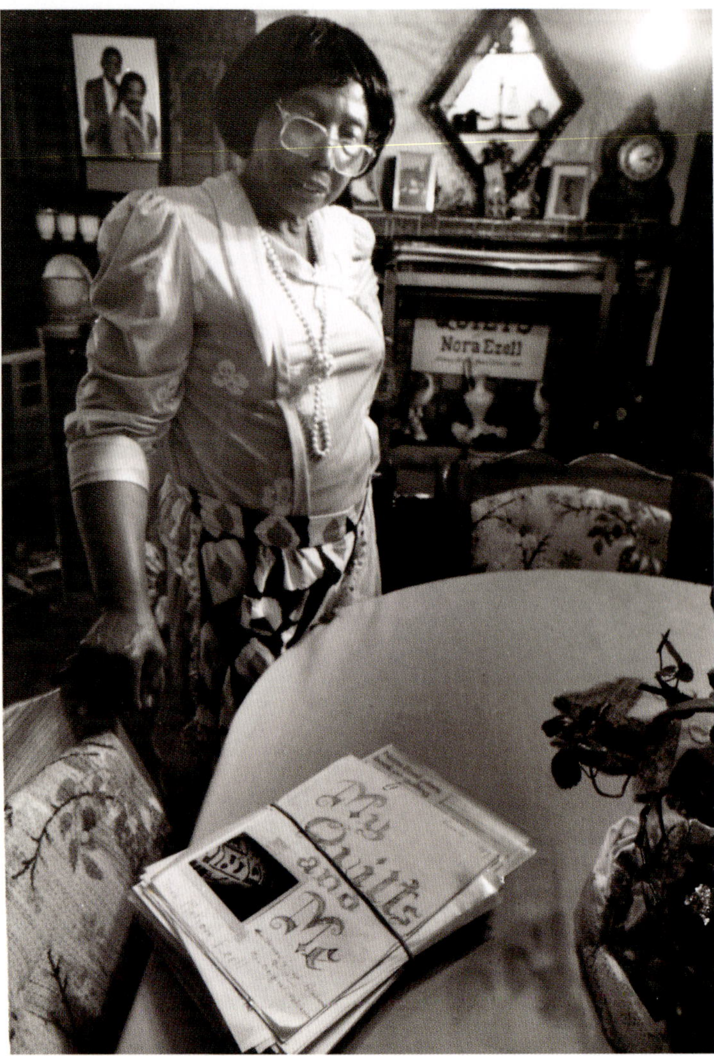

Mrs. Ezell shows a visitor the original manuscript of this book. She plans to have it bound, along with the original snapshots and newspaper clippings, into a permanent keepsake for her grand- and great-grandchildren.
Photograph by Patricia Miklik. Courtesy of *The Montgomery Advertiser.*

Editorial Notes and Acknowledgments

When Mrs. Ezell finished her manuscript in 1992, she first showed it to University of Alabama Press director Malcolm McDonald (now retired). McDonald was unable to acquire the book for UAP, but he admired the manuscript and encouraged Mrs. Ezell to send it to Randall Williams of Black Belt Press. Hank Willett of the Alabama Center for Traditional Culture subsequently introduced Williams and Mrs. Ezell and helped Black Belt to acquire the work.

The original manuscript is enlivened by scores of instant snapshots, newspaper clippings, and ribbons won at exhibitions. Mrs. Ezell even glued a protractor and a 6-inch ruler into the pages of her book! She says that her original intent was to make only one copy of the book; she wanted someone to bind her project into a permanent record of her work. It is the hope of many of Mrs. Ezell's friends that her original manuscript will eventually find its way into the archives of the Center for Traditional Culture or another suitable repository where it may be enjoyed by many.

As Williams and editor Mary Elizabeth Johnson began work on the project, it became apparent that enthusiasm for Mrs. Ezell's talent was shared by countless admirers. It also became evident that Mrs. Ezell's customers have become her friends, and each was eager to do whatever they could to contribute to Mrs. Ezell's book. Collectors of her quilts shipped them to Black Belt Press for photography (although not without some trepidation about letting go of their masterpieces for even a short time). Those in the various government agencies who have worked with Mrs. Ezell through the years searched their records, photographs, and memories. Especially helpful were the following individuals:

Gail Trechsel, now the Director of the Birmingham Museum of Art, was extremely generous with her personal photographs, quilts, notes and tapes of meetings with Mrs. Ezell. She also provided an insightful preface.

Joey Brackner, folklorist for the state of Alabama through the Alabama State Council on the Arts, was untiring in his efforts to locate original photographs of Mrs. Ezell that had been published in the newspapers and in ASCA journals. Mrs. Ezell keeps her newspaper and magazine clippings in the original manuscript, and we tried whenever possible to find the originals of those photos to include in this book. Joey Brackner also allowed us to accompany him and a National Endowment of the Arts representative to Mrs. Ezell's home for video documentation of a follow-up interview they were doing for NEA grant recipients.

Georgine Clark, Hank Willett, and Anne Kimzey, all of the Alabama State Council on the Arts, were most helpful in locating the addresses and telephone numbers of the collectors who had bought Mrs. Ezell's work. Many of these collectors loaned their Ezell quilts to be photographed. Hank Willett also wrote the foreword for the book, detailing his experiences as one of the panelists who chose Mrs. Ezell for her NEA fellowship. Anne Kimzey lent a tape of field interviews with Mrs. Ezell.

Robert Cargo, an early and faithful supporter of Mrs. Ezell, shared research, personal reminescences, notes, quilts, and photographs. He also contributed a poignant essay on his long-time relationship with her.

Fervent collectors of Mrs. Ezell's work, such as Jim Hedges, Anne Miller, and Jim Sokol, were extremely generous in loaning their quilts to be photographed. Each had something they wanted to say in tribute to Nora, as well. It seemed that everyone who collects Mrs. Ezell's quilts wanted the opportunity to pay tribute to her talent and to their friendship with her by doing something for her book.

Although every effort was made to locate all the owners of the quilts, and to retrieve those quilts for photography, we were not able to be 100 percent successful. Without doubt, some of the missing owners will emerge after the book is published.

Jim Carnes made careful suggestions regarding the editing of the text; his wife, Erin Kellen, worked with Black Belt to make sure that Mrs. Ezell's voice rings true throughout the book. They have the advantage of knowing Mrs. Ezell personally, so their help was particularly valuable.

Breuna Baine, the designer of the book, and Jeff Slaton, Black Belt's managing editor during most of the time the book was in production, both took an interest in the book that went far beyond the mere responsibilities of their jobs.

Mrs. Ezell herself, though out of patience with the amount of time it takes to publish a book, was nonetheless always willing to go back through her memories and mementoes to double-check a fact or search for a name. She has lost touch with some people, such as the owner of *The Baseball Quilt*, but there was never any doubt about who had which quilt. She knows exactly who is tending to the offspring of her needle.

Finally, publication of this book was delayed several times by the cost of the project and the burden such capital requirements place on a small, independent press. Toward the end of the process, financial assistance was provided by Alabama novelist Daniel Glover, to whom we are grateful.

The Editors

Suggested Reading

To read more about African-American quilters in general and story quilters in particular, consult the following publications:

Benberry, Cuesta. *Always There: The African-American Presence in American Quilts.* 1992; The Kentucky Quilt Project, Inc., Louisville.

Callahan, Nancy. *The Freedom Quilting Bee*; 1987; The University of Alabama Press, Tuscaloosa and London.

Fry, Gladys-Marie. *Stitched from the Soul: Slave Quilts from the Ante-Bellum South.* 1990; Dutton Studio Books, in association with the Museum of American Folk Art, New York.

——— "Not by Rules But By the Heart: The Quilts of Clementine Hunter," in *Clementine Hunter, American Folk Artist*, catalog to an exhibition of the same name organized by the Museum of African-American Life and Culture, Dallas. Published by the Museum of African-American Life and Culture in 1993.

Lyons, Mary E. *Stitching Stars: The Story Quilts of Harriet Powers.* 1993; Charles Scribner's Sons (Books for Young Readers), McMillan Publishing Company, New York.

Mashuta, Mary. *Story Quilts: Telling Your Tale in Fabric.* 1992; C & T Publishing, Lafayette, Calif.

Ringgold, Faith. *Tar Beach*; 1988; Crown Publishers, New York.

Vlach, John Michael. *The Afro-American Tradition in Decorative Arts*; 1990; a Brown Thrasher Book by The University of Georgia Press; Athens and London.

Wahlman, Maude Southwell. *Signs and Symbols: African Images in African-American Quilts*; 1993; Studio Books in association with The Museum of American Folk Art, New York.

Watts, Katherine with Elizabeth Walker. *Anna Williams: Her Quilts and Their Influences*; 1995; American Quilter's Society, Paducah, Ky.